W9-BFQ-869

*A remembrance
to the Library*

By

Polly Pittman
'66

April 1986

OGS OREGON EPISCOPAL SCHOOL

The Twentieth Century

The Cambridge History Library

The Cambridge Introduction to History
Written by Trevor Cairns

The Cambridge Topic Books
General Editor Trevor Cairns

The Twentieth Century

Upper Division Library
Oregon Episcopal School
6300 S.W. Nicol Road
Portland, OR _ 97223

Trevor Cairns

Published in cooperation with Cambridge University Press
Lerner Publications Company, Minneapolis

Editors' Note: In preparing this edition of *The Cambridge Introduction to History* for publication, the editors have made only a few minor changes in the original material. In some isolated cases, British spelling and usage were altered in order to avoid possible confusion for our readers. Whenever necessary, information was added to clarify references to people, places, and events in British history. An index and a list of maps and diagrams were also provided in each volume.

LIBRARY OF CONGRESS CATALOGING IN PUBLICATION DATA

Cairns, Trevor.
  The twentieth century.

  (The Cambridge introduction to history)
  "Published in cooperation with Cambridge University Press."
  Includes index.
  Summary: Presents main themes in twentieth-century life, including military confrontations, booms and depressions, political ideologies, and technological developments.
   1. Civilization, Modern — 20th century — Juvenile literature.
  [1. Civilization, Modern — 20th century] I. Title.
  II. Series: Cairns, Trevor. Cambridge introduction to history.
  CB425.C25 1984b   909.82   84-12564
  ISBN 0-8225-0810-9 (lib. bdg.)

This edition first published 1984 by Lerner Publications Company
by permission of Cambridge University Press.

International Standard Book Number: 0-8225-0810-9
Library of Congress Catalog Card Number: 84-12564

Manufactured in the United States of America

This edition is available exclusively from:
Lerner Publications Company, 241 First Avenue North, Minneapolis, Minnesota 55401

2 3 4 5 6 7 8 9 10 93 92 91 90 89 88 87 86

Contents

The most important century of all?

Sometimes we think of history as a long road leading up to the present day. Looking back over the past, unable to see the future, we may easily feel that we are standing at the highest point that mankind has yet reached. Certainly the latest century has been different from any that have gone before, in many important ways:

– The world's population has grown far larger.
– Travel and communications have become extremely fast; so, in effect, the world that once seemed enormous now seems small.
– As a result, events in one place can quickly affect the whole world; this century has suffered world-wide depressions, rivalries and wars, and has seen the formation of world organisations trying to keep peace.
– Science and technology have developed faster than ever; 'advanced' nations have become enormously rich and comfortable, compared with all peoples of the past and many of the present.
– Science has also given a few people the power to destroy, at one blow, the whole of civilisation and perhaps all mankind.
– Human beings have learned to fly, to leave the surface of the world where people have lived for their entire existence and to reach towards other worlds.

Often we take all this speed and power for granted, but the changes have been so great that this century may well be a turning point in the history of mankind. Certainly it is the first century when all the peoples of the world have been linked so closely that we can see world events as one vast story, as well as the separate stories of nations and civilisations.

This book tries to explain the outlines of that story. Within it there are many major themes:

– When the century began the great powers of Europe led the world. They had the most advanced techniques, the strongest armies and navies, and – or so they mostly believed – the most humane civilisation. It would be possible to relate the history of the twentieth century as the tale of Europe's downfall, devastated by self-inflicted wars and bereft of empires.
– Alternatively, this could be seen as the story of the liberation of the coloured peoples of the world from white domination, and how they claimed a full share in world affairs.
– Or the theme could be how two superpowers grew and struggled for leadership of the world.
– Or we could concentrate on the political creeds that have divided and united peoples, the ideologies or 'isms' that have sometimes seemed the new religions of the modern world.
– Or the theme could be how science and inventions have improved our standard of living.
– Or how war has become more destructive.
– Or we may prefer the attempts to prevent war and encourage co-operation between nations, either within single continents or throughout the world.

All these themes are woven together in the general history of the world in the twentieth century, and at different times one or another will stand out. Sometimes, too, one particular country will be most prominent, either because it influenced many others or because it was typical. It is not always easy to decide what is true or to pick out the threads in so large and complicated a pattern. But it is worth trying, for most of the stories are still going on and we may be in them.

below: *On 25 July, 1909 Louis Blériot won the £1,000 prize offered by the London 'Daily Mail' for the first airplane flight across the English Channel. It was this flight more than anything else that made the British public begin to realise that the airplane might become an important force in the new century. This is the scene after Blériot's landing near Dover, and in the background is one of the other machines that would reshape life in the twentieth century, an automobile.*

"All Right—John."

"I'll be half an hour late"

"His Master's Voice"

top right: *The telephone, introduced in the 1870s, was becoming quite normal in 'advanced' countries. In this American telephone advertisement we catch a glimpse of the sort of people the telephone company thought likely to buy their instruments. The office manager speaks from his desk, while behind him the clerks work beneath the electric lights; his wife replies from beside the window of their home in the country, or perhaps an outer suburb. It was possible also to capture sounds, and play them back on machines small and cheap enough for average homes. The trademark of 'His Master's Voice' (right), with its combination of a fashionable gadget, a family pet, the hint of a story and a touch of humour, was cleverly designed to attract potential customers.*

1   The world before the war

Progress and promise

In 1901 Edward VII came to the British throne. The Victorian age was over. The new king was a portly man of fifty-nine who liked good food and drink, elegant ladies, horse racing and cards. Afterwards, when people looked back from the misery of the Great War, they often saw his ten years as 'the good old days' when everything had been safe, prosperous and cheerful.

There was some truth in this vision. The rich were led by a glittering aristocratic extravagant 'high society' but there was plenty of fun for all the people, too. Popular songs were lively and good-humoured; stars such as Marie Lloyd and Vesta Tilley, Harry Lauder and George Robey kept the music-halls full of mirth. *The Merry Widow*, from Vienna, was the queen of all operettas but there were popular and tuneful British musical comedies like *The Arcadians* or *A Country Girl*, and younger people were taking to an energetic new rhythm from America

Edwardian society – the wealthy and elegant, with expensive car and liveried servant – pictured in the West End of London, outside Harrods, the department store that prided itself on its reputation for selling only the best to the best. The picture is from the Harrods catalogue for 1909.

called 'ragtime'. Mass entertainment had arrived. Thousands flocked to the local soccer ground every Saturday. Tobacco and drink were cheap and plentiful – too plentiful, some said. Popular newspapers, cheap, easy-to-read and sensational, were mixing entertainment with information in a spicy new way, and prospering; Alfred Harmsworth's *Daily Mail* was founded in 1896 and in four years became the first British daily paper to achieve a circulation of a million.

The firm center of the British people was the middle class. It was large and varied, from skilled workmen and small shop-keepers to bankers who hobnobbed with the aristocracy. The typical middle-class family lived in a solidly built terraced house, rather heavily furnished, with a piano in the sitting-room where they would often gather in the evening. Many had one of the new gramophones as well, and some were replacing their gas lights with electricity. A few private houses even had telephones. They could look forward to a century of progress. Most of their new comforts came from inventions of the previous twenty or thirty years, but already the twentieth century was producing fresh marvels such as radio and airplanes.

Britain was possibly the richest and most powerful country in the world. She had been the first to become industrialised in the nineteenth century. She had used this advantage to become 'the workshop of the world' and its financial center, and to build an unequalled world-wide empire with an unrivalled navy to protect it and the vital trade routes. Yet Britain was also typical of the other leading countries of the world. Indeed, Germany and the USA were already overtaking Britain in some important industries, though neither had a great overseas empire.

The leading nations were proud as well as confident. Nationalism had grown during the nineteenth century into the main driving force in European politics. As their countries became richer and stronger, peoples easily came to feel more important and even aggressive, and governments were tempted to encourage and exploit such emotions. Except for the USA and France, all the foremost nations had emperors or kings, and a monarch was a natural focus for loyalty, pageantry and splendid military displays. The pomp and ceremonial, the gold lace, scarlet coats and spiked helmets may seem to belong to a world that was past, very different from the world of radio, electricity, cars and airplanes that the new century

A British patriotic postcard of the years before 1914. To the music of one of the 'Pomp and Circumstance' marches composed by Sir Edward Elgar (1857–1934), words were written by A.C. Benson (1862–1924), and the result became almost a second national anthem. About this time the new German fleet was seen as a challenge to Britannia's naval might, and political speakers and newspapers were constantly calling for more and bigger battleships.

promised; but it all went to create a shining image of those few years that the British remembered as 'Edwardian' and the French as *la belle époque*, the beautiful time.

Social strains and national tensions

We have painted a rosy picture. It is all true, but it is not the whole truth. We could just as easily paint a dark one.

In Britain there were still masses of people living in semi-starvation and dirt. Some writers called them 'the submerged tenth', the people whom the rest of society ignored, neglected and despised, but there may have been many more. In 1899 war broke out with the Boers in South Africa, and the British government got two bad shocks. First, the Boers did so well against the British troops that it looked as if the mighty British Empire could be driven shamefully out of South Africa by a bunch of farmers. Secondly, when the government called for volunteers to form a big army for the duration of the war, very many of the men who offered themselves had to be rejected at their medical examinations; they were weak or diseased because they had been born and brought up in poverty. Some politicians asked themselves what sort of glory there was in an empire that could not feed its citizens, and how long it could last when they were not fit to fight for it.

Britain was still very much ruled by the upper classes. Three Parliamentary Reform Acts in the nineteenth century (1832, 1867, 1884) had given many men the vote, but many other men and all women had no say in electing Members of Parliament. Besides, since MPs received no pay, only men with other sources of income could afford to sit in Parliament. There were two great political parties that struggled for power, the Liberals and the Conservatives. On the whole, the Liberals were more ready to introduce reforms and the Conservatives were more anxious to conserve what was good and successful in British life, but both parties had passed important acts to improve housing, public health and conditions in factories over the last fifty or sixty years.

It was not enough. Probably they meant well, but these comfortably-off men could never really understand what problems the poor faced. A growing number of people argued that the whole economic system was wrong. *Capitalism*, as it was called, was based on the principle that people worked best for their own profit, and if they were entitled to keep what they could get in competition with others. Capitalism had been working for at least five centuries and its supporters claimed that it caused people to try hard and produce new things and that eventually this improved life for everybody. But its critics said that it just made a few people richer and more powerful while the poor remained downtrodden. They preferred *socialism*, which taught that all the main sources of wealth – such as land, mines, factories, railways – ought to belong not to private capitalists but to all the people; in prac-

A working-class couple in their home in the East End of London, December 1912. The room does not look miserable or dirty, but it is not affluent either; it seems cramped, and is probably their only living room. Clothes hang from the ceiling, the floor has rugs but no carpet or linoleum, and the cane seat of the chair on the left needs mending. The fireplace is small – the man almost hides it – but we can see tins, teapot and plates standing on the mantelshelf. The table is set for tea – possibly a reminder of how much the diet of the poorer British consisted of tea and bread. Many more of the British people resembled this man and woman than the ladies and gentlemen outside Harrods.

tice, this would mean that the state would be the owner and the government would manage all these industries and use the profits on behalf of the public. Basically it was a simple idea but in practice socialism could be very complicated and there could be many different varieties; for instance, some socialists would allow a certain amount of capitalism to carry on, or some would rather see the workers in an industry, not the state, owning the resources and organising co-operative management. Socialism was not a new idea, but by about 1900 it was growing much more popular in most European countries, and socialist parties were gaining strength in European parliaments.

There was only a tiny number of working-class MPs in the British Parliament when, in 1900, the Trades Union Congress decided to form, with some socialist groups, a new political organisation, the Labour Representation Committee, that would truly represent ordinary working people. In 1905 the Liberals came to power, and, in alliance with the small but growing LRC, won a general election in 1906. After this election the LRC MPs took the name of the Labour Party.

The new government set about doing more for the welfare of the weakest and poorest. In 1909 old age pensions began; they were small, but saved many old men and women from having to end their lives in the workhouse. This sort of welfare was not at all revolutionary. Germany and New Zealand, for example, had done something similar several years before. But in Britain it caused trouble because the Chancellor of the Exchequer, David Lloyd George, tried to raise the money for it (and for some new battleships) by sharply increasing the taxes on the rich. The Conservatives were enraged. They called it confiscation and robbery. The House of Lords refused to pass the Budget. It was a constitutional crisis, Commons against Lords, but after the Liberals won two general elections in 1910 the Lords were forced to give in. In 1911 the Lords lost the power to reject bills that the Commons had passed; they could only delay them for a limited time. The victorious Liberals went on to devise a compulsory national insurance scheme to protect people who lost their jobs or fell ill.

But prices were rising faster than wages, and workers were becoming more discontented. There were waves of strikes, and some of them were very serious, especially the railwaymen's in 1911 and the miners' in 1912. Women were complaining, too. For many years some of them had been demanding the right to vote on the same terms as men, and now a small number decided that peaceful argument had failed so they must use violence. They attacked MPs, damaged public property, chained themselves to railings and caused disturbances wherever they could; when arrested they often tried to starve themselves. To make their behaviour even more shocking, the leaders of these 'suffragettes' were well-bred ladies. What was British society coming to? King Edward VII died in 1910 and it looked as if the new king, George V, was inheriting a deeply divided and dissatisfied society.

Social problems were trouble enough, but nationalism was even worse. The Irish wanted Home Rule. Irish MPs in the British House of Commons had been demanding it for many years, and the Liberals were prepared to grant it. But every time a Liberal government had tried to pass a Home Rule Bill the Lords had rejected it. Now the Lords had lost the power to do that, and the Liberals promised a new bill which would give the Irish Home Rule at last. But if this pleased most of the Irish, who were Catholics, it had exactly the opposite effect on the Protestants of Ulster in the north. These people were the

Another piece of propaganda using the Union Flag, but this time it is linked with the Red Hand of Ulster, and its 'patriotic' appeal is for armed resistance to the British government's plans for Irish Home Rule in 1914.

descendants of Scottish and English settlers who had been 'planted' there three centuries before and had driven out many of the Catholic Irish to the barren lands of the west. The hatreds of those days had never been forgotten or forgiven. Now the Protestant Ulstermen swore that they would never accept Home Rule, because it would make them subject to the Catholic Irish. 'Ulster will fight, and Ulster will be right' was their cry, and they meant it. They smuggled in weapons and began to drill. By the summer of 1914 the British government was pledged to go ahead with Home Rule, but faced a civil war in Ireland if it did. To make matters worse, there was a lot of sympathy in Britain for the Ulstermen, especially among the upper classes, and several army officers let it be known that they would resign if they were ordered to use force against Ulster.

Britain's troubles could be described broadly as social discontent and nationalist grievance. The other great powers of Europe all suffered from one or both of the same ills.

The German Empire was the foremost military power in Europe. The people were prosperous, hardworking, well-educated and orderly. Germany was thirty years ahead of

Britain in looking after the aged and sick. But the German parliament, the *Reichstag*, did not have nearly as much control over the government as in Britain, and the emperor, Kaiser William II, had far more power than the British king. William gloried in military display, boasted and made warlike noises from time to time, and carried many Germans along with him, so that Germany got the reputation of being very fond of war. But many Germans thought that the Kaiser's militarism was an absurd and wasteful game, and wanted to see the Reichstag, not the Kaiser, control the government. In spite of several attempts by various ministers over many years to suppress them, the socialists became steadily more popular. By 1912 the German Socialist Party was the biggest single party in the Reichstag, and many members were sure that if the Kaiser did eventually involve Germany in a war, the mass of the German people would refuse to fight their fellow-workers of other nations.

The French Third Republic was less industrialised than Britain or Germany, but there was even more discontent among the industrial workers. From 1900 onwards there was a succession of big strikes, sometimes with sabotage and vio-

William II; born 1859, German Emperor 1888, abdicated 1918, died 1941. He presents a martial appearance though the left arm that rests on his sword-hilt had been crippled from birth.

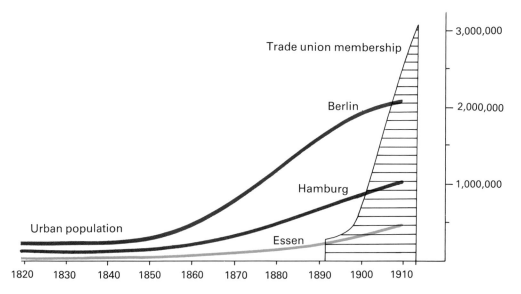

Rise in German trade union membership and urban population growth

lence, and some of the strike leaders hoped that these would grow into a general strike that would bring about a revolution.

There were plenty of people who said that French society was rotten at the top, behind its fashion and elegance. There were many cases of corruption, but the worst scandal of all was the Dreyfus affair, which lasted from 1894 to 1906. Dreyfus was an officer convicted of selling military secrets to Germany and sent to Devil's Island. But a few people noticed that there were one or two flaws in the evidence, and that Dreyfus was a Jew, came from Alsace, which was now part of Germany, and was personally disliked by other officers – just the man who could easily be 'framed'. Had Dreyfus been made to take the blame for the crime of somebody else? Accusations began to fly about, and there was an enormous political storm that went on and on. Dreyfus was given a pardon in 1899, but it was another seven years before he had his commission restored; the real culprit was a popular, fashionable, aristocratic officer with important friends.

What made such affairs so bitter was a tradition of hatred between political parties. It dated back to the massacres and executions of the French Revolution in the 1790s and had been kept alive by the bloody street fighting of the 1848 Revolution in Paris. More recently there had been the suppression of the Paris Commune of 1871, when both sides had slaughtered prisoners. The more conservative groups, the so-called Right, had never really accepted the idea of a republic and would still have preferred a king; they included most of the old nobility, the heads of the army and the Catholic clergy. Against them were the parties of the Left, republicans of various shades from moderate liberals to extreme socialists.

Possibly the only thing that united French society was another memory of 1871. Just before the Commune, France had been crushed and humiliated by Germany in the war of 1870–1. Most of the French still feared and hated Germany, and would unite in a war of *revanche*, revenge.

The Austro-Hungarian Dual Monarchy was another deeply divided state, though here the divisions were mainly between different nationalities. The two leading nations were the German-speaking Austrians, whose empire covered the western half, and the Hungarians or Magyars, whose kingdom covered the east. (The same man, Francis Joseph of the old Imperial Habsburg family, was both Emperor of Austria and King of Hungary.) The minority nations included Czechs,

'There is the enemy!' declares a French anti-clerical paper, with a vampire priest perched on the new Sacred Heart basilica. This had been built on the summit of Monmartre, Paris, to atone for the crimes of the Communards of 1871, but the Left protested angrily that in fact it was the Church's own Right-wing friends who had done most of the killing. Such memories made politics very bitter in the Third Republic.

Slovaks, Poles, Romanians, Croats, Serbs and Italians. Some of them were reasonably content, for the government was usually fairly easy-going, but there were always men who tried to stir up nationalist feelings among their own people and enlist sympathy abroad by means of speeches, newspaper articles and books. A few formed conspiracies. Though it was true that the Habsburg Empire had lasted as a patchwork of many peoples for several hundred years, it was also true that nationalism had become a much stronger feeling in all parts of Europe during the past hundred years, and there was no sign that it would die down. The Austro-Hungarian government had good cause to be worried, and looked suspiciously across the frontier to neighbours, especially the Serbs and the Russians, who might try to take advantage of unrest.

The Russian Empire was the biggest but, in some ways, the weakest of the great powers. It possessed vast lands, populations and resources, but its very size made it difficult to govern. In 1900 it was still a society of peasants and landlords, ruled by the tsar with absolute power; there was comparatively little industry, except in a few big cities, and no parliament. The tsar's ministers argued that they needed complete power, with censorship and secret police, to control such a huge empire; they remembered what had happened to Alexander II, 'the Tsar Liberator', who had freed the serfs in 1861 and intended gradually to introduce a form of parliament – his reward had been to be blown up by a revolutionary's bomb in 1881. At the back of their minds, the Russian upper classes dreaded a repetition of the peasant risings, 'senseless and merciless' as the poet Pushkin called them, that had blazed across the land in the seventeenth and eighteenth centuries. But some of them argued that Russia must make a real effort to catch up with western Europe, and that the best way to prevent revolution was to start a steady series of reforms, moderate but solid.

In 1904 war broke out with Japan. The tsar's government hoped that it would bring quick victories and rally all the people behind the tsar. But things went badly, trade slumped and prices rose. It was a miserable winter, most of all for the factory workers in the big cities who were wretchedly poor even at the best of times. In the capital, St Petersburg, on Sunday 22 January 1905, thousands of poor people came in procession to the Winter Palace to ask for help. They thought of the tsar as 'little father', and were sure that if only he knew what they were suffering he would do something for them. They came peacefully, led by a priest and carrying religious pictures. But the tsar was not even in St Petersburg and the square in front of the palace was lined with soldiers. They opened fire, the crowd panicked, hundreds were killed or injured – nobody knows how many. This was 'Bloody Sunday', and it set off what was nearly a revolution.

A Russian propaganda print of the Russo-Japanese War. The peasant soldier, summoned to join his regiment, kneels to receive the blessing of his family – father, wife, even smallest child – before going to fight for 'Holy Russia'. The title, printed in colloquial Russian such as peasants used, means: 'My child, you too must bless your father.' The artist does not disguise the poverty of the peasant's home, a simple wooden cottage with little furnishing beyond a big stove.

There were indignant, shocked protests all over Russia, but the government seemed too busy losing the war with Japan to realise the strength of feeling that all classes of Russians were expressing. By October 1905 there was a big wave of strikes, and at last the government saw that it would have to make real concessions. It promised to set up a *duma*, or parliament. By now this was not enough for many Russians. *Soviets*, or workers' councils, were formed in the main cities to organise more strikes, and there was a rising in Moscow. These actions were inspired by revolutionary socialists. They all failed, and their effect was to frighten more moderate reformers into accepting what the government offered. So from 1906 Russia had a parliament of sorts, though the tsar's ministers did not allow the duma much power. There were some improvements – better education, for example, and help for peasants who wanted to buy their own farms or migrate to Siberia. There was still dis-

'Bloody Sunday', 22 January 1905. A film reconstruction that emphasises the unfeeling grandeur of the Winter Palace, the blank expanse of snow, the menace of the dark, disciplined line of soldiers; and catches the moment of alarm and confusion as the crowd begins to flee. It was because so many Russians thought that the tsar's government had nothing to offer them but the cold repression shown in this picture, that there was nearly a revolution in 1905.

content, riots sometimes, and terrorist murders, but on the other hand many Russians now hoped that the country had begun to move in the right direction.

The Russian government also had problems with the non-Russian peoples in the empire. The native Siberian tribes were few and peaceful, and the Muslim nations of Central Asia, who had been conquered only about forty years before, were closely watched by the tsar's officials and soldiers. In Europe it was more difficult. The Poles, the Finns, the small Baltic nations and the Ukrainians all had more or less noisy independence movements that demanded concessions of varying importance, from the use of the native language instead of Russian on official documents to complete independence.

But if nationalism was in some respects embarrassing to the Russian government, it could also be useful. Like the Russians themselves, most of the nations of eastern Europe belonged to the great Slav family of peoples. Many of the smaller Slav

nations, especially if they felt threatened or oppressed, looked to Russia for support. This gave Russia many opportunities to intervene, if the tsar chose, across the eastern half of Europe.

These were the five great powers of Europe. Some other European states also played a considerable part in international affairs, and the kingdom of Italy, though not as large, rich and strong as the others, was often ranked with the great powers. Between them, they were the masters of the world at the beginning of the twentieth century.

The world outside Europe

In many lands across the oceans far from Europe there were European nations. They had grown from colonies. Most of them were Spanish-speaking or English-speaking. Among the latter, Canada, Australia, New Zealand and South Africa were self-governing countries that stayed in the British Empire because they wanted to. In these countries the whites had not inter-married with the original peoples, but treated them generally as inferiors who could either live their own lives on reservations or do unskilled jobs for the whites. The Spanish-speaking countries of South America, and Portuguese-speaking Brazil, had become entirely independent of the 'mother country' during the early nineteenth century, but on the whole they had not settled down very easily into peaceful and prosperous states. In these countries there had been a great deal more inter-marriage between different races and a high proportion of the people were *mestizo* – mixed – though the whites tended to remain in charge, and Latin-American civilisation was firmly rooted in the civilisation of Spain and Portugal.

The United States of America, alone among the ex-colonies, had grown big enough to rank with the great powers. However, the USA refused to become involved with Europe. She was prepared to intervene in the Pacific or in South and Central America, because her own prosperity and safety could be at risk if anything went wrong in those areas; but the USA was still preoccupied with absorbing millions of new citizens rather than with looking for new empires. The Americans were a rich mixture of European nations. Most of the earlier immigrants had come from the British Isles, Scandinavia and Germany, but by the early twentieth century the flood was from the Mediterranean and eastern Europe. They all learned to speak English and accept the Constitution that the thirteen original states had agreed upon soon after their War of Independence. They had all come to the USA because they thought that here they would have the freedom and opportunity to make their fortunes by working hard and using their brains. Though many Americans remained miserably poor, that was still the belief of most of them. In Europe, where the old aristocratic families still set the standards of correct behaviour and good manners in almost every country, people often made jokes about the boastful, clumsy Yankee. But they had to recognise that the USA was the busiest and most inventive place in the world, and European aristocrats were ready enough to marry the daughters of American millionaires.

That world was undoubtedly a white man's world, because the white man was so strong, and he was strong because of his industries and technology. This was particularly true in war: as the English poet Hilaire Belloc remarked,

'Whatever happens, we have got
The Maxim gun, and they have not.'

But was it possible for other races, brought up in civilisations so different from the European, to adopt their ways and become equally powerful technically and industrially?

Japan was the first to try. Almost from the first time that Americans and other Westerners forced their way in, during the 1850s and 1860s, Japan's leaders faced the unpleasant fact that Japan must learn Western technical skills in order to survive. By 1900 Japan had an efficient Western-style civil service, army and navy, and her industries were growing well. She joined the Western nations almost as an equal in bullying and robbing China. Finally, in the Russo-Japanese War of 1904–5, she fought one of the great powers and won. It was a victory that sent an electrifying message through Asia and beyond; a coloured people could beat the whites with their own weapons.

China had been obstinately slow to learn, and paid the price. The emperor and his mandarins had honestly believed that all foreigners were inferior barbarians, with nothing to teach the Chinese. So China had suffered one humiliating defeat after another, and had been forced to hand over great ports to the 'foreign devils' and to allow them to behave almost as masters of the country in large areas that were known as 'spheres of influence'. Naturally, Chinese of all classes, from the Dowager Empress (who was the real power behind the emperor) to the peasants and coolies, resented the foreigners bitterly; but the Boxer Rising in 1900, which was intended to drive the foreigners out, only proved that the Chinese were too weak to do it.

Meanwhile, though, a growing number of Chinese realised that they must learn Western ways. Hundreds, then thousands of students went to Europe or the USA; some remained there, but very many returned to China and convinced their friends that big changes were needed if China were to survive. Even some generals and ministers, and at one stage the emperor himself, tried to 'modernise' in various ways. But the Dowager Empress and her friends were far too strong for the reformers.

At last, in 1908, she died, and a small boy was left as emperor. The reforming ministers and princes seized control. They reorganised the civil service, the army and the educa-

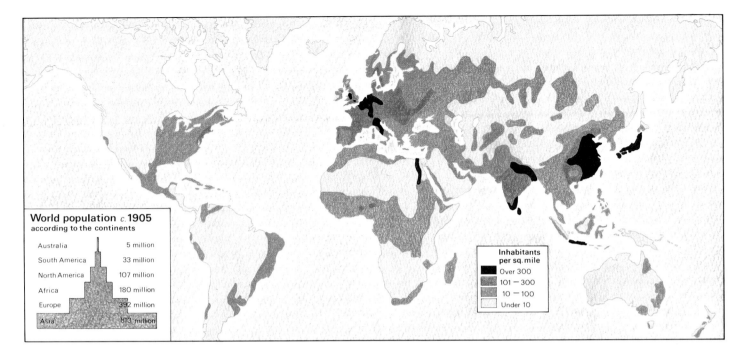

World population _c._1905
according to the continents

Australia	5 million
South America	33 million
North America	107 million
Africa	180 million
Europe	392 million
Asia	813 million

Inhabitants per sq. mile
- Over 300
- 101 – 300
- 10 – 100
- Under 10

World trade at the beginning of the twentieth century

Annual imports 1904

CHILE
ROMANIA
PORTUGAL
MEXICO
NORWAY
BRAZIL
EGYPT
TURKEY
SWEDEN
SPAIN
DENMARK
ARGENTINA
JAPAN
SWITZERLAND
CHINA
RUSSIA
ITALY
AUSTRIA–HUNGARY
BELGIUM
FRANCE
NETHERLANDS
USA
GERMANY
UK

Annual exports 1904

PORTUGAL
NORWAY
ROMANIA
TURKEY
CHILE
MEXICO
EGYPT
SWEDEN
DENMARK
BRAZIL
JAPAN
SPAIN
CHINA
SWITZERLAND
ARGENTINA
ITALY
AUSTRIA–HUNGARY
BELGIUM
RUSSIA
NETHERLANDS
FRANCE
GERMANY
USA
UK

Trends in world trade
Trade was increasing rapidly. Britain still had the largest share, but Germany and the USA were catching up.

	1885	1905
Total value of world's trade	£2900 million	£5400 million
Britain's share	18.1%	15.0%
British Empire's share	12.8%	10.8%
Germany's share	10.0%	11.3%
France's share	9.9%	7.1%
USA's share	9.3%	10.5%

(Imports from and exports to the United Kingdom are shown in red)

0   50   100
£million

tional system along Western lines. They built railways and encouraged modern industries. They set up local and provincial councils, and a national advisory assembly which met in Beijing (Peking) and planned to make way for a full Chinese parliament in 1913. They even managed to reduce the national disease of opium-smoking to a fraction of what it had been. And all this in a couple of years.

It was not enough for some of the Western-educated Chinese. Over the previous twenty or thirty years they had formed many small political groups, often in secret for fear of arrest or murder by government agents. They believed that reforms would not do. The whole imperial system of government must be swept away. There must be a republic. In the late 1890s a doctor called Sun Yat-sen, living in exile, succeeded in bringing many of these groups to agree to form one big movement that would be guided by three principles: nationalism, democracy, socialism. These people were not going to be satisfied with the imperial government's efforts.

The Chinese Revolution happened in 1911, almost by accident. In October government officials discovered the revolutionary movement's headquarters in Wuhan (Hankow). The revolutionaries either had to start a revolution immediately, or wait to be arrested. They decided to try to seize the local government offices – and there was no resistance! Nobody really cared enough about the old system to fight for it. The revolutionary take-over swept across the whole of southern China and an assembly met at Nanjing (Nanking) and elected Sun Yat-sen president. He now reorganised his movement as the *Guomindang* (*Kuomintang*), or Nationalist Party.

Northern China, however, did not accept Sun. The advisory assembly in Beijing that was preparing for the parliament preferred to appoint General Yuan Shikai (Yüan Shih-k'ai) as prime minister and then president (the boy emperor was declared to have abdicated). Obviously there was a danger that China would split into two rival republics, north and south. To prevent this, Sun recognised Yuan as the legal president of China, but he still remained the leader of the Guomindang.

So far everything had been remarkably peaceful, but it remained to be seen whether a parliamentary system could work in such a huge country that had not been prepared for it. Yuan called a Chinese parliament in 1913 but quickly dismissed it. He announced that he would remain president for ten years, and had plans to make himself emperor, but found he did not have enough support. Yuan died, disappointed, in 1916. It was beginning to look as though the reformers and revolutionaries had managed to wreck old imperial China,

'The Yellow Peril' as displayed in a picture made for Kaiser William II. St Michael, the warrior angel, summons the powers of the West to resist evil darkness spreading from the East. With drawn sword, Germany takes the lead, Austria supporting her and France at her side. Despite Russia's encouragement, Britain is not eager to play her part – probably a reference to the British friendship with Japan.

which had been collapsing anyhow, without being able to set up a new system that the whole of China would obey.

One thing was clear. The gigantic bulk of China was stirring. Japan had shown what an Oriental nation could achieve, and Japan was comparatively small. What if China and other Eastern countries, with their enormous populations, were to rise up and turn against the West? Some people in Europe talked nervously about 'the Yellow Peril' and of a threat to Western civilisation worse than the barbarian destruction of the Roman Empire. Britain was the only great power to have shown friendship for Japan during the Russo-Japanese War, but Britain had always feared Russian ambitions in Asia. Britain especially feared that Russia threatened India. In fact, the only serious threat to Britain's Indian empire came from the Indians themselves.

India, unlike China and Japan, had never been one united empire. It had been a sub-continent of many warring kingdoms and of rival cultures and religions when the British imposed their *raj* (or rule) in the eighteenth and nineteenth centuries. The British claimed that they were bringing peace and Western knowledge, but there had always been many Indians who did not seem to want them. The Great Rebellion of 1857, which the British called the Indian Mutiny, had come perilously close to smashing the British hold. The challenge in the early 1900s, though, was peaceful.

A great number of Indians were now educated in the British style, but the British still did not treat them as equals. These Indians saw no reason why they should not govern themselves, and in 1885 the Indian National Congress Party was founded, to work peacefully to persuade the British to give more power to Indians. But most of the members of Congress were Hindus, and Muslims distrusted them. In 1906 the Muslim League was founded; it sometimes acted with the Congress Party, but there was no love lost between the two.

The British, who boasted of their traditions of freedom and parliamentary government, could hardly deny the claims of the Indians. They took more of them into government jobs, and allowed a certain amount of local self-government by the Indian Councils Act of 1909. But they said that it would not be safe to go any further, because it was only British power that prevented Hindus and Muslims, for instance, from attacking each other. So they tried to impress everyone with the might and splendour of the British Raj by building a spectacular new

The Coronation durbar of George V at Delhi, 12 December 1911. It was such an overpowering mixture of Eastern and Western ceremonial that the Gaekwar of Baroda was confused and forgot to retire backwards from the King-Emperor's presence – he just walked away normally, to everybody's consternation. This magazine illustration of the incident was drawn from a newsreel that had been rushed at top speed to London and shown in the cinemas there as early as 30 December.

capital, New Delhi, near the old Mogul capital of Delhi, and by holding a very lavish coronation celebration, or *durbar*, when George V came to India in 1911. This did little to satisfy the Congress Party, or the growing number of Indian factory workers whose demands and strikes for better pay could easily be confused with anti-British demonstrations.

Of all the overseas possessions of the European nations,

Britain's Indian empire was by far the greatest and richest. What happened there might set the example for the rest. The British government had no intention of giving it up.

A worn-out civilisation?

If we had to decide which picture of Europe gave the truest understanding of how it was at the beginning of the century – strength and confidence, or doubt and division – we ought to bear in mind what the leading artists and scientists of the time were thinking and doing.

In Paris, which had become the most lively artistic center in Europe, many artists said that traditional European art had nothing more to offer, was dying of old age. They must break away, find something fresh. Some tried to begin again with art that was primitive and barbaric, not yet corrupted by civilisation. Some tried to get away from painting pictures that showed what people and things looked like – a camera could do that – and tried to reveal the geometrical shapes behind every thing (this idea was called Cubism), or to express their feelings with violent splashes of colour. Often such ideas could over-

lap; for example, one of these artists found a West African carving, 'a crude figure, a rough wooden cylinder whose arms and legs were four supplementary cylinders, surmounted by a globe in which were cut two slits for eyes. It had a squat nose, protruding thick lips chopped arbitrarily . . .' He showed it to his friends, saying that it was almost as beautiful as the Venus de Milo. They disagreed; one said it was just as beautiful; another said it was more beautiful. This last was a young Spaniard named Pablo Picasso, who was to become the most famous artist of the century.

below left: 'Self-portrait' (1907) by Pablo Picasso, 1881–1973, the most famous artist of the twentieth century. The apparent crudity of line and colour was intended to be a fresh, forceful method of artistic expression.

below: 'Cossacks', sometimes known as 'Battle' (1910–11) by Wassily Kandinsky, 1866–1944. Though it is possible to identify two mounted, sabre-wielding men on the left and three standing on the right (two holding spears) in front of a castle, this is mainly an abstract painting. The artist is trying to express ideas, feelings and atmosphere by the way he arranges lines and colours.

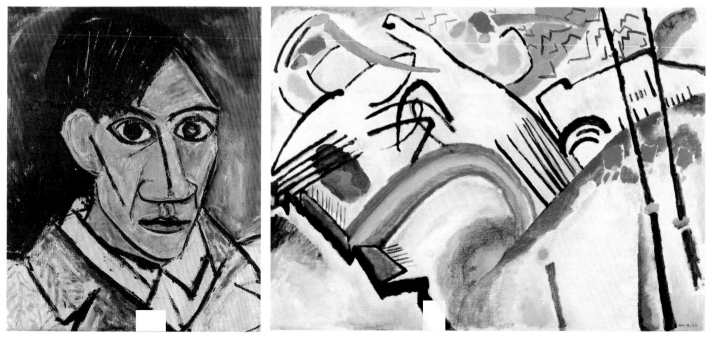

'Nude Descending a Stair, No. 3' (1912) by Marcel Duchamp 1887–1968. In an effort to interpret movement the artist took three successive photographs of the model as she came downstairs and then worked over them with ink, crayon, pastel and water-colour. He also tried to give Cubist solidity to the shapes in the picture. When this picture was exhibited in New York in 1913 it was furiously criticised as a grotesque distortion.

Other artists went to the opposite extreme, and worshipped the powerful machines that were going to shape the future – dynamoes, racing cars, battleships. They called themselves Futurists and delighted in noise and destruction. Their leader, an Italian named Marinetti, was so inspired by the beauty of the bombardment of Adrianople in 1912 that he wrote a poem:

TZANG – TUMB – TUUMB
Taratata ta pic-pac – pum – tumb
Pluff-pluff – flic-flac – tzing tzing – crooc-craac –
BOOM
TZANG – SITTTTT
TUMB – TZANG – TUMB – TUUUMB

Musicians too were trying to find new ways of expressing themselves, with strange, irregular rhythms and with sounds that were weird, harsh and discordant to audiences accustomed to Mozart or Beethoven. A few of them even gave concerts where the noise was intended to provoke the audience to riot; if the theatre got wrecked, the concert was a success.

Of course most people thought they were mad.

But what do you mean by madness? Scientists were raising some disturbing questions in their studies of psychology. The Russian, Pavlov, experimented with methods of changing the way dogs instinctively behaved in certain circumstances. These reflex actions had seemed to be part of the dog's nature, but Pavlov was able to 'condition' them to do something different. Would it be possible for psychologists to change a human in the same way? The Austrian Sigmund Freud suggested a new explanation of human behaviour which many people thought shocking. Freud had been trying to help patients suffering from hysteria, and developed a method of treatment known as psychoanalysis. It involved probing deep into the patient's mind, below what the patient was aware of. Freud believed that a person's actions and feelings and conscious thoughts were really formed in a deep, hidden part of the mind that he called the subconscious, and down here were all sorts of emotions and memories that the conscious mind had forgotten and buried. In the subconscious there could be fear, guilt or desire, for example, often associated with sex. Freud argued that when people tried to bury such things in their subconscious, the memories sometimes forced their way back in a twisted form that caused mental illness. Many people believed that Freud and other psychologists were bringing valuable new insights into the human mind, but others accused them of degrading man into some sort of creature that was not responsible for its actions. Where did this leave the old ideals of European civilisation?

Then the German scientist Albert Einstein undermined the

interpretation of the universe that Isaac Newton had put forward two centuries before, which everyone had accepted as the truth. Newton had shown a solid universe, with everything held in balance and working by unchanging scientific laws. (Newton also believed that the universe and its laws were the creation of the supreme intelligence, God.) Now Einstein said that nothing was fixed, except perhaps the speed of light. According to Einstein, we can understand one thing only in relation to other things, by comparing it with them. To take a very simple example, it is not accurate to say that a thing is big; what we mean is that it is bigger than some other things. That is what Einstein meant by *relativity*. It was when he applied this idea to everything that the scientific laws which had seemed permanent began to look a great deal less certain. At first only a small number of scientists fully understood what Einstein was suggesting, but it did not take long for the idea to spread among educated Europeans that scientists did not believe any longer in a reliable, clockwork Newtonian universe.

Even the solid earth was solid no longer. All matter was made of tiny atoms; most people had accepted this calmly for a long time. But was there really such a thing as solid matter? Einstein argued that matter was in fact a form of energy, and that atoms were held together by tremendous concentrated energy. If atoms could be destroyed, this would release the energy as a vast outburst of heat and light. Most people who heard about this idea had only a vague notion of what 'splitting the atom' or 'the mighty atom' meant, but some of the world's cleverest scientists took it as a fascinating challenge. Could it be done? Could they find out how to unlock such a terrific power?

During the opening years of the new century there were good reasons why Europeans should feel optimistic. They were well off and there was progress all around. The rest of the world respected and obeyed Europe. But there were also signs that the great powers were not as steady and strong as their rulers liked to proclaim. There was discontent among industrial workers, and socialist parties were growing rapidly. There were nationalist movements within states, and rivalries between them. Outside Europe there were signs that other peoples might not be willing to accept European superiority much longer; the East was learning Western skills. Finally, perhaps most important of all, some of Europe's most active minds in the arts and the sciences were trying to upset what had been accepted as obviously right.

2 The Great War of 1914–18

The descent into war

'The lamps are going out all over Europe; we shall
not see them lit again in our lifetime.'

The words are those of the British Foreign Secretary, Sir
Edward Grey. He said them on 3 August 1914. For a hundred
years there had been no great European war, but one was
beginning now.

Who was to blame? The argument still goes on, but probably there can never be a straight answer because the causes
were so complicated.

The map shows the main international rivalries and
alliances before 1914, but not how bitter the ill-feeling was
between some nations. France craved revenge for 1870–1
(page 11), and many other people disliked the militaristic
arrogance that Germany displayed. Britain resented the way
Germany was challenging her everywhere – in trade, by plant-
ing colonies in Africa and, most blatant of all, building a very
powerful navy. Germany resented the way Britain seemed to
think she had a right to the lion's share of everything. In eastern Europe Austria and Russia had been rivals in the Balkans
for a century; Austria feared Russia's habit of acting as 'big
brother' to other Slav peoples, while Russia feared that she
would lose prestige if she failed to help them when they were
in trouble.

On the other hand, governments did not allow such traditional likes and dislikes to decide their policies. Austria and
Italy were old enemies, and so were the ruling families of
Austria and Germany, the Habsburgs and the Hohenzollerns;
but Germany, Austria and Italy thought it wise to form the
Triple Alliance, to defend one another from possible attacks
by others. Britain and France had been enemies since Norman
times and had nearly fought again as recently as 1898, over
territory on the Upper Nile; but after 1904 they formed an
Entente (understanding). Both countries boasted of their love

The German satirical journal 'Simplicissimus' printed this
cartoon. Germany is shown resting comfortably, with pipe and
beer, reading the newspaper. Dangerous beasts crowd round
his bed, most obviously the British lion, the Russian bear and
the French cock. But are they real? The German caption says:
'Undisturbed by scaremongering in the sensational papers,
Germany is better able than ever to view the future with
complete tranquility.' Yet there were many Germans who did
believe that they were being 'encircled' by hostile powers.

of liberty and regarded Russia as the home of tyranny; but
France had been allied to Russia for ten years as a counter to
Germany and Austria, and soon they brought Russia into the
Entente.

The two groups of great powers were defensive, and did not

21

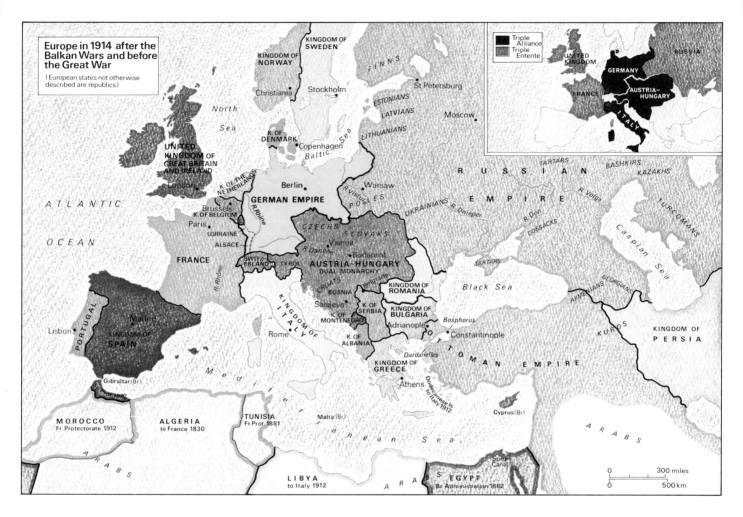

Europe in 1914 after the Balkan Wars and before the Great War
(European states not otherwise described are republics)

make war inevitable. However, whenever there was a big international dispute they tended to behave like opposing teams, and each time the losers felt less like giving way next time. One trouble-spot was Morocco, which France wanted to add to her North African empire and where Germany had valuable trading links; there were international crises about it in 1905–6 and 1911, and the Entente gained most from both of them. Another trouble-spot was the Balkans. In 1908 Austria formally annexed Bosnia, which she had been occupying for many years; Russia objected, but this time Austria and Germany won.

Another possible source of danger was the size and readiness of European armies. Except for Britain, which relied on the Royal Navy to prevent invasion as it always had done, every great power conscripted its young men for a year or two's military training, so that in time of war it would be able to mobilise huge numbers of trained men into the army. Generals believed that wars were won by size and speed. To have a chance of victory, a country must mobilise a big army quickly and strike hard. There was no time to spare, so detailed plans must be worked out in advance, to meet any possible enemy. For safety, the great powers made ready to fight, and this involved the whole public. In Britain, for example, speakers and newspapers stirred up a 'scare' that German spies were everywhere, and there were popular novels about the future war with Germany.

There were attempts to lessen the danger. International conferences to try to reduce armaments were held at the Hague in 1899 and 1907. They failed in their main aim, but they produced the Hague Convention which limited the methods of warfare that civilised states were supposed to use, and they set up the International Court where states could take their disputes to be settled by arbitration.

It may be that some Europeans were attracted by the idea of war, but few would have denied that the most fiery of all were the Balkan peoples. Ever since the Greek War of Independence in the 1820s European statesmen had been bothered by what they called the Eastern Question – what was to happen to the different parts of the Ottoman Empire as it cracked apart. By 1900 most of the Christian nations of the Balkans were free from the Turks, but not satisfied; they all thought themselves entitled to lands that some of their neighbours had got. Their latest outburst was a complicated scrimmage known as the Balkan Wars, 1912–13, which left Turkey and Bulgaria brooding over their losses while the Serbs, Greeks and Romanians were cock-a-hoop over their gains. It was a Serb who began the events that led directly to the Great War.

On 28 June 1914, Archduke Francis Ferdinand, the heir to the Austrian throne, visited Sarajevo, the chief town of Bosnia. He was murdered by a student called Gavrilo Princip. Princip had been trained by the Black Hand, a secret society sworn to bring all Serbs together within a greater Serbian state; their motto was 'Unity or death'. So was this crime the work of a mere terrorist gang, for which nobody else could be blamed? The Austrian government thought not. They had good reason to believe that the Serbian government had known about the plot and had done nothing to stop it. The Serbs had been annoying the Austrians for many years and it was time to teach them a lesson. Austria demanded heavy compensation, with humiliating conditions attached. Serbia agreed to some of the terms but not all, and began to mobilise her army. Austria accepted the challenge and declared war on 28 July.

Russia felt bound to save Serbia. Germany must support Austria. Every European statesman saw the danger. The events of the next week have been studied by historians hour by hour and minute by minute, and still it is not clear why war

Archduke Francis Ferdinand, heir to the Austro-Hungarian throne, with his wife Sophie, smiling and gracious as they visited Sarajevo on a fine summer day in 1914. Soon afterwards they were both dead – as it turned out, the first deaths of the Great War.

could not be prevented. Perhaps the critical moment was when the first big mobilisation began, because then nobody dared risk delaying. Russia began mobilising on 30 July, Austria on 31 July, France and Germany on 1 August. Leaders on all sides were sending urgent messages with suggestions to stop things slipping further, but each one seemed to arrive just too late. The generals may have been willing to fight – after all, that was their duty – but the politicians seem to have had the nightmare feeling of sliding, despite their struggles, down a slope where none wanted to go.

On 1 August Russia failed to reply to a German ultimatum, so Germany declared war on her. Two days later Germany declared war on France and German armies swept westwards, into Belgium.

The opening attacks

Germany put herself completely in the wrong by invading small, neutral Belgium, and it was probably this that finally made the reluctant and divided British government decide

The Schlieffen Plan
The idea that France or Germany might attack through the Low Countries had often been discussed by the military experts. The French High Command judged that their Plan 17, a direct attack on Lorraine and Alsace, would bring them victory if Germany attempted any such movement.

1st Army
2nd Army
3rd Army
4th Army
5th Army
6th Army
7th Army

NETHERLANDS
BELGIUM
LUX.
GERMANY
LORRAINE
ALSACE
R. Seine
R. Aisne
R. Marne
Paris
Verdun
French main forces
FRANCE
SWITZERLAND

⇦ Approx. German lines of advance proposed by Schlieffen, 1905: 36 corps in the great wheeling attack, only 5 to hold Lorraine and Alsace.
← Approx. lines of advance in Aug. 1914: 5 armies in the wheel, 2 to hold Lorraine and Alsace (and allowed to attack after repelling French offensive)
···· Line of trench warfare

just enough time to scrape together reserve armies. On 5 September, as the Germans, tired and somewhat disorganised, reached the River Marne, almost within sight of Paris, the French attacked and drove them back. They retreated to the River Aisne, and then held their ground. The Schlieffen Plan had come very near success, but when it failed Germany lost her chance of a quick victory.

As soon as the armies came to a standstill they started to strengthen the positions they found themselves in. The soldiers had learned by bloody experience how easily magazine rifles, quick-firing artillery and, most of all, machine-guns could massacre troups on open ground. The only sensible thing was to dig in. Each army rapidly constructed lines of trenches from which its own soldiers could safely shoot down any enemy foolish enough to charge against them.

Each side naturally tried to get round the other's flank, and neither succeeded. The effect was that both sides extended their positions sideways, and the armies were so big that the trenches soon stretched virtually unbroken from the Channel to Switzerland. It was going to be very difficult for either side to move.

There was no decision in the east either. The Russian attack was smashed by the forces of the veteran General Hindenburg, who became the idol of Germany. Further south the Russian and Austrian armies seemed to be fairly evenly matched, and the Austrians failed to finish off the Serbs in their native mountains. Neither side had much reason to celebrate as 1914 ended.

When the war began there had been cheering in the streets of all the capitals. The French cried 'To Berlin!' and the Germans 'To Paris!' They all expected to have won by Christmas. A few people refused to fight, for conscientious reasons, but many more were sure that their war was righteous and that God was with them. Some socialists said that the war was only a struggle between the ruling classes, greedy, rich capitalists trying to grab more wealth, and that workers should not shoot their fellow-workers of other nations. But most, whatever they may have said before the war, were loyal to king and country when the fighting started. Now they had to get used to the idea that it was not going to be brisk glorious adventure but a long squalid test of endurance.

With the five leading states of Europe locked in war, several other countries decided that they had most to gain by joining

to declare war on 4 August. Why did Germany do it? The reason was the Schlieffen Plan. General Schlieffen, Chief of Staff of the German Army from 1891 to 1905, had worried about what Germany could do if she had to fight a powerful enemy on the east and on the west at the same time – Russia and France together. He could see only one answer – knock out one quickly, and then deal with the other. Russia was too big to be overwhelmed quickly, but France was not. However, France was well prepared along her frontier with Germany. The only possible solution was to outflank the French defences by striking through the Low Countries. There were practical difficulties and it was morally wrong, but it gave the best chance of saving Germany and ending the war quickly, which would save thousands of lives.

Schlieffen's plan had been modified by other generals so that the striking force was made weaker; and now more troops were withdrawn from it to go and stop the Russians, who were attacking in the east quicker than had been expected. Then the Belgian army and the British Expeditionary Force that had been rushed across the Channel put up a stout resistance and delayed the German advance. This gave the French

in. Turkey sided with the *Central Powers* (as Germany and Austria were known) in October 1914; this meant that Russia and Britain would now have to fight along the Caucasus and the Suez Canal respectively, and that the sea route between Russia and her western allies by way of the Black Sea and Bosphorus was closed. On the other side, Italy withdrew from the Triple Alliance in May 1915 and attacked Austria, opening another new front along the southern edge of the Alps. Later the other Balkan states joined in, Bulgaria with the Central Powers and Greece and Romania with *the Allies* (as Britain, France and Russia were known). Portugal also decided to help her old ally, Britain. Thus it was certainly a great European war. Because the great powers of Europe had empires and other interests all over the world, other parts of the world were drawn in too, and it became known as the World War. However, the fighting in other continents was slight and unimportant compared with the struggle of the gigantic armies in Europe, and nobody doubted that it was there that the war would be decided.

Stalemate and attrition

Along the European fronts, especially in France as we saw, the war took on the appearance of a vast siege as modern weapons gave the defenders an enormous advantage over the attackers. Neither side could advance. It was stalemate unless somebody could think of a way of getting round or smashing through the enemy lines.

The Allies were much stronger than the Central Powers at sea, and this gave them a chance to choose a new place to attack. They dared not risk a landing on the German coast, but they thought that Turkey would be less formidable. Their plan was to force a passage through the Bosphorus to the Black Sea and link up again with Russia, to take Constantinople and to knock Turkey out of the war. It might have worked, but it was hopelessly mismanaged. The Allied forces failed to pass through the very first strait, the Dardanelles, and failed to take the peninsula that commanded it, Gallipoli. For most of 1915 British, Australian and New Zealand troops tried vainly to break through, suffered heavy losses and at last sailed away. The Allies could not get round the Central Powers.

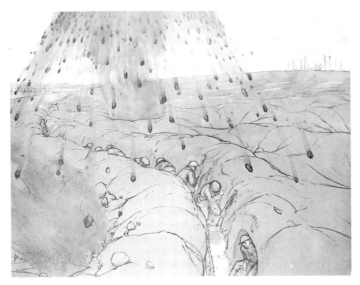

above: *War artists were officially appointed to record the scenes of what was being called the greatest war in history. In this picture the desolate landscape, the danger and the miserable conditions of trench warfare on the Western Front are caught by the British war artist H.S. Williamson.*

right: *One of the new weapons intended to break the deadlock of trench warfare. A British tank going into action; drawing by war artist Muirhead Bone.*

Airplanes could be used both to scout and to photograph what they discovered. Here are two air photographs of the same place, a farm on the Western Front with the rather confusing name of Gallipoli. The first is dated 26 June 1917; the second, where nothing remains but shell-holes, is dated 3 September 1917.

Could more and better arms overcome the trenches? On both sides scientists and technicians strove to improve equipment and invent weapons. Motor cycles, cars, trucks and ambulances were made in thousands. Armoured cars had been thought of long before, but British engineers had the idea of giving them caterpillar tracks, and invented the tank. It was an excellent idea, and tanks did rumble and crash their way through German trench systems; but they were too few and too liable to mechanical breakdowns to deliver the mighty blows needed to break the stalemate.

Under the pressure of war, aircraft were also developed rapidly. The long-range airships designed by Count Zeppelin dropped bombs on London and other cities, but they were clumsy and vulnerable, and their bombs were too small and inaccurate to damage important targets. Airplanes proved much more useful. Fast, agile little machines were built to scout and fight, and bigger planes with greatly increased range and endurance to carry bombs. Airplanes caught people's imagination, and the fights in the sky had a sporting and chivalrous spirit that was sadly lacking in the trenches below. But, with all their improvements, aircraft were still too weak to decide battles on land or sea.

There were other new weapons, including poison gas and flame-throwers, which surprised and terrified the enemy at first. But the enemy always found a way of dealing with them, and their only effect was to make war on both sides even more horrible. Mainly the generals had to pin their hopes on 'more and bigger'. If they could batter the enemy hard enough, they must surely break his line somewhere. Both sides thought the same. They drafted every fit man into the army and blazed away fantastic quantities of shells and bullets. The destruction and slaughter were immense, far more frightful than any previous war in history. But neither side could break through.

So the war became simply a matter of the two sides wearing each other down. This was called attrition. What it meant was that sooner or later one side would lose so many men that it would not be able to fight any longer. The Allies had more men than the Central Powers, so their leaders felt sure of winning. But it turned out that the Central Powers were rather better at this bloody contest than the Allies, and so it dragged on while hundreds of thousands died.

'The Harvest of Battle', by British war artist C. Nevinson.

There was another way in which the Allies could try to wear down the Central Powers – blockade. They could use their sea power to stop all overseas supplies. Sooner or later the Central Powers would run short of munitions and food, and would be starved into surrender.

The new German navy was strong, but not strong enough to defeat the British. The two main fleets fought a battle only once, on 31 May 1916; the British called it Jutland, the Germans the Skaggerak. The Germans fought well, and actually inflicted heavier losses than they suffered, but they were lucky and glad to escape to their harbours and never risked another battle. The German navy's real answer was to develop a new form of naval warfare by using submarines to blockade Britain. Before the war nobody had guessed how far it would be possible to range in the improved submarines, but they were soon able to surround Britain and wait ready to sink any ship heading for a British port. The Germans' difficulty was that a U-boat (Unterseeboot) was very weak when on the surface, and many merchant ships as well as warships now carried guns. So the German government announced that their U-boats would not surface and warn their victims; they would sink without warning any ship heading for Britain, whatever the ship's nationality.

Unrestricted submarine warfare, as it was called, broke internationally agreed rules of sea warfare. The German government argued that these rules had been drawn up before submarines were developed, and did not cover the new situation. They also said that the British blockade of Germany was illegal, because it was starving civilians as well as soldiers. Whatever the legal rights, though, it was the Germans who were actually sinking neutral ships, while the British were only stopping them. Feelings began to mount in the USA as their ships, sailors and passengers went down. Germany knew the danger that this might eventually bring the USA into the war, but also knew that Britain was becoming perilously short of food and supplies. In 1917 she decided to take the risk, and renew an unrestricted U-boat blockade.

In fact, this was 'total war', a fight not just between armies but between whole nations. Every man who was not fighting was doing essential work, and women were employed in all sorts of jobs that men used to do – the armament factories depended on thousands of women filling shells with explosives

TWELVE MONTHS OF "KULTUR."

("There are already, thanks to William the Bloody, in Europe more than 5,000,000 corpses and nearly 7,000,000 wounded. What will the victorious nations do in this war?" Le Matin.)

ENLIST

far left: *This British cartoon uses a 'horror' technique to cast blame and hatred upon the Kaiser personally and the German nation; after a year of war, the Kaiser glories in the death and destruction he has caused – this is true German* Kultur, *civilisation. From 'The Passing Show', 21 August 1915.*

left: *This American recruiting poster of 1917 uses a 'tear-jerking' technique to arouse pity and indignation, and to convince doubters that the USA was righteous in declaring war. The drowned mother and child are helpless, innocent victims of Germany's lawless and cruel U-boats.*

and making fuses. With nations straining like this, and with the casualty lists growing until there was hardly a family that had not lost a father or son in the trenches, people blamed the whole enemy nation and hated them all. In Britain, for example, some people refused to listen to music by 'evil' composers like Beethoven; shops owned by people with German-sounding names were wrecked; and the royal family adopted the name of Windsor, while some of their relatives changed from Battenberg to Mountbatten. The Russians changed St Petersburg to Petrograd and the Germans sang a 'Hymn of Hate' against the wicked British. This sort of nationalist hysteria was deliberately whipped up by propaganda, especially 'atrocity stories' about the cruelty of the subhuman enemy. Probably the civilians hated the enemy more than the soldiers did. The common soldiers in the British and German armies often felt respect and sympathy for each other; after all, they were both being forced to go through the same horrors.

The fall of empires

1917 was the year of crisis. Every nation was feeling the strain. Britain was within a few weeks of running out of food. In Germany there were strikes because of the food shortage. After heavy defeats there were mutinies in the French army and the Italian army nearly fell to pieces. But the Russians were suffering worst of all. Russian soldiers had a well-deserved reputation for brave, patient loyalty, but they had suffered appalling losses because they were short of weapons, medicine and food, and were often badly led; at last even they began to lose faith. At home, as the shortages became worse, the poor were in a desperate plight; the duma, usually meek and mild, began to speak out and accuse the tsar's government of bringing ruin on Russia.

On 8 March in Petrograd workers went on strike and there was rioting. Troops were ordered to fire on the rioters; they refused. The tsar was away, attempting to rekindle confidence among the troops at the front. He tried to get back to the capital, but everywhere he found that the soldiers would not obey him. They had had enough – of hardship, of war, and finally of the tsar. Nicholas II had always believed that there was an unbreakable bond of trust and love between him and the Russian people, especially the soldiers. At first he could not believe that they would reject him. When he saw that they had, he was helpless. The duma announced that it did not recognise the tsar's government any longer, and set up a Provisional Government of its own. Broken and bewildered, Nicholas II abdicated on 15 March. In one city, in one week the Tsardom of all the Russias had been thrown down.

The Provisional Government was a mixed group of liberals and moderate socialists, full of good intentions but with no experience of running a country. They promised land to the peasants, self-government to Poland and Finland – everyone would be free and prosperous. But first the war must be won. That was their fatal mistake.

Other groups claimed to speak for the Russian people. Soviets (page 12) had sprung up again in many cities. They claimed to have the workers and soldiers behind them, while the Provisional Government was made up of the middle class who understood nothing and cared less about ordinary people. Within the soviets the more extreme socialists gained influence, and among them were many revolutionaries who had been living in exile and who now flocked back to Russia. Vladimir Ilyich Ulyanov, was one of the best-known of these; it was usual for revolutionary writers and conspirators to assume nicknames, and his was Lenin. He led a branch of the socialists who called themselves *Bolsheviks*, meaning the majority.

Everything went wrong for the Provisional Government. There were more defeats at the hands of the Germans, the army and the workers could not see much improvement since the fall of the tsar, and meanwhile the tsar's supporters recovered from their shock and plotted to restore him to power. In Petrograd nobody trusted the Provisional Government any more, and most people probably did not know what to believe or how things could be made better. But Lenin and the Bolsheviks knew exactly what they wanted. The Petrograd soviet, under their control, had called a national congress of representatives from all soviets to meet early in November.

Bolsheviks storm into the Winter Palace – the most dramatic incident of the October Revolution, as reconstructed in the Soviet film 'October'. There was in fact very little fighting.

On the night of the 7th, their men stormed into the Winter Palace, where the Provisional Goverment were still talking about what to do, and took them prisoner; there was very little fighting, because few soldiers were willing to defend the government. Next day the congress of soviets met and declared that the Bolshevik Party was now the government of Russia; Lenin's men moved into the main government offices and started to give the orders.

This swift take-over has become famous as the October Revolution. Russia was still using the Old Style or Julian calendar, so that what the rest of Europe called 7 November was 26 October in Russia. Those few days in Petrograd changed the whole course of world history, but for the moment we shall look only at the effect on the Great War.

Lenin knew that he must have peace at any price, and so did the Germans. At the Treaty of Brest-Litovsk, 3 March 1918,

Germany forced Russia to give up Finland, Estonia, Latvia, Lithuania, Poland, the Ukraine and Transcaucasia; in theory these were now free to set up as independent states, in practice Germany intended them to supply much of what she needed, like wheat from the Ukraine. Many German troops had to stay to make sure of this, but many could now be transferred from the Eastern to the Western Front.

But though the Central Powers had knocked out Russia, the biggest of the Allies, they could see that they would soon be hopelessly outnumbered. In April 1917, mainly because of the U-boats (page 27), the USA had joined the Allies. Very soon US ships were helping the British navy to escort merchant ships across the Atlantic, and as the convoy system developed the U-boats lost any chance of starving Britain. It would be just as hopeless for the Central Powers on land as at sea, once the Americans organised themselves for war and sent big armies to the Western Front. In March 1918 the German generals made a desperate attempt to snatch victory before this could happen. The sudden attack caught the British off guard, and for a few days it looked as though their front might collapse. But the German army could not keep up the pressure long enough; between March and July they made great ad-vances but did not destroy the Allies, so now only a miracle could save the Central Powers from defeat.

The smallest, Bulgaria, gave up first. Then it was the turn of the Ottoman Empire which had never had the resources and efficient organisation necessary in a modern war of this size. Also, the Arab peoples who lived in the southern part of the empire were eager to get rid of Turkish rule. As British forces advanced from Egypt into Palestine, desert warriors from Arabia helped them to drive the Turks northwards. On 30 October 1918 the Turkish government signed an armistice with the Allies; by this time the Arabs were setting up independent states and it was clear that the Ottoman Empire was shattered beyond repair.

Austria-Hungary went next. Here again the 'subject peoples' proved a fatal weakness. Many soldiers of these nationalities had no intention of dying for the Austrians or Hungarians, and were glad to surrender or desert to the Russians or Italians when they got the chance. Thousands of these men enlisted in the Polish, Czech or Yugoslav (mainly Serb) legions, fighting for the Allies, who promised to make their nations fully independent. At last the strain was too much for the Habsburg monarchy. The government signed an

Allied and Central Power deaths during World War I

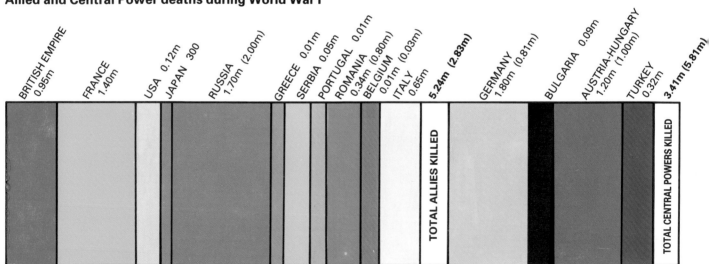

BRITISH EMPIRE 0.95m · FRANCE 1.40m · USA 0.12m · JAPAN 300 · RUSSIA 1.70m (2.00m) · GREECE 0.01m · SERBIA 0.05m · PORTUGAL 0.01m · ROMANIA 0.34m (0.80m) · BELGIUM 0.01m · ITALY 0.65m (0.03m) · TOTAL ALLIES KILLED 5.24m (2.83m) · GERMANY 1.80m (0.81m) · BULGARIA 0.09m · AUSTRIA-HUNGARY 1.20m (1.00m) · TURKEY 0.32m · TOTAL CENTRAL POWERS KILLED 3.41m (5.81m)

Figures in brackets show civilian deaths. The 5.81 million civilian deaths among the Central Powers includes 4.0 million killed during civil wars in Turkey.

armistice on 3 November, the emperor abdicated and the empire fell apart. The Czechs and Slovaks set up the new republic of Czechoslovakia. The southern Slav peoples were grouped with the old kingdom of Serbia as the new kingdom of Yugoslavia. Italy and the new republic of Poland got those lands where most of the people spoke Italian and Polish respectively, and the people of Transylvania voted to join Romania. This left Austria and Hungary as two separate small republics. The Habsburg Empire vanished, leaving the Danube basin as a region of small states with new, sometimes unsettled, frontiers.

Germany, which had become more and more the driving force of the Central Powers as the war went on, was last to give in. The German Empire consisted only of Germans, and did not fall to pieces. But the army was being pushed back steadily by the Allies, the navy was in a state of mutiny and civilians were on the verge of famine. Many German politicans had been arguing for peace, and now the generals agreed with them. Some of them proclaimed on 9 November that the Kaiser had abdicated and a republic was being formed. The Kaiser accepted the situation, and fled to the Netherlands. On 11 November, at 11 a.m., the Armistice between Germany and the Allies came into effect, the Western Front fell suddenly silent and the Great War was over.

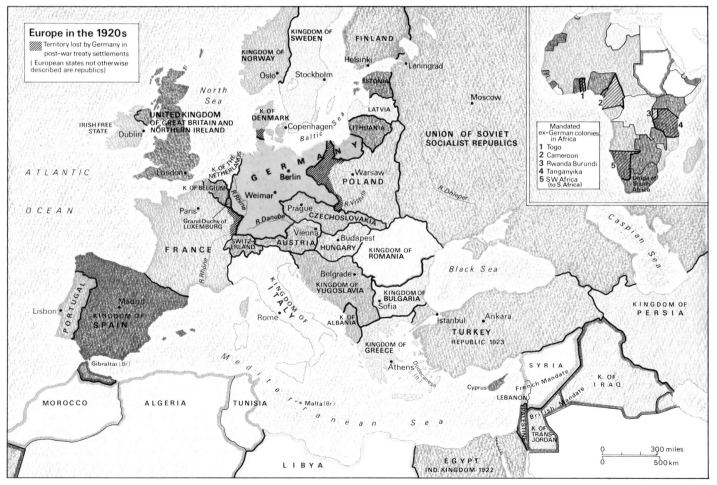

Europe in the 1920s

////// Territory lost by Germany in post-war treaty settlements
(European states not otherwise described are republics)

Mandated ex-German colonies in Africa
1 Togo
2 Cameroon
3 Rwanda Burundi
4 Tanganyika
5 S.W.Africa (to S.Africa)

The peace settlements

Never again! That was the feeling throughout Europe and America, and the man who most fully expressed it was the American President, Woodrow Wilson. A former professor of constitutional law and history, he tried to lay down principles that would ensure that the peace would be just and would last. He listed the famous Fourteen Points in January 1918. Both the Allies and the Germans accepted these on paper in November 1918 as the basis of the Armistice and future peace settlement. Wilson's main ideas were:

- Every nation should be independent, and should include all people speaking the national language. (Wilson mentioned by name several of the states that were springing up from the wreckage of the old empires.)
- The seas must be free and safe for merchant ships, and customs fees should be reduced.
- Claims to colonies must be discussed and settled fairly, bearing in mind what would be best for the natives of the colonies.
- Armaments must be reduced.
- Secret deals between governments must end; from now on international diplomacy should consist of 'open covenants openly arrived at'.
- Finally, all this should be upheld by a League of Nations preserving peace and protecting each of its members.

But many of the Allies thought that the best way of ensuring peace was to punish those who had begun the Great War and make them powerless to fight again. Austria and Turkey were broken to pieces but Germany, the most dangerous of all, remained united. Those who thought this held the whole German nation responsible for the war and all the terrible losses; with a sense of perfect justice, they set out to hurt and humiliate the Germans.

The German peace treaty was signed in 1919 at Versailles. The place had been chosen deliberately because that was where the German Empire had first been proclaimed in 1871. Germany had to give lands to France, Belgium, Denmark, Poland and Lithuania – and lost all her colonies. The German army and navy lost all heavy weapons and were reduced in numbers, so that they could do no more than watch the borders and keep order inside Germany. Over the next thirty

From 1914 to 1918 the 'Daily Mail' had tried harder, probably, than any other British newspaper to inflame war fever and hatred of the Germans. As this poster shows, its attitude had not softened in 1919, when peace was being signed.

years Germany must pay huge amounts of money and goods as 'reparations' to the Allies for all the losses she had caused them. For the next fifteen years Allied troops would occupy the Rhineland, and German troops must never again be stationed there, so close to Belgium and France. Finally it was declared that Germany was guilty of starting the war and waging it in a barbarous manner, and the ex-Kaiser and other leading Germans should be tried for these crimes (this, in fact, was never done). In vain the German delegates, who represented the new republic, protested. They were forced to sign

At the treaties of St Germain and Trianon peace was signed with the new small republics of Austria and Hungary respectively, and the new arrangement of their former empire was recognised. Turkey was more difficult; the sultan's government had to put up with the loss of their empire at the Treaty of Sèvres in 1920, but when Greeks tried to take part of the Turkish homeland of Asia Minor fighting broke out again. The Turks drove out the Greeks, and peace was eventually agreed at Lausanne in 1923. By then the sultan had been deposed and Turkey too was a republic.

On 3 June 1919, 'Simplicissimus' printed a German view of the peace 'negotiations'. Germany, like a condemned criminal, is about to be guillotined by a man who had never concealed his desire to smash Germany, the French Prime Minister Clemenceau. The British Prime Minister, Lloyd George, looks on sternly, holding the peace treaty which gave his country so much. The American President Wilson, garbed as a clergyman, explains to the victim with unctuous hypocrisy: 'You, too, still have a right of self-determination: do you want to have your pockets emptied before or after your death?'

When the war began, all of central and eastern Europe and the Middle East had been dominated by four great empires. Now all were gone. Of the old great powers only Britain and France remained, battered but victorious. Austria-Hungary had ceased to exist, Germany was crushed, Russia was slipping from revolution into civil war. The great imperial ruling families had fallen, too. Was there to be a new Europe, setting an example of democracy, freedom and peace to the world?

Some such feeling was behind the setting up of the League of Nations in 1920. With its headquarters at Geneva in neutral, peaceful Switzerland, the League would provide a sort of international parliament where representatives of the member nations could discuss problems and reach agreements. There would also be special offices, like departments of an international civil service, to administer some duties that the League would undertake – looking after refugees, for example, trying to stop the smuggling of drugs, and, through the international Labour Organisation, comparing and improving working conditions in many parts of the world. The League could also entrust particular duties to member countries, and it handed over Germany's former colonies and some parts of the former Turkish Empire as *mandates,* mainly to Britain and France; this meant that the territories did not become parts of the British or French empires, but that the British and French should train the natives to rule themselves and become independent as soon as possible.

It was a bold, ambitious scheme. For the first time in history there was an organisation that aimed to look after the peace and prosperity of the whole world. It depended entirely on good-will. The hope was that all nations would eventually join, and that the strongest ones would lead and give most help. One weakness was that the League had no military force behind it, but people hoped that no nation would feel able to defy world opinion. A vote in the Assembly of the League, they hoped, would probably cool hot tempers. Another weakness was that many countries did not belong to the League, so that it did not in fact speak for the whole world. Even the USA refused to join; rejecting Wilson, the Americans decided that it was not their duty to get involved in other people's problems and opted for an attitude known as 'isolationism'. There was nothing that the League could do to compel nations, because the League was founded on the idea that every nation was free.

Despite its lack of force, the League began well. During the first few years it settled a number of border disputes among small countries, and there were various international agreements to restrict armaments and not to attack one another. Pious hopes, perhaps; but it was also possible that 1914–18 had taught statesmen that modern warfare had become too destructive to be used again.

Who started the Great War?

Was it one particular nation state?

(Accusations in the left-hand column;
Defence arguments in the right.)

1 SERBIA

A Serbia encouraged fellow Slavs to revolt against Austrian rule because she hoped to break up the empire and enlarge her own territory.

B Serbia knew of, and did not prevent, the plot to murder Francis Ferdinand.

C Serbia provoked war by rejecting the most important terms of Austria's ultimatum.

A It was only natural that Bosnians and other Slavs wanted freedom from Austrian rule.

B Some Serbians may have encouraged the plotters, but the government was not involved.

C Austria's demands would have destroyed Serbia's independence.

2 AUSTRIA – HUNGARY

A Austria seized the opportunity to force war on Serbia in order to crush what she had long regarded as a threat to the empire.

B Austrian demands were encouraged by the army; Conrad von Hötzendorff, Chief of Staff, was particularly keen on decisive action.

A The assassination threatened both Austrian and European stability. Austria had to take firm steps to get at the root of the trouble and check Serb nationalism.

B The soldiers saw this as a purely local problem, with no reason for other powers to step in.

3 RUSSIA

A Russia wanted to preserve her power in the Balkans, and her influence in Serbia, particularly after her failure in 1908.

B Russia's mobilisation to support Serbia against Austria forced Germany to stand by her ally, thus widening a local conflict.

A Russia could not let down her ally and allow Austria to bully a small Slav nation, as she had been forced to in 1908.

B Russia was concerned only to check Austria, which was already bombarding Belgrade. There was no need for German alarm.

4 GERMANY

A Germany had sought to dominate Europe by military strength since 1871, and especially under Kaiser William II.

B Germany also sought naval dominance, upsetting Britain and creating tension.

C Germany's Triple Alliance started the division of Europe into armed camps, which only needed an incident to cause widespread conflict.

D Germany's Schlieffen Plan for war meant involving France and other neutral countries in an east European conflict.

E Germany encouraged the Austrians to solve their problems by crushing Serbia, promising German support if Russia came to Serbia's aid.

A Germany sought only her rightful place in the center of European politics. Since she was dangerously encircled she needed strong forces.

B Germany needed colonies and naval strength just as much as Britain.

C Germany's alliances were defensive only.

D In her weak, encircled position, Germany must end the danger of war on two fronts by destroying one enemy as speedily as possible.

E It was Germany's duty to help preserve the Austro-Hungarian Empire in the face of Serbian and Russian threats, which could lead to its break-up.

5 FRANCE

A France encouraged and financed Russia because she sought *revanche* and the recovery of Alsace-Lorraine.

B The French-inspired Entente encircled and threatened Germany.

A Alsace-Lorraine was part of France, and she could not abandon the people there.

B France and Russia created the Entente in response to Germany's aggressiveness and alliances.

6 BRITAIN

A British commercial, colonial and naval interests resented Germany's growing industrial strength and naval building program.

B Britain joined France and Russia in 1914 in a quarrel that was none of her business, helping to prevent a quick victory for Germany.

A Germany's rapid naval build-up and the Kaiser's determination to interfere in areas where Britain had traditional rights alarmed Britain.

B Britain had promised naval help to France, and British public opinion was horrified by the attack on Belgium. Germany's war plans were devised without taking account of Britain anyway.

Was it one particular class in all nations?

7 CAPITALISTS

Those who profit from armaments and from exploiting overseas possessions naturally welcome war, and encourage warlike policies.

Those with most money and property have most to lose. Industry and trade will be disrupted. Few capitalists welcome war.

8 IMPERIALISTS

Rivalry between the great powers over overseas possessions, trade, railways, naval power, etc. caused tension and conflict in many areas and prepared everyone for war.

There have always been clashes over colonies. But the war began in Europe, not overseas, and the first countries concerned had no colonies.

9 MILITARISTS

Armies and navies were growing ever larger, more highly skilled and expensively equipped. Chiefs of Staff like Conrad von Hötzendorff in Austria, von Moltke in Germany and Fisher in Britain hoped to use these powerful weapons at the best possible moment from their own point of view. This tight planning and emphasis on striking quickly prevented statesmen from taking time to seek a peaceful solution.

Armaments, mass armies and careful planning of possible campaigns showed fear of others, not aggressiveness. It was the politicians who used the weapons, not the military.

10 THE PEOPLE

The half-educated prejudices of the common man influenced policies in democratic states, and even the most autocratic ruler had to respect public opinion, which had no time for the subtleties of diplomacy and demanded clean, forceful solutions.

Popular attitudes were the product of government leadership and propaganda, and of the media controlled by capitalists and warmongers.

11 THE PRESS

Most people now could read, but were not well enough educated to be critical. Journalists and novelists made money by providing sensations, stirring up national pride and hatred of foreigners.

Writers only provide what the public wants.

12 DIPLOMATS

The system of secret alliances and understandings brought about war before anyone realised the danger.

The war was an outcome of many different causes, not one alone.

The next-of-kin of British soldiers and sailors killed in the Great War were given bronze plaques like this, 12 cm (5 in.) across and suitable for setting into a memorial stone. As on the 'Land of Hope and Glory' picture (page 7) Britannia and the lion are the most prominent part of the design, but the mood has changed.

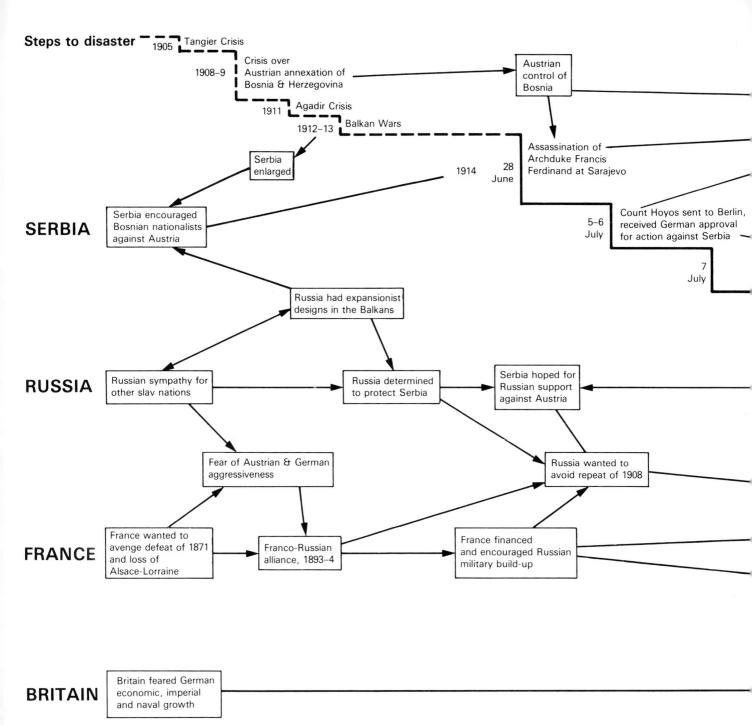

Steps to disaster

1905 Tangier Crisis

1908-9 Crisis over Austrian annexation of Bosnia & Herzegovina

1911 Agadir Crisis

1912-13 Balkan Wars

Austrian control of Bosnia

Serbia enlarged

1914 28 June

Assassination of Archduke Francis Ferdinand at Sarajevo

5-6 July Count Hoyos sent to Berlin, received German approval for action against Serbia

7 July

SERBIA

Serbia encouraged Bosnian nationalists against Austria

Russia had expansionist designs in the Balkans

RUSSIA

Russian sympathy for other slav nations

Russia determined to protect Serbia

Serbia hoped for Russian support against Austria

Fear of Austrian & German aggressiveness

Russia wanted to avoid repeat of 1908

FRANCE

France wanted to avenge defeat of 1871 and loss of Alsace-Lorraine

Franco-Russian alliance, 1893-4

France financed and encouraged Russian military build-up

BRITAIN

Britain feared German economic, imperial and naval growth

AUSTRIA

GERMANY

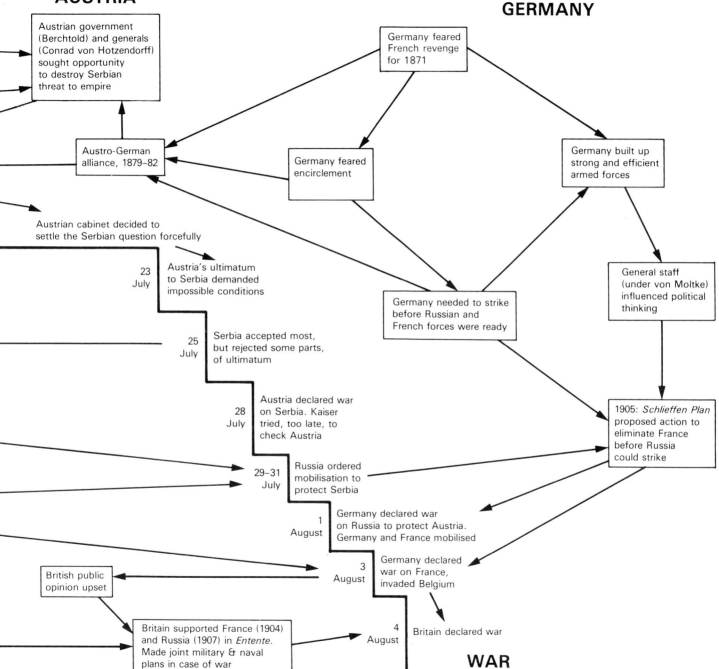

Austrian government (Berchtold) and generals (Conrad von Hotzendorff) sought opportunity to destroy Serbian threat to empire

Germany feared French revenge for 1871

Austro-German alliance, 1879–82

Germany feared encirclement

Germany built up strong and efficient armed forces

Austrian cabinet decided to settle the Serbian question forcefully

23 July — Austria's ultimatum to Serbia demanded impossible conditions

General staff (under von Moltke) influenced political thinking

25 July — Serbia accepted most, but rejected some parts, of ultimatum

Germany needed to strike before Russian and French forces were ready

28 July — Austria declared war on Serbia. Kaiser tried, too late, to check Austria

1905: *Schlieffen Plan* proposed action to eliminate France before Russia could strike

29–31 July — Russia ordered mobilisation to protect Serbia

1 August — Germany declared war on Russia to protect Austria. Germany and France mobilised

British public opinion upset

3 August — Germany declared war on France, invaded Belgium

Britain supported France (1904) and Russia (1907) in *Entente*. Made joint military & naval plans in case of war

4 August — Britain declared war

WAR

The peace treaties and their consequences

What did the peace treaties achieve?

Like most important questions, this one can only be answered if we look at other questions first.

1 What exactly did the treaties lay down? **(The terms)**
2 Why did they make these terms? **(The origins)**
3 What did the terms lead to? **(The results)**

This table deals with these questions for each of the treaties.

The treaties

Terms	Origins	Results
BREST-LITOVSK 3 March 1918 Russia and Germany		
Russia gave up Poland, Finland, Baltic states, Ukraine and Transcaucasia.	Germany determined to weaken Russia and to get control of the resources in the territories that Russia gave up. Lenin determined to make peace at all costs in order to preserve Bolshevik power in what was left of Russia.	The Bolsheviks held on to power. They rejected the Treaty as soon as Germany was defeated. Ukraine was reoccupied, 1919, and Transcaucasia soon afterwards. A new frontier with Poland was settled after a war in 1920, but in 1939 eastern Poland was reoccupied after agreement between Stalin and Hitler. The Baltic states were re-absorbed in 1940. Finland remained independent, though it ceded territory to Russia in 1940.
VERSAILLES 28 June 1919 Germany and the Allies		
1 The Covenant of the League of Nations 'to promote international co-operation . . . peace and security.'	President Wilson's plan for an international peacemaking organisation.	USA refused to join. The League had little real power, and never worked well in dealing with major international problems.

2 *Territory in Europe*
  2.1 Alsace & Lorraine returned to France.
  2.2 Eupen & Malmédy ceded to Belgium.
  2.3 Schleswig's future to be settled by plebiscite.
  2.4 Upper Silesia to be partitioned by plebiscite.
  2.5 Parts of eastern Germany transferred to give Poland a corridor to the Baltic Sea.
  2.6 Danzig became a free city under the League of Nations.
	France determined to regain 1871 losses. Compensation for Belgium's sufferings. Wilson's ideas of national self-determination. Poland needed this industrial area.
	
	Wilson's '14 Points' had promised Poland access to the sea.
		This was clearly revenge for France and Belgium, and punishment for Germany. Plebiscites took place only when they were likely to go against Germany. She argued that Germans elsewhere had the right to opt for German rule. Many Germans lived in the Corridor and Danzig. Disputes over these led to Germany's invasion of Poland and the Second World War in 1939.

3 *Territory outside Europe* Germany surrendered all her colonies.	Old imperialist rivalries, together with Wilson's ideas about self-determination for colonial peoples.	Ex-German colonies became League of Nations mandates, with special rules to ensure good government. Began general move towards decolonisation. Germany complained she had been unfairly penalised.

Terms	Origins	Results
4 *War Guilt, Clause 231* 'Germany accepts the responsibility . . . for causing all the loss and damage . . . as a consequence of the war imposed . . . by the aggression of Germany and her allies.'	The bitterness of war, and determination to make Germany pay for all the loss and suffering. Wartime propaganda assumed Germany alone was responsible.	As historians revised ideas about the causes of war, Germany could claim that the whole peace settlement had been based on a lie. Many people in other countries sympathised with Germany, so the 'appeasers' agreed that the treaty should not be enforced.
5 *Reparations* 5.1 Germany had to pay for all the losses and damage of the Allies, eventually assessed at £6,600 millions. 5.2 Germany to hand over merchant shipping, coal supplies and farm stock to countries which had lost their own through the war.	This followed from the assertion of Germany's guilt, the loss and suffering of the war, and the idea that making Germany pay would prevent her financing rearmament.	These clauses soon appeared not only unfair but economically unsound. They helped wreck both the German and the Allied economies. They led to breakdown of German industry, inflation, and support for extremists like the Nazis. Elsewhere they helped add to unemployment. Germany asked for postponements and loans, and never paid most of the reparations.
6 *Disarmament* 6.1 German army limited to 100,000. 6.2 No conscription. 6.3 No air force. 6.4 Naval ships strictly limited in number and size; no submarines. 6.5 The Rhineland to be occupied by the Allies for 15 years, and permanently demilitarised. 6.6 Germany never to unite with Austria.	This was intended both to avert the danger of Germany launching another war, and as a starting-point for general disarmament. 6.4 preserved Britain's naval lead. 6.5 gave France a protective barrier.	Germans complained that they were deprived of the means of defence, but no one else gave up forces or weapons. The clauses were difficult to enforce, and very soon the Germans found ways to avoid them. From 1933 Hitler openly defied them, reintroducing conscription (1935), building up the air force, navy and submarines, and marching into the Rhineland (1936).

St GERMAIN   10 September 1919   Austria and the Allies

1 Recognised the break-up of the Austro-Hungarian Empire and the independence of Czechoslovakia, Hungary, Poland, Yugoslavia. 2 Army limited to 30,000; reparations to be paid. 3 Union of Austria and Germany forbidden.	Serbia had long sought South Slav (Yugoslav) independence under her own leadership. The Allies during the war encouraged Czechs and Poles to seek independence to weaken Austria. Leaders like Masaryk (Czech) had already brought these new states into existence by the end of the war. Wilson's ideas on national independence encouraged them. The other clauses punished Austria for war guilt and made sure she would not quickly recover strength.	Eastern Europe was left with many new states, frontiers and problems. Austria became a tiny state, with one-third of its people living in Vienna and railways that led nowhere. Much economic disruption. All the new countries suffered from problems of minority nationalities, causing disruption. They needed protection, and sought to make alliances among themselves and with powerful countries.

NEUILLY   27 November 1919   Bulgaria and the Allies

Bulgaria gave up its outlet to the Aegean Sea, paid reparations, limited its army.	Balkan rivalries; Greece and Serbia (now Yugoslavia) gained at Bulgaria's expense.	Bulgaria only too ready to ally with Hitler's Germany to recover her losses.

Terms	Origins	Results

TRIANON   4 June 1920   Hungary and the Allies

Hungary separated from Austria, lost three-quarters of its territory to Czechoslovakia, Yugoslavia, Romania.	Nationalist movements within the former empire. Czech encouragement of Slovak nationalism, and Serbian encouragement of Croats.	Hungarian resentment at being dismembered in order to create artificial new states led to willingness to side with Hitler's Germany, particularly in demolishing Czechoslovakia.

SÈVRES   20 August 1920   Turkey and the Allies

1 Turkey gave up the Arab lands in the Middle East: Hejaz became independent under Arab rule; Syria became a French mandate; Mesopotamia (Iraq), Palestine and Transjordan became British mandates. 2 Cyprus given to Britain. 3 Rhodes and Dodecanese Is. given to Italy. 4 Thrace and Smyrna given to Greece.	The Arabs had been encouraged to revolt during the war, and promised their own kingdoms after it. France and Britain had long-standing strategic interests in the Middle East, and oil was becoming important. They had already made a provisional partition of the area in 1916. Greece and Italy demanded their share of the pickings from the destruction of the old Ottoman Empire.	Arab hostility soon turned against the mandatory powers. Iraq won independence, 1927; Syria, 1945. Palestine was split by Arab-Jewish hostility. In Turkey, a nationalist movement led by Mustafa Kemal rose against the government that accepted the humiliating peace terms, particularly the handing over of some of Asia Minor to the Greeks. The nationalists drove out the Greeks.

LAUSANNE   24 July 1923   Turkey and the Allies

Turkey accepted most of the Sèvres terms, but did not have to cede land to the Greeks.	Nationalist defeat of the Greeks and threat to fight the Allies rather than accept humiliating terms.	A success for Kemal's nationalist dictatorship, set a pattern for inter-war dictators and use of force.

Europe faced many problems in the years between the wars

How far were they a result of the peace treaties?

The war itself caused economic disruption, destruction of industry and resources, and loss of the most useful manpower. Some economic problems like trade depression would have arisen even without a war, but the peace treaties were directly responsible for many problems:

1 resentment over loss of territory, one-sided disarmament restrictions, and the burden of reparations;
2 border disputes;
3 national minorities placed under foreign rule;
4 interference with patterns of trade and transport, so that producers had no markets and railways led nowhere.

One result was that many countries turned to dictatorship as the most effective way to solve the problems.

Why were these mistakes made?

1 Partly because the peacemakers claimed to be guided by high principles, but could not overcome their own and their people's hatred and fear of Germany. So what they did was often contradictory and seemed hypocritical.
2 Partly because the peacemakers were subjected to many pressures and had to accept what had already happened. For example, new states had already emerged from the old Austro-Hungarian Empire even before the war ended. Many countries in desperate need of economic help towards recovery expected to get it from the resources of defeated Germany.
3 Partly because the peacemakers disagreed on what they were trying to do. Wilson thought the old Europe should be

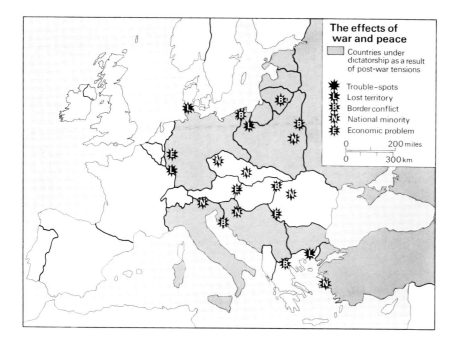

The effects of war and peace

Countries under dictatorship as a result of post-war tensions

Trouble-spots
Lost territory
Border conflict
National minority
Economic problem

0   200 miles
0   300 km

replaced by one redesigned on sound principles of national self-determination and democratic, peaceful co-operation. Clemenceau and the French people were anxious that Germany should never again be able to threaten the peace of Europe or the security of France. Lloyd George sought a realistic settlement that would satisfy as many people as possible; but the British Press and electorate wanted to squeeze Germany 'till the pips squeak'. All wanted to preserve Europe from the dangers of future war and from unrest that might lead to the spread of Bolshevik revolution. The result was a compromise settlement. So nobody was completely satisfied, nobody really believed in the peace settlement, and some were left with deep grievances.

Was the settlement unfair?

Germans thought so. Clause 231 said Germany had caused the war, so she must be made to pay and given no chance to make war again. The Germans never believed that. German historians investigated the causes of the war, and were soon able to argue convincingly that it was not wholly Germany's fault. Soon, many people, even in the victorious countries, came to agree that Germany had been unfairly blamed and unfairly punished. So they made efforts to 'appease' the Germans when they complained, instead of enforcing the peace terms. Germany was therefore able to disregard first the

reparations clauses, then the disarmament clauses, and finally the boundary changes. And that led to the Second World War.

Many other countries thought the treaties were unfair because they did not get all they hoped for and all they had suffered for in the war. Italy had been promised control of the Adriatic Sea. The Arabs had been promised their own states. Some nationalities found themselves under foreign rule, for although the Allies seemed to be promising self-government to all nations it was not possible to draw a simple line on a map separating one from another. Germans were left under Polish or Czech rule. Hungarians were under Czech or Yugoslav rule. Ukrainians were under Polish, Czech or Russian rule. Croats and Austrians were under Yugoslav or Italian rule.

But could any treaty have been fairer to all these without being unfair to others?

Could any treaty have been 'fair'?

Would it have made a difference if Germany had been treated more generously, as defeated France was treated in the Treaty of Vienna of 1815?

Would it have made a difference if Germany had been treated more severely, carved up and ruined economically, as she was after the Second World War?

Certainly, very soon almost everyone was blaming the peacemakers for their mistakes, their hypocrisy and humbug. Perhaps the peacemakers helped to bring about the Second World War; but perhaps also those who condemned them and wanted to change what they did helped to bring it about.

Why was there an October Revolution?

The name may be misleading – it was really the Bolsheviks seizing power in a revolution that was already eight months old. And for many years before, Russia had been full of fears – and hopes – of revolution.

Why?

The full answer lies far back, in the way Russian society evolved over the centuries. By the nineteenth century it was roughly like this:

The materials of revolution – Russian society in the nineteenth century

The whole vast empire was almost entirely rural, sometimes primitive.

THE TSAR was a complete autocrat; he did not need the consent or advice of anyone; his will was law.

But there were important towns, and in a few places industries were developing.

THE OFFICIALS existed to carry out the tsar's commands. Besides the army and navy, there was a vast civil service, including secret police and censors. This bureaucracy was often slow and sometimes corrupt, but Russians were always aware that it was there.

THE NOBLES were obliged to serve the tsar in the forces, diplomatic and civil services; the tsar could make or break any of them. But they enjoyed great privileges and power over the peasants on their estates.

THE MIDDLE CLASSES included merchants and craftsmen, lower officials and smaller landowners, and now a growing number of factory owners. Compared with the middle classes in western Europe, they had little influence. But they were often well educated and were growing more numerous and wealthy.

THE PEASANTS were the vast bulk of the Russian people. Most were miserably poor. They had few rights against the government or their landlords – many were serfs until 1861. The population was growing, so they had more mouths to feed and their desire for land became more urgent. Farming methods were mainly old-fashioned, but they lacked the money and the knowledge needed for improvements. Riots against local landowners were not uncommon, but they revered their tsar and Church.

THE INDUSTRIAL WORKERS were becoming much more numerous in the late nineteenth century, though they were still very few compared to the peasants. They were often crowded together in big cities, with poor pay and under squalid conditions.

Any society, being made of people, is constantly stirring and adjusting. This was true of Russia, even if it seemed a rigid, unchanging place when compared to western Europe. Even if very many Russians had cause to want improvements, did this make revolution inevitable? Or could there be steady, gradual reforms instead?

The pressure increases, 1825–1905

The early nineteenth century was the great age of liberalism, romanticism and revolutions (1820, 1830, 1848) throughout Europe. Educated Russians shared these feelings.

> **1825** The Decembrists, the earliest Russian revolutionaries; a group of army officers tried to seize power in St Petersburg to make Russia a constitutional monarchy. It was ill-planned and a complete fiasco.

But the new tsar, Nicholas I, was alarmed. From now on any sort of criticism was sternly suppressed. Political parties were not allowed, police spies were everywhere and even the mildest disagreement with the government earned a term of exile in Siberia.

> All this forced opposition underground, and led a number of educated Russians, especially students, to think that there was no chance of reform and that violent revolution was the only way forward. Some of them believed that murder and terrorism were right, in order to destroy the tsarist state.

The reforming tsar, 1861–81

Nicholas I's iron grasp held Russia quiet while the rest of Europe was swept by revolutions in 1830 and 1848. But when he died in 1855 the next tsar, Alexander II, thought that reforms were needed, and that he would use his power to change Russia from above. **1861** saw the emancipation of the serfs. Later the tsar reformed the system of justice, set up local councils (*zemstvos*) and planned to introduce a limited form of parliament.

> Discontent continued, however. Freedom did not make the peasants less poor – sometimes they were worse off, with rents and repayments to make. Many nobles and officials disapproved of the reforms, many would-be reformers said they were not enough, and extreme revolutionaries feared that the reforms might succeed and thus prevent a revolution.
> **1881** Alexander II, 'the Tsar Liberator', was murdered by revolutionaries.

Silver 10-kopeck piece of 1861, with the double-headed imperial eagle on one side. (Diameter 1.8 cm, 0.7 in.)

Repression, 1881–1905

From now on the tsars and their ministers felt sure that reforms would merely be seen as weakness, and they clamped down hard. But they also tried to make practical improvements: railways, more industry and peasant emigration to Siberia were encouraged.

> Whatever the government did made no difference to the revolutionary groups, but demands for reform became steadily stronger among the middle classes as they became richer yet saw no sign of getting their voices heard. By the beginning of the twentieth century the three most important illegal political parties were:

> THE SOCIAL DEMOCRATIC PARTY, founded 1898, held the socialist theories of Karl Marx, believed that the capitalist system was bound to collapse and the industrial workers (or proletarians) take control. They tried to spread their ideas among these workers – they themselves, like most of the revolutionaries, were usually educated and middle class. The leaders were almost all exiled abroad, but kept their influence through their writings. **1903** the party split between the MENSHEVIKS (minority – though actually there were more of them) and the more extreme BOLSHEVIKS (majority) led by Lenin.

> THE SOCIAL REVOLUTIONARY PARTY was formed in 1901 from several old-established revolutionary groups. Their main concern was for the peasants, though they were not peasants themselves and found it hard to organise recruits in the countryside. They believed in terrorism, and murdered many prominent people.

> THE UNION OF LIBERATION, organised in 1903, brought together middle-class liberals who wanted reforms but not revolution. While the SDs and SRs were small parties, this was large and contained many wealthy and respected people.

NICHOLAS II became tsar in 1894; pleasant, well-meaning, convinced that it was his duty before God to rule as an autocrat for the good of his people, he was much influenced by his wife. The tsar's secret police infiltrated most of the revolutionary groups and sometimes even encouraged them as a way of keeping a sort of direction over their activities and making them less dangerous.

Revolution and reform, 1905–14

As the twentieth century began there was no sign that the tsarist government was softening, nor that the revolutionaries were giving up, while the reform movement was stronger. There seemed to be a balance, or stalemate. Could this go on indefinitely, or could a sudden extra strain produce a breakdown?

1904: the Russo-Japanese War broke out.

The government hoped that it would inspire the people to rally behind the tsar, and that some quick, glorious victories would strengthen the tsar still more.

> Instead there was nothing but defeats, while hardship increased for workers and peasants.
> **22 January 1905**: 'Bloody Sunday' in St Petersburg, when troops shot people peacefully trying to petition the tsar.

The Revolution of 1905

> Indignation blazed all over Russia, and the protests turned into strong, persistent demands for reform.

March: the government gave way, a little. The reforms it offered included a *duma* (parliament), but with no powers beyond giving advice.

> It was too little. Demands for reform grew louder. There were workers' strikes and peasant riots.
> **October**: general strikes in many areas paralysed the main cities. In St Petersburg the first *soviet* (workers' council) was set up.

The government offered more concessions in its October Manifesto, including a duma with real powers.

> This satisfied many, though not all of the liberals. The revolutionary groups tried to go on with strikes and risings.
> **December**: rising in Moscow, several days' fighting and many hundreds dead before troops put it down. The continued violence caused more moderates to back the government in restoring order.

Thus the government now felt secure enough to use troops freely to put down disorder and to allow the 'Black Hundreds', pro-government volunteers, to terrorise districts where there had been risings.

Tsar with duma, 1906–14

May 1906: just before the first duma met, the government felt strong enough to proclaim its Fundamental Law, which stated that the tsar still had full autocratic powers and restricted the part a duma could play. Next year it altered the electoral system, to give more representation to the wealthier people, less to peasants and workers.

But at the same time the chief minister, Peter Stolypin, carried out limited but solid reforms that improved agriculture, industry and education.

> New moderate parties formed from the Union of Liberation decided, after some doubt, to sit in the duma and try to push the government to make more reforms. A few had socialist views, but they did not publicly admit to any connection with SDs or SRs.

> Social Demoorats: the the Bolsheviks kept up their revolutionary propaganda from exile, the Mensheviks were more ready to get sympathisers into the duma.

> Social Revolutionaries went on as before. One of them shot Stolypin in 1911.

Was Russia now becoming a reformed tsarist state, so that the demand for revolution was dying away? Or were the reforms too little and too late? There were some strikes and peasant riots, but nothing like 1905; the most serious discontent had nothing to do with social conditions – it was the growing demand for self-government by minority nations in the empire, such as Finns and Poles.

So was the 1905 Russian Revolution now safely over, or had its final stages merely been postponed?

We cannot know the answer to the last question, because the Great War made everything so much worse.

Silver rouble issued in 1913 to mark the third centenary of the Romanov dynasty. It bears the portraits of the first Romanov tsar and of Nicholas II, who was destined to be the last. (Actual size.)

War and revolution, 1914–17

The impact of war, 1914–17

As in 1904, the government in 1914 expected a great surge of patriotism. At first they were proved right.

The duma gave its full support to the fight against Germany and Austria-Hungary.

Socialists were bitterly disappointed that Russian workers put their nation first. The Bolshevik exiles practically gave up hope.

The war went very badly. In 1914, 1915 and 1916 the Russians launched offensives which began with victories and ended with shattering defeats and gigantic losses. At the same time the imperial court was losing its subjects' respect; the tsarina was completely under the influence of religious cranks, especially a wild, disreputable monk named Gregory Rasputin. In December 1916 some nobles murdered Rasputin, which only increased the feeling that things were falling apart.

Dismay and disgust made the duma bold; it challenged the government openly and forced some ministers to resign. Meanwhile hardship and shortages were making the poorer people desperate, and the repeated disasters were making the soldiers distrust their commanders.

The revolution of 1917

March (February Old Style): strikes and riots broke out in Petrograd, and troops refused to stop them.

The tsar abdicated.

The duma appointed a Provisional Government. This assumed power.

The revolutionary groups had not planned this. They were surprised, like everybody else.

The tsarist system was ended. A new elected government had taken authority. The revolution had happened. Why did Russia not settle down now under the new government?

The Provisional Government was unprepared, inexperienced, composed of different parties who kept arguing. It intended to carry out reforms, giving more land to the peasants, but put them off while it tried to win the war.

Soviets were formed in many cities. They were encouraged by revolutionary groups who argued that the new government and the duma represented the middle classes, not the workers and peasants.

April: Bolshevik leaders returned from exile; they had been allowed to cross Germany in a sealed railway coach, as the German government expected them to damage Russia's war effort. They worked to get their people into the soviets and become their leaders.

June–July: the Russian offensive began well, ended in disaster – the same old story. Troops and people felt that nothing had really changed.

July: the Petrograd soviet, led by the Bolsheviks, tried to take over the city. The rising was put down by troops loyal to the government, and the Bolshevik leaders imprisoned.

Kerensky, a socialist, was now head of the Provisional Government. He feared a revival of support for the tsar among army officers, and hoped to use the Bolsheviks against them.

September: General Kornilov tried to take Petrograd to 'rescue' the government from the soviet, but not enough troops supported him.

Kerensky released the Bolsheviks and gave arms to workers in order to resist Kornilov.

By now hardly anybody trusted the government or thought it was strong enough to survive.

Meanwhile the Bolsheviks under Lenin had learned from their mistake in July, were under determined leadership, knew exactly what they wanted and had a strong force of armed workers – the Red Guards.

7 November (26 October OS): the October Revolution – Bolsheviks took the key positions in Petrograd and arrested the Provisional Government. **8 November**: meeting of the All-Russia Congress of Soviets in Petrograd; anti-Bolshevik members stayed away or kept quiet, the rest declared the Bolsheviks to be the government of Russia.

Though the Bolsheviks were now the government, elections had been organised by the Provisional Government for a Constituent Assembly which would decide on the future constitution of Russia. The Bolsheviks did not win a majority. 18 January, 1918: meeting of the Constituent Assembly in Petrograd. It was broken up and dispersed by Red soldiers.

The Bolsheviks gained and held power by the well-planned and ruthless use of force.

3 The world made safe for democracy

The good things of life

The Great War was something that people wanted to put behind them, but could not and would not forget. Every town and village had its war memorial engraved with the names of all those ordinary men who had gone from their everyday work to the trenches and never come back. In Britain, at 11 a.m. on every 11 November, the whole nation stood in silence remembering their dead; in their coats they wore artificial Flanders poppies, sold to help the blinded and crippled. They would not believe that all the suffering had been useless. They wanted to think of the dead as 'heroes' who had 'laid down their lives' for freedom, honour or simply their motherland. During the war, politicians had promised that the sacrifices would win a better, happier life after the war: Wilson saw 'a world safe for democracy' and Lloyd George, now Prime Minister of Britain, 'a fit country for heroes to live in'.

We shall use Britain again as an example of what took place in most of the richer countries during the next twenty years. What people wanted above all was to get back to normal life, earn a living in peace and dwell in comfort. In many ways they got what they wanted. Daily life was transformed; the changes that had begun before the war, some of them quickened by the war itself, ceased to be marvellous novelties and became commonplace. The age of coal and gas gave way to the age of oil and electricity. Streets became bright with big lights and neon signs. Filling stations mushroomed along the roads, which were beginning to rumble with trucks, buses and cars – little cheap cars that ordinary people could afford. Even on farms the horse was being replaced by the tractor. The fuel for all this came from distant oilfields, mainly in the Middle East, and was carried along the seaways in long ungainly tankers, while ships of all sorts were changing from coal engines to oil.

The most exciting part of the new transport revolution was the air. In 1919, only ten years after Blériot had first flown

The war memorial at Margate, Kent. Like every other town in Britain, Margate had lost many soldiers and sailors; unlike most of the others, it had also suffered air raids and had seemed a likely landing-place if the Germans were to attempt an invasion. That may explain why the inscription is rather longer than most:

IN MEMORY OF THOSE WHO DIED AND SUFFERED FOR THEIR COUNTRY IN THE GREAT WAR EARNING PRAISE AND HONOUR THAT CAN NEVER DIE, OF THOSE TOO WHO WERE DONE TO DEATH IN THIS TOWN, AND AS A SIGN FOR ALL TIME OF THANKFULNESS TO ALMIGHTY GOD FOR THE SAFE HOME COMING OF SO MANY OF THEIR FIGHTING MEN, AND OF THE DELIVERANCE OF THEIR TOWN FROM MANY PERILS FROM THE AIR AND FROM THE SEA THIS CROSS WAS RAISED BY THE PEOPLE OF MARGATE A.D. 1922 DEATH IS SWALLOWED UP IN VICTORY

over the English Channel, Alcock and Brown crossed the North Atlantic in a converted Vickers Vimy bomber. During the twenties air lines gradually spun a web across the continents. At first it was a great adventure for the few rich passengers who flew, cold and uncomfortable, on the London–Paris service, but by the late thirties giant flying boats, like airborne hotels, were cruising over the oceans.

Out from the crowded cities sprouted suburbs and 'dormit-óry' towns as 'commuting' to work became easier. Builders bought tracts of land to make 'estates' of small houses, each with a garden and, of course, space for a garage; so the typical house was 'detached' or, much more often, 'semi-detached'. Local councils also created large housing estates. At first the idea was very much to rehouse people from slums, but before long many councils believed it was their duty to provide as many houses as possible for any people who wanted to rent them.

Within their homes people enjoyed new comforts. Electricity provided far more than light – it powered all sorts of gadgets from vacuum cleaners to toy trains. Refrigerators were still a luxury but telephones were becoming more common, and by the thirties the normal home had its radio receiver: already wireless had grown into a huge system of channels through which broadcasting companies poured an endless flow of music and talk.

Even the suffragettes were satisfied. Women got the vote in 1918 (for those over thirty – at the same time all men over twenty-one got the vote) and 1928 (for those over twenty-one), and some were elected to Parliament. After the work women had done in the war, it was no longer possible to argue that they were not as fit as men to have the full rights of a democratic citizen.

Developments in the USA were bigger and faster than what was happening in Britain and other European countries. This was partly because the USA was so big and go-ahead before the war, partly because the war had stimulated the Americans without exhausting them. American industries used mass-production methods to turn out astonishing amounts of goods quickly and cheaply. They wanted to go on making more and more, and thus everybody would have more. To keep the wheels of industry turning faster and faster, goods had to be sold to more people, and customers had to be persuaded to throw away what they already had and buy something new. This was a society built on the belief that it was good to *consume*, so advertising became one of the biggest and most important industries of all. Advertisers used every technical and psychological trick to make people buy – one of their most brilliant successes was the invention of Mother's Day, with its

above: *A British suburban sitting room, or 'lounge', of the late 1930s, as reconstructed in the Geffrye Museum, London. With its fitted carpet and three-piece suite it seems typical of middle-class standards of the time. Electricity is heavily used – lights, fire, radio – and there are modernistic geometrical designs and modern materials – metal tubes, chrome, bakelite. At the same time such things as the many knick-knacks, the frilly lampshade and the stained glass in the window suggest older-fashioned ideas of domestic cosiness. The television receiver on the left would have been a very unusual feature, for at that time television was only in its experimental stages.*

right: *A British newspaper advertisement of 1929. The advertisers seem to be aiming at the sort of people who might live in the house above – sedate but reasonably fashion-conscious middle class who go to one of the more lavishly appointed cinemas for an evening out, perhaps once a week.*

suggestion that anyone who did not spend lavishly should be ashamed of himself. American energy and optimism, the attitude that 'the sky's the limit', the drive always to break records, to be biggest and fastest, hit the newcomer the moment his ship came into sight of New York's fantastic skyline of skyscrapers. This was the land of jazz and cocktails – and gangsters too. Though older Europeans might sneer, many young people felt that America was the most exciting place in the world. They copied American manners and music and expressions. The USA was beginning to set the fashion for the rest of the world.

It was the cinema that taught everybody else what the Americans were like. The pictures may not have been very accurate, and it has been said that in the twenties and thirties Hollywood was the capital of a dream empire. In fact it is impossible to be sure what effect the films had on the millions who watched them. Sitting in upholstered darkness, gazing at visions of daring and romance, most of them knew perfectly well that it was just commercial entertainment. All the same, many of them may have come to accept, unconsciously, some of the opinions and attitudes of people they saw on the screen, and to feel familiar with what they believed to be the American way of life.

48

Depression and state intervention

As we saw in the years before the war, there can be a dark side as well as a bright side, and the twenties and thirties are often remembered as a time of distress and anxiety.

To begin with, the European nations faced the difficulties of readjusting to peace. All of a sudden, the government was not making desperate demands for food, clothes, weapons and ships, and was no longer organising everybody to do war work. Merchants, manufacturers and farmers were left to try to return to the markets they had supplied before the war, or find new ones. They had to repair or replace buildings and machines worn out during four hard years, not to mention damage and destruction. At the same time millions of men were being demobilised from the armed forces and looking for jobs. Often the returning 'heroes' found that jobs were few and poorly paid. All this was only to be expected after a great war – it had been much the same after the Napoleonic Wars – but the governments and the employers had not been able to make effective plans to solve the problems. The French and British particularly reflected bitterly that this was not much of a reward for victory.

Why wasn't Germany paying? The answer was simple. Germany was even worse off. In Germany, prices had been rising even before the war, then there had been the shortages caused by the blockade, and now the Allies were carrying off great quantities of German goods as reparations. *Inflation* (that is, the rise in prices) increased madly until money was virtually worthless. Germans put all the blame for this on the reparations though in fact the reasons were much more complicated, and the government declared that it could not pay the Allies what it owed them. The French government replied in January 1923 by sending troops into the Ruhr, the most important center of German heavy industry, to seize by force what was owed, and at the same time tried to persuade the Rhinelanders to break away from Germany and form a separate state under French protection. These tough tactics failed. But Germany's financial condition got worse, and now came alarming signs that it would drag down other nations' currencies. The French franc began to lose value. The governments of the victorious countries were discovering a hard fact: trade, finance and industry between nations were so entangled that the total collapse of one of the main economic powers would have dire effects on the rest. For their own good, the Allies reduced reparations under the Dawes Plan of 1924, and provided a large loan to help Germany to found a national bank and a new currency.

There was also another reason for saving the Germans from total misery: the danger that they might go the same way as Russia. There the Bolsheviks had won a vast, ferocious civil

German inflation of the early 1920s as shown in the cost of a loaf

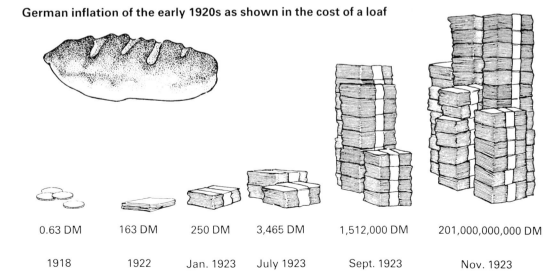

| 0.63 DM | 163 DM | 250 DM | 3,465 DM | 1,512,000 DM | 201,000,000,000 DM |
| 1918 | 1922 | Jan. 1923 | July 1923 | Sept. 1923 | Nov. 1923 |

war and set up what they called a *Communist* system of government (described in the next chapter). They tried to abolish all private property and suppress religion, and they ruthlessly punished anyone who disagreed; hideous tales were told of the cruelty of the 'Red Terror'. This was the specter that frightened governments, the rich, and millions of ordinary people all over Europe. The Bolsheviks believed in world revolution; what had happened in Russia could not be complete until it had happened in every other country too. In many other countries Communist parties existed, closely in touch with Moscow, and just after the war there had been serious attempts to follow the Russian example, notably in Hungary and parts of Germany.

The danger was in reality less than it seemed. Socialist parties grew stronger than before the war in many countries – in Britain, the Labour Party replaced the Liberals as the great opponent of the Conservatives – and communism was an extreme form of socialism. But most European socialists believed in parliamentary democracy, wanted change to be peaceful and detested violent revolution. For example, the British Trades Union Congress called a national general strike in May 1926 to support the coal-miners, whose employers were trying to force them to accept lower wages; they hoped that this might paralyse the country sufficiently to make the government intervene in the dispute. But when the government showed no sign of giving in after a week, and volunteers from the better-off classes kept trains, buses and trucks running, the strike leaders called it off. They would not risk its dragging on until hatred grew and rioting broke out. Fortunately in most industrial countries trade picked up, prosperity returned as the twenties went on, and there was more money for people to spend on going to the pictures, buying a wireless or even a small car.

Then the Wall Street Crash came, and after it the depression of the thirties. It is not easy to explain why it happened, but economists have tried. During the prosperous years in the USA, anyone with money to spare was eager to buy stocks and shares in companies that were making good profits. As trade flourished and as there was such demand for shares, so their value increased and people were more than ever glad to own shares. But in the autumn of 1929 a few people began to fear that this steady rise could not go on forever and that some companies were not worth nearly as much as their shares were

valued at. So a few people started selling their shares, then more decided that it would be wise to get rid of theirs before the value dropped, and soon everybody was trying to sell shares. Of course this was the very thing to bring about what they feared. Shares slumped. Without financial support, businesses went bankrupt and factories closed. Thousands, then millions, of Americans lost their savings and jobs.

The crash began in Wall Street, the center of stock-broking in New York, and spread round the world. It has been argued that the financial collapse could not have damaged agriculture, industry and trade so badly had it not been for their other weaknesses, such as producing more food and products than people could buy. Whatever the exact causes, millions of men and women were soon without work or money, or hope of finding any. In May 1931 the Kreditanstalt Bank in Vienna failed, and a new wave of business collapses went through central Europe.

Those years were long to be remembered in Britain as the time of the dole and the means test. The dole was the money handed out to the unemployed every week by the government; it came principally from the funds that the workers and employers had been made to contribute as insurance (page 9). Anyone who could not manage on this, and asked for extra relief, had to prove that he had no other means of supporting himself – no possessions that he could sell, for instance – before getting help. This means test and the officials who carried it out were loathed, naturally, but the people really responsible for it were the government.

Was there anything else the government could do? The situation was so grim that many of the Labour Party and all the Conservative Party agreed to forget their differences and form the National Government, as it was called, under the Labour leader Ramsay Macdonald. Their idea was to try to spend very little, to encourage people to 'Buy British' and support their own industries; like a family that had got into debt, the whole nation must tighten its belt and work hard until it was paying its way again. As an alternative the economist John Maynard Keynes believed that the important thing was to get people buying again, so that industries would have customers and be able to employ more workers again, who would themselves now be able to buy more goods, and so on. So he said that the government ought to spend more, not less, even if it meant borrowing still more money until prosperity returned. Though

'Street Scene, 1935' painted by L.S. Lowry, 1887–1976. This is George Street, Pendlebury, Lancashire. The place and people look dingy and joyless, with the harsh bulk of the Acme mill dominating everything. The few touches of colour only emphasise the drabness of the rest. In the years of severe unemployment such a place must have been depressing indeed.

the government thought this idea rash, it did see the need to try to encourage new industries. One of the most worrying things about the depression, as far as Britain was concerned, was that the hardest-hit industries were the big old ones such as coal, iron and cotton, where Britain had led since the Industrial Revolution. Quite apart from the depression, it seemed that these industries themselves were out of date. New fuels, materials and methods were being developed, and Britain was too slow in changing. So the government did a little to help new factories on 'trading estates', making, for example, specialist electrical equipment or motors. These enterprises, though, could not take up more than a small fraction of the unemployed. For the most part Britain's policy was to hang on and hope that world trade would revive.

In the USA, where the depression had started, industry had never been old-fashioned or slow to adapt. Now the mood was summed up in a popular song: 'Brother, can you spare a dime?' But still most Americans did not want the government to interfere. They still held to what has become known as 'the American dream'– that in the USA riches and happiness can be won by anyone prepared to work hard enough. The free enterprise of businessmen working hard to enrich themselves had made the USA grow and prosper for a century, and it would do so again. Government help would make the government more powerful and the people less free and self-reliant; it would be the beginning of socialism, and that, they argued, would make them all slaves of the state. So the government was content to raise tariff barriers against the importing of foreign goods, and give a little support to banks and railways because everything else needed them. Anyway, it seemed likely that the American Constitution could be interpreted as forbidding government interference in trade.

Franklin Delano Roosevelt took office as President of the USA in 1933, and just as he did so a new financial crisis struck

Working on the Norris Dam, Clinch River, Tennessee. The TVA's first dam, begun in 1933 and completed in 1936, it is 81 metres (265 feet) high and 567 metres (1,860 feet) long. It has two 50,400 kilowatt power units.

the country and banks began to close. Roosevelt had always been against government interference, but this was an emergency. Unless the banks could be trusted to provide credit, businesses could not carry on, and the country's huge reserve of gold might have to be used up. The President sent officials to take charge of banks that were in difficulties, so that their customers would feel confident that their money was safe and business would go on normally.

Now that he had started to intervene, Roosevelt decided he ought to do much more, and the result over the next few years was a complicated mass of projects known as the 'New Deal'. Its main ideas were:

– *Support vital industries.* Banking and farming were in danger. The President took powers to control the use of credit, gold and silver; and allowed people to insure money they deposited in a bank. Farmers who had fallen into debt were helped to raise new loans and keep their land and machines until the next harvest. Many farmers were in difficulties because they had been producing too much of some crops, not enough of others; government

experts were sent round to advise them on what to grow.

– *Improve working conditions.* The government told employers that they would get more co-operation from their workers if they recognised trade unions, accepted a set of rules for settling disputes and set up pension schemes.

– *Help the needy.* The Social Security Act, 1935, attempted to organise welfare schemes for the old and disabled, for children in need of protection and even, to a limited extent, people who had lost their jobs.

– *Create more useful jobs.* Some tasks were too big for even the biggest private enterprise, but not for the government. The Civilian Conservation Corps employed two million people reforesting wide tracts of the USA that generations of settlers had heedlessly stripped, and the Works Progress Administration employed four million on public works of all kinds. The most famous single project was the Tennessee Valley Authority, which irrigated and brought hydro-electricity to a huge area that included parts of seven states.

Roosevelt had to face furious criticism. His schemes cost money and meant higher taxes, which fell mostly on the rich; but they, the President said, held 'an unjust concentration of wealth and economic power'. His opponents succeeded in getting the Supreme Court to rule that some of the government's attempts to improve working conditions were an interference with liberty and against the Constitution. But there was no doubt what most Americans thought when they re-elected Roosevelt in 1936 with an overwhelming majority.

The New Deal posed some serious questions. Things soon began to improve in the USA, but was this because of the New Deal or just because trade was reviving generally? There is no certain answer. Naturally, governments claimed the credit when things improved, but perhaps the truth was that industry and trade had become so complex, and some big businesses had become so powerful, that governments simply had to intervene, to protect their people. Was what Roosevelt had done very different from socialism? And was there a danger that a government strong enough to do all this would be too strong for the people to change in elections? Could a well-organised state still be a democracy?

Colonies and freedom

There was another difficult question that faced some democracies: how could a state that boasted of its freedom rule over an empire? Britain had by far the largest empire, and the British answer was that any colony able and willing to look after itself could have independence whenever it wished. The dominions had once been colonies, but now they were completely self-governing and only remained with Britain because they wanted to; in 1926 the Imperial Conference in London agreed that the dominions were fully equal to Britain within the empire. What had been a colonial empire could grow into an association of free and equal nations.

So far this 'growing up' had happened to colonies where the people were predominantly white. The only serious trouble had been in Ireland, which was quite different from the rest: it was certainly a much older colony than any other, and it could be regarded as part of Britain. The threat of civil war in 1914 (page 10) became a reality during and after the Great War. In 1922 Britain recognised most of Ireland as the self-governing Irish Free State, but Ulster remained part of the

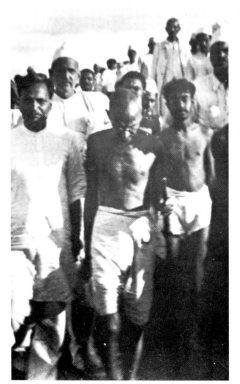

Non-violent opposition to British rule in India. Salt was a state monopoly; everyone had to buy it from official shops, and the profit went to the government. Gandhi encouraged his followers not to buy. Instead, in the spring of 1930, he led a three-week march from his home to the sea, where they could evaporate water and make salt, illegally but peacefully. Here he is on the 'Salt March'.

United Kingdom; a feeling of great bitterness remained between the leaders of the two parts of Ireland, and many of their people.

The other part of the British Empire where a demand for self-government had been growing before the Great War was India (page 17), and here the British government continued to argue that the peoples of India were too divided by race and religion to be able to govern themselves peacefully. Therefore, although committed in principle after 1917 to eventual self-government for India, they gave only a few concessions at first; and they tried to give an impression of strength by putting down any sort of disorder very firmly and arresting Indian leaders who seemed to be stirring up discontent.

One of these leaders was Mohandas Gandhi, usually known as *Mahatma*, the great soul. He believed that he could prove the British wrong by purely peaceful means, emphasising the part of the Hindu religion that taught that bloodshed and violence were evil. He organised strikes and marches and told his followers not to co-operate with the British authorities – they might refuse to pay a tax, for instance. But they must never be violent. If the police charged them, wielding iron-bound *lathis*, Gandhi's followers must not resist; they must allow themselves to be struck down, injured or even killed. Gandhi himself used another form of self-sacrifice, the hunger strike. For example, he forced Hindu leaders to agree to treat the despised Untouchables as fellow human beings and fellow-Hindus, by starving himself almost to death. He was astonishingly successful, both in winning what he wanted with his own hunger strikes and in persuading enormous numbers of Indians to adopt his methods of non-violent resistance to British rule.

The British had no answer. They knew how to deal with riots and murders, and there were still many of these, for Gandhi's methods did not appeal to all Indians. Sometimes, indeed, the British accused Gandhi and other Congress leaders of being the real cause of riots, with their speeches and writings, and put them in prison. But the sheer quiet persistence of vast masses of people, never striking back but never giving in, gradually made the British realise that India did not accept them any longer, and that it was just a matter of time before they would have to leave. By the late 1930s most agreed that India would soon have self-government, but there were deep disagreements among Indians as well as British about how it should be organised and who should have power. The India Act of 1935 gave Indians more power in local government, and planned to convert the Indian empire into a federation; but there was so much dispute about how the federation should work that this part of the Act never came into force.

There were demands for independence in some other colonies, but nowhere nearly as strong as in India. So the colonial governments (British, French, Dutch and Portuguese mainly) were able to claim that most of the natives of their colonies were contented and loyal, and that those who were agitating for freedom were no more than a handful of ambitious would-be politicians and trouble-makers. Indeed, they had more difficulty with old-fashioned tribal feuds or religious outbursts than with people claiming democratic rights such as elections and parliamentary government.

Practically all Africa was divided into colonies, and it was remarkably peaceful. This may have been partly because most areas had been colonies for only about thirty or forty years, and the people were still awed by the power of the white man's machines and weapons. But a growing number of them were now learning European languages and technical skills, and black students were becoming more common at European universities. They were learning fast.

Islam and the modern world

Across North Africa, the Middle East and Western Asia the people were almost all Muslims. They belonged to many different races; they included nomads of the deserts, farmers of the river valleys, merchants and craftsmen of the great cities. They often fought among themselves, and many of their wars were religious, between different branches of the Muslim faith. But they all were conscious that they belonged to the religion and civilisation of Islam which arose from the teachings of the Prophet Muhammad thirteen centuries before; that this should be the most important, the only important thing in their lives; and that it made them very different from all other peoples.

Many of them were Arabs. This was a loose name, covering far more peoples than those who dwelt in Arabia, but they all used the Arabic language. It was from Arabia that the Muslim faith had spread, and it was towards Mecca in Arabia that all Muslims turned in their daily prayers. The Arabs were proud of this, but for hundreds of years they had been under the Ottoman Empire, and had to accept the Turkish sultan as *caliph*, successor of the Prophet and leader of all true Muslims. With the collapse of that empire (page 32) some Arabs set up independent kingdoms, but others were kept under League of Nations mandates (page 33); and those whose countries were parts of European empires saw no change. Most of the Middle East was poor, much of it desert, but Europeans were interested partly because it was just over the Mediterranean and there had been trade or war between Europe and the Middle East since the beginning of history; partly because it lay across the routes to the Far East; and partly for a new reason that was becoming more important every year – oil had been found there. The Arabs did not want the Westerners, and many of them still thought of all Europeans as 'Franks', Christians who had been the enemies of Islam ever since the Crusades. But they were weak, without the industries and technical know-

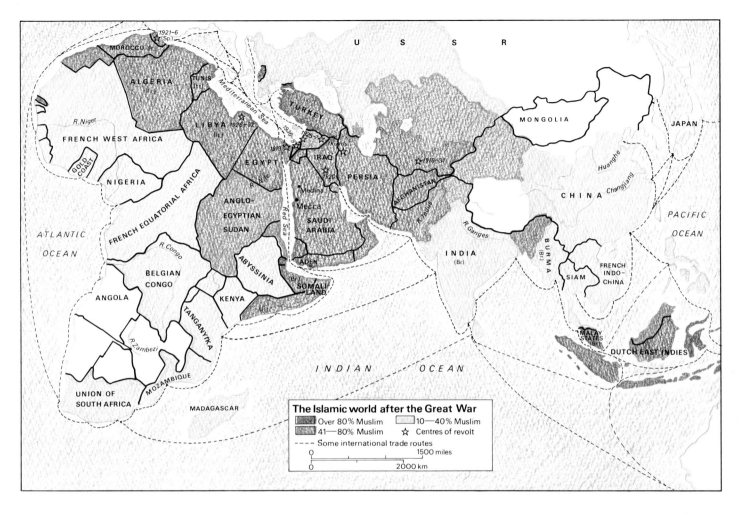

The Islamic world after the Great War

Over 80% Muslim
41—80% Muslim
10—40% Muslim
☆ Centres of revolt
--- Some international trade routes

0 _____ 1500 miles
0 _____ 2000 km

ledge that made the Europeans so powerful; there were some determined risings, like that of the Druses in Lebanon or of Abd-el-Krim in the Riff mountains of Morocco, but they all failed eventually.

There were problems and disputes in many parts of the Middle East, but one of the worst was in Palestine, where Britain ruled under a League of Nations mandate. The difficulty was that Britain had promised the land to two different peoples: the Arabs who had been living there for many centuries, and the Jews who had been driven from it by the Romans. Since their *diaspora* (scattering) the Jews had been a nation held together by their religion but without a

homeland. They had often been ill-treated, mainly by Christians who thought of them as enemies of Christ, and *pogroms* (anti-Jewish riots) were still going on in Russia at the end of the nineteenth century – this was one reason why so many east European Jews fled to the USA. In the 1890s some Jews began a movement known as Zionism, which aimed at giving the Jews once more a homeland where they could be safe from persecution. Naturally, they wanted to go to their holy land. Many non-Jews in Europe and America sympathised, and during the Great War several Allied statesmen were grateful for the support of influential Jews. So in 1917 the British Foreign Secretary, A.J. Balfour, declared his support for a

Different leaders in the post-war Islamic world

Abd el Krim of the Rif, c.1882–1963, well-born Berber tribesman. Worked as newspaper editor and senior legal adviser under Spanish authorities, 1906–19. Feared European intentions to exploit minerals and defraud people. Led revolt against Spanish and French, 1921–6, trying to unite tribes into independent Rifian state. After many victories, overwhelmed and exiled to French island of Réunion. Allowed to go to Egypt, 1947, where he remained an honoured guest until his death.

Fuad of Egypt, 1868–1936, member of Khedival (viceregal) family which ruled Egypt on behalf of Sultan of Turkey. 1914, Britain declared Egypt her protectorate. 1917, Fuad succeeded to title of Sultan of Egypt. 1922, Egypt recognised as independent kingdom; Fuad king, with a parliamentary constitution – but a strong British garrison remained. Throughout his reign, had to cope with pressure from *Wafd* (nationalist) party on one side, British on the other.

Ibn Saud of Arabia, c.1880–1953, member of exiled ruling family. Returned and won leadership of *Wahabis* (strict Muslim sect) in Nejd, eastern Arabia. Extended power in that area, joined Arab fight against Turks 1914–18. Conquered Hejaz (western Arabia, including Mecca) 1919–26; proclaimed king. Renamed kingdom Saudi Arabia 1932. Maintained good relations with Britain throughout. Signed first Saudi agreement authorising oil prospecting, 1933.

Mustapha Kemal Ataturk, 1881–1938, professional soldier, became famous 1914–18. Joined Turkish Nationalist Party, was elected president of its Congress, 1919. Defeated Greek invasion of Asia Minor, 1922, and obtained revised peace treaty from Allies, 1923. Ended Turkish sultanate and caliphate, was elected president of the republic and regularly re-elected for the rest of his life. Tried to force Turkey to become a non-religious, modern, Western-style state.

Jewish national home in Palestine, and this was written into the conditions of the mandate in 1920. Nobody foresaw serious trouble with the Palestinian Arabs, though Britain had given Arab leaders to understand that Palestine would be an Arab state, in accordance with Wilson's Fourteen Points and in gratitude for the help that the Arabs had given the Allies.

If only a few Jews had come, perhaps there would have been no trouble. But many came. They were clever and hardworking, they irrigated poor land and made it prosperous, and soon the Palestinian Arabs feared that Zionists were going to take the whole country. Armed gangs of Arabs began to attack Zionist settlements. Zionists organised their own armed bands to strike back. The British, being in the impossible position of having supported both Jews and Arabs, tried to keep order and failed. By the later 1930s Arabs and Jews were virtually involved in a guerrilla war, with the British looking uncomfortable and absurd in the middle.

The former rulers of the Middle East, the Turks, were at least freed from such problems when they lost their empire, but they were in serious difficulties. The sultan's government had long been notorious for corruption and inefficiency, and after its disastrous defeats in the Great War seemed to be de-moralised and helpless. Greece, Turkey's old enemy, saw this as her opportunity. She claimed that the people living on the Aegean coast of Asia Minor were mainly of Greek stock, and sent an army to seize that part of Turkey. It was the shock of this invasion of their own homeland that revived the Turks. They turned furiously on the Greeks, beat them back to the sea and slaughtered them. Their leader was a general called Mustapha Kemal who had first become famous for defending the Dardanelles against the Allies (page 25). After his victory he made himself the master of Turkey. He showed the Allies that the Turks were ready to fight again, and so got better terms in the peace treaty that was at last signed in 1923 (page 40). That same year he dismissed the sultan and declared Turkey a republic. When he ended the sultanate, he also ended the caliphate. Turkey, he believed, could never become

Men of the Transjordanian Arab Legion. Most of them were from Bedouin tribes, and learned the skills and disciplines of modern warfare from British officers without losing the traditions of the desert. The British officer here is John Glubb, who served in various posts in Iraq and Transjordan from 1920, and was appointed to command the Legion in 1939. (Conditions changed after the Second World War, and in 1956 he was suddenly dismissed by the King of Jordan – as the country was renamed in 1949 – to satisfy Arab nationalist demands.)

Turkish women in the late 1920s; a photograph that was obviously posed specially to illustrate the transformation that Kemal was trying to effect. The three on the left are still concealing themselves beneath their traditional gowns and veils, while the two on the right are thoroughly modern in appearance, even to the handbag and wristwatch.

a modern power while it was steeped in religion and the ancient customs of Islam. He made the Turks write their language in Western letters, not in Arabic script. He tried to encourage modern industry and business methods. Most astonishing of all, he ordered Turkish women to stop hiding themselves in long black gowns and veils, and to dress like Western women and come out into the world; this went against one of the most deep-rooted customs of the Islamic world. Kemal also wanted to emphasise that the Turks were now a self-contained nation, not the heads of a multi-national empire; he changed the capital from Istanbul, the former Constantinople or Byzantium, on the Bosphorus, to Ankara deep in the Turkish heartland of Asia Minor. Kemal remained master of Turkey until his death in 1938. He took the name of *Ataturk,* father of the Turks, and there was no doubt that he did his best to create a new Turkish nation. He had to sweep aside all opposition ruthlessly, but there were many who doubted if it was either right or possible to cut off the nation so suddenly from the Islamic culture that had been at the center of Turkish life during all the centuries the Turks had lived in the Middle East.

The Chinese republic

Perhaps China was too big for anyone to seize and modernise as Ataturk was attempting to do with Turkey. In any case, many of the leading 'modernisers' believed in Western-style parliamentary democracy, which did not fit well with the idea of driving everybody, willy-nilly, to live and work in new ways. Whatever the reason, China lacked a strong central government. After the death of Yuan (page 16) Sun Yat-sen remained the main influence in the south, at the head of the Guomindang, but many provinces fell under the control of men who became known as 'war-lords' because they relied on private armies to protect themselves and enforce their authority. Sun tried to get the main leaders to agree to keep China united, and he was still negotiating for this on a visit to Beijing when he died in 1925.

Now there was discord in the Guomindang itself, for some of its members said that Sun had been convinced before his death that Communism was the best thing for China, while others said that he had remained a firm believer in parliamentary democracy. The latter group won the struggle for control of the party. Their leader was General Chiang Kai-shek, an able man who admired the USA. During the next few years he defeated or made agreements with other war-lords until in

Chinese peasants paying their rent. They bring part of their harvest, and the landlord makes them winnow it in his machine so that he can get full weight in solid grain, with no chaff. In this scene one of the landlord's men has knocked down a small boy for picking up some grain, and the child's grandfather is trying to explain that he did no harm. This is part of a series of 114 life-size clay sculptures arranged in six scenes around a former rent-collecting yard in Tayi, Sichuan. They were made in 1965 and are avowedly Communist propaganda, but there is no doubt that during the 1920s and 1930s peasants were in fact often treated harshly.

1931 he could claim to be the acknowledged head of the Chinese republic. He announced a new constitution; on paper, the biggest nation on earth was a Western-style democracy.

Could it possibly work? Many Chinese now were educated in Western ways, and understood Western politics, technology and business very well. But these were only a handful compared with the vast mass of the Chinese people, the peasants who lived as they had done for thousands of years, toiling hard for a frugal living and enduring floods and droughts, heavy rents and taxes from landlords and officials, and pillage from undisciplined soldiers or rebels. To these people the constitution would only mean something if it gave them solid pro-

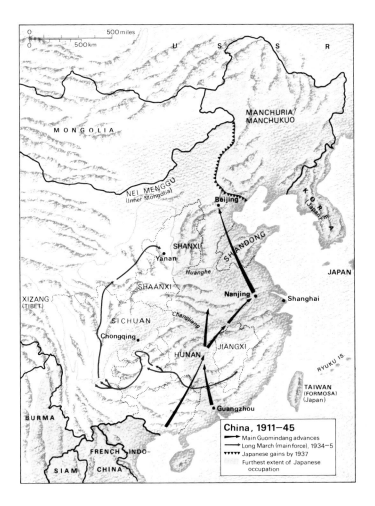

China, 1911–45
→ Main Guomindang advances
→ Long March (main force), 1934–5
ᴠᴠᴠᴠ Japanese gains by 1937
░ Furthest extent of Japanese occupation

had been defeated the Communists would not give in. They retreated from their base in Jiangxi (Kiangsi) province to the mountains of Shaanxi (Shensi). The retreat was called the 'Long March'; their route covered about 9,660 kilometres (6,000 miles) and they lost about 70,000 men on the way, and it took from October 1934 to October 1935, but at the end the Communists were still a fighting force and in a strong position. Their leader was called Mao Zedong (Tse-tung).

Japan was an even greater threat. In 1931 the Japanese troops stationed in Manchuria to protect the railway – Japan had been the dominant foreign power in this part of China since the Russo-Japanese War (page 12) – claimed that they had been attacked, and took control of the whole province. In 1932 Japan declared Manchuria to be a separate country from China, gave it the name Manchukuo and placed on its throne, as their puppet, the man who had, as a boy, been the last Emperor of China and had been deposed in 1911 (page 16). The League of Nations condemned this, but Japan took no notice. She developed Manchukuo as an industrial area to supplement Japanese industries. Even this did not satisfy the Japanese leaders. In 1937 they moved into the rest of China, using the rivers and railways to thrust deep and seize the big cities. Japan never declared war; this was just 'the China incident'. In reality, it was war on a huge scale. The Guomindang and the Communists made a truce with each other so that both could resist the Japanese. The Japanese were efficient and ruthless. They won most of the battles and over-ran great areas, but China was enormous. It looked as if this struggle could go on for a very long time.

tection against natural disasters and human oppression. Chiang was hardly able to offer this. It would take years for his government to find or train enough officials to govern the country well, and to find the money to help the peasants to improve their crops and to bring relief in time of famine. And perhaps he never would, because he had done deals with a great number of people who expected to be rewarded, and the only way to reward them was by giving them jobs and letting them take bribes. Whatever the constitution said, the Guomindang government was bound to be corrupt and inefficient.

Anyway, he never had a chance. The Chinese Communist Party had a large army, and continued to fight. Even after they

The twenty years after the Great War brought the winners some of the rewards they had expected. Technical progress went on apace, and made life easier for millions; but there were also what appeared to be world trade slumps that brought massive unemployment, and governments did not know what to do or how much they ought to interfere. Ideas of freedom and democracy seemed to be spreading round the world, and non-European peoples were learning much from the West. But this too brought problems, since some colonial peoples were asking for more than their rulers wished to give them; and in other countries, including the biggest in the world, the conditions were so difficult that Western methods of parliamentary government would not work.

The world depression of the interwar years

What caused it?

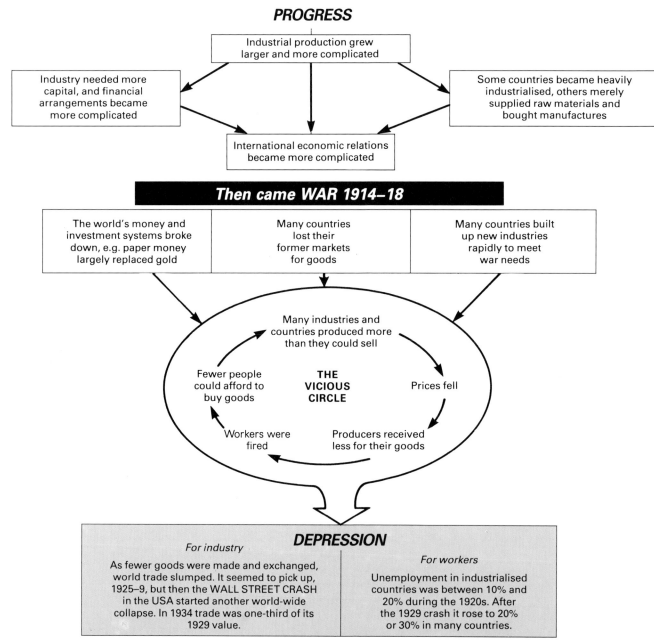

PROGRESS

Industrial production grew larger and more complicated

Industry needed more capital, and financial arrangements became more complicated

Some countries became heavily industrialised, others merely supplied raw materials and bought manufactures

International economic relations became more complicated

Then came WAR 1914–18

The world's money and investment systems broke down, e.g. paper money largely replaced gold

Many countries lost their former markets for goods

Many countries built up new industries rapidly to meet war needs

Many industries and countries produced more than they could sell

Fewer people could afford to buy goods

THE VICIOUS CIRCLE

Prices fell

Workers were fired

Producers received less for their goods

DEPRESSION

For industry

As fewer goods were made and exchanged, world trade slumped. It seemed to pick up, 1925–9, but then the WALL STREET CRASH in the USA started another world-wide collapse. In 1934 trade was one-third of its 1929 value.

For workers

Unemployment in industrialised countries was between 10% and 20% during the 1920s. After the 1929 crash it rose to 20% or 30% in many countries.

What were its consequences?

Experts suggested different explanations for the depression, and different cures:

1 CUT government spending, wages, and prices. Save money and get out of debt. The usual, orthodox solution.	3 BUSINESSMEN should be helped and encouraged to compete with as little interference as possible to get industry going again.
2 SPEND more, and borrow more, to increase employment, spending, demand, production, employment, spending . . . This was J.M. Keynes' solution.	4 THE STATE must step in to control imports and exports, prices and wages, employers and workers. It must start large enterprises itself to create employment.

Different countries were hit by depression in different ways, and tried different cures:

USA	BRITAIN	GERMANY	USSR	OTHER COUNTRIES
Business boomed, 1925–9. Optimists bought shares, sending share prices up until in 1929 investors began to realise industry's weakness. The Wall Street Crash brought failure for investors and businesses. 12 million unemployed. Roosevelt, 1933, offered New Deal to restore finance and industry by large-scale government schemes.	Decline of coal industry caused General Strike, 1926. 23% unemployed by 1931. National Government took over, ended Free Trade and imposed import duties. 1932, Ottawa Agreement to protect Commonwealth trade.	30% unemployed. Strikes, disorder, and businessmen demanding strong government. Growth of extremist political parties. NAZIS came to power, 1933, promising sweeping measures and tight controls to restore German power and prosperity.	The government cut Russia off from most trade with the rest of the world. It planned industrial growth and directed all labour. Industrial production grew, but Russian workers and peasants suffered terrible hardship and shortage because of government mistakes.	In many countries emergency governments or dictatorships came to power, promising firm action to restore trade, industry and employment. Some tried similar methods in foreign policy. Some, like Japan, saw war as a solution to their problems.

So how different was the world that emerged from depression?

Everybody wanted to avoid ever having the same terrible experience again, but nobody was sure of the way to avoid it.

The world was split up into a number of trading blocks. Each one had its own currency – dollar, pound or mark.

Many governments started rearmament programs to develop industry and because war seemed nearer. But did rearmament help bring war closer still?

Increased international tension and conflict.

4 The dictatorships: Communism, Fascism and Nazism

All democracies, in their separate ways, had governments that depended on elections in which different political parties competed for the people's votes. All sorts of opinions were tolerated; people were free to believe and argue whatever they wished, short of bloodshed and robbery. The state was there to serve the citizens and guarantee their freedom, and the law was there to protect every individual equally. These ideas, often called liberal, spread through many countries during the nineteenth century, and by the 1920s most members of the League of Nations seemed to assume that this was the only way to run a modern civilised nation. But now liberal democracy was challenged and defeated in some of the most important countries of Europe.

Lenin and Communist Russia

The Bolsheviks officially changed their name to the Communist Party in 1918. They had no respect for liberal freedom, which left the rich free to oppress the poor and the poor free to starve. They said that wealth was the key to everything, and they must see that everybody had an equal share. So the state would become the owner of all wealth, and allow to each person enough to satisfy his or her needs. There would be no rich and no poor.

Accordingly, Lenin decreed that all land, houses, shops, factories and machinery belonged to the state, and money was no longer to be used. All businesses would be managed by state officials – Communist Party members if possible – and workers would receive ration cards which entitled them to so much food and clothing from state stores.

The scheme failed. It was easy to force owners to hand over their businesses, but hard to keep the works running smoothly, with goods and materials getting to the right place at the right time, now that inexperienced men and women were in charge. The wartime shortages had not eased, people were cold and hungry, and there was bartering and black market trading and bribery that no amount of punishment could prevent. In the towns the Communists could keep a grip on the people because they controlled the workers' soviets and the security police. In the country, though, the village communities had their own ideas. The peasants thought that the revolution meant that the land now belonged to them, not to some distant thing called the state, so they took possession of the fields they worked on. When Communists from the towns came to give orders and take away most of the crops, they got a very rough reception.

At the same time the Communists had to fight for their lives. After the Bolsheviks made peace with the Germans early in 1918, the Allies sent expeditions to co-operate with the non-Bolshevik forces that were rising all over Russia. These forces wanted all sorts of different things, some to restore the tsar to full power, some to have parliamentary government, some to set up independent states, like the Ukrainians or the Don Cossacks; but they all agreed that the Communists must be overthrown.

Since the French Revolution, red had been the colour that stood for revolution, white for royalism. The Communists carried a red flag; their soldiers called themselves the Red Army. All their enemies were lumped together as Whites. Though most of the soldiers on both sides probably only fought because they were forced to (as happens often in civil wars), the Reds were heavily outnumbered. Yet they won. Why? One reason is that they were united under a firm leadership, discipline was strict, and some of them were fanatics. Among young Communists especially, there was an almost religious faith that they were going to build a wonderful new civilisation, with equality and brotherhood between all men. Another reason was strategic. The Reds held the real center of Russia, Moscow and Petrograd and the area between, while their enemies were dispersed over great distances around the edges. Then the

A Red view of the civil war. In this 1919 cartoon the principal White leaders are depicted as savage dogs owned by the USA, France and Britain. From left to right the 'dogs' are:
General Denikin, who threatened Moscow from the south;
Admiral Kolchak, 'Supreme Ruler' in Siberia;
General Yudenich, who thrust from the Baltic provinces.

Allies withdrew; the governments were unwilling to do so, but when the Great War ended their peoples demanded that the soldiers be brought home and the Russians left to settle their own affairs. What the Russians suffered in the civil war is not accurately known. One moderate estimate is that the deaths by battle, massacre, famine and disease numbered about fourteen million.

By the end of 1920 the Communists had won, and Lenin could turn all his attention to building the new society. He soon realised that there would be no society at all if he did not act quickly. Everything was scarce, especially food. Peasant revolts and factory strikes were constantly breaking out. Most alarming of all, the sailors at the naval base of Kronstadt, outside Petrograd, who had always been the staunchest of Reds, mutinied and were only put down after very severe fighting. Lenin decided that he must relax the 'pure' Communism of 1918, and announced the New Economic Policy. The NEP allowed peasants to own fair-sized farms and to keep what they grew, after paying a tax to the state. It permitted people to buy and sell; new coins were minted. Shops could re-open,

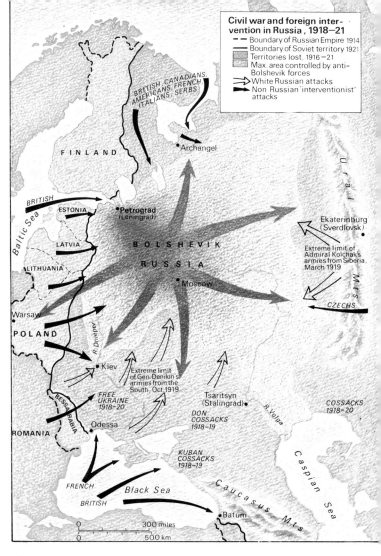

Civil war and foreign inter-vention in Russia, 1918–21
- - - Boundary of Russian Empire 1914
Boundary of Soviet territory 1921
Territories lost, 1916–21
Max. area controlled by anti-Bolshevik forces
→ White Russian attacks
➔ Non Russian 'interventionist' attacks

Early Soviet currency – a silver half-rouble (50 kopecks) of 1926, with communist symbols replacing the eagle (page 43). The inscription means: 'Proletarians of all nations, unite!' (Actual size.)

63

Lenin explaining the GOELRO map, 22 December 1920; the scene as imagined by the Soviet painter L. Shmatko. GOELRO (short for Government Electrification of Russia) was the ambitious Bolshevik plan to provide power to modernise the whole vast country. As Lenin described it to the Eighth All-Russia Congress of Soviets, a coloured light appeared on the map marking the site of each new power station when he named it. The trick caught the imagination of the delegates, who were mainly peasants, workers and soldiers. Prominent among the leading Bolsheviks in the front row is Stalin, gazing up at Lenin like an inspired disciple; it is not difficult to guess who was ruling the USSR at the time the picture was painted.

and even small factories could be privately owned. The NEP succeeded. The Russians managed to grow, make and trade enough to survive – but only just. There was a terrible drought in 1921–2 which spread death over southern Russia, but in this crisis food was sent by other countries, especially the USA; gradually food supplies improved until the danger of total breakdown faded.

The next task was to organise the government of the Russian Empire. All the different nations inside its borders were declared separate republics, but they all had to be governed the same way – as soviet republics, run by local and central soviets. Members of the soviets were elected by the people, but there was only one political party, the Communists. All important jobs were in fact filled by Party members. The soviet republics were no longer under the old empire, but they were held together in the Union of Soviet Socialist Republics, and the Russian Soviet Republic was far the biggest and strongest in the union. So, in effect, the whole USSR was ruled by the Russian Communist Party. This party obeyed a small political committee, the *Politburo*, which was dominated by Lenin.

The USSR was under a dictatorship. Communists would argue that it was a dictatorship of the proletariat, the workers,

and that a dictatorship which had the support of the vast mass of the people was more truly democratic than the parliamentary system of western Europe and America. Anyway, it was only temporary. At present the government needed all its powers to educate the people (only a quarter could read) and make the vast backward land prosperous. Once this gigantic task was accomplished, the powers of the state would be allowed to wither away.

There was also the rest of the world to consider. There were no other Communist countries, but there were many where the rulers believed in capitalism, as in the USA (page 47). These were the richest and most powerful countries in the world. Communists believed in world revolution, and some of the events in Europe after the Great War had frightened non-Communists (page 50). Yet the USSR needed these other countries to send goods, loans and technical experts to help to build Soviet industries. Lenin decided that it would be best to say as little as possible about world revolution, and try to have normal diplomatic and trading relations with the capitalists whom he wished eventually to destroy. So the USSR exchanged ambassadors with other countries, sent representatives to an international economic conference as early as 1922, and generally tried to give the appearance of an ordinary

Lenin presides over the first meeting of the Third International, held in Moscow, 2 March 1919. At that time he and the other Communist leaders believed that the Russian revolution was just the start of a world revolution in which the Third International would take the lead.

member of the international community. But suspicion remained on both sides, and the USSR did not join the League of Nations until 1934.

Except for those official contacts, the USSR tried to prevent foreign influences from reaching the people. Moscow, deep inside Russia, was capital once more, not Petrograd which Peter the Great had built specially to make contact with the West easier. Foreigners were allowed into the USSR only under strict supervision, and Soviet citizens were hardly ever allowed to travel abroad. Of course all newspapers and books were tightly censored, to protect the people against harmful ideas. One of these was religion, which Karl Marx had called 'the opium of the people'. The Church had always been on the side of the rich and powerful, and against revolution; so it would be well to break the hold of the priests on the people and stamp out any 'superstitious' belief in God. According to Soviet law, all citizens had freedom of religion. In fact, everything possible was done to discourage religion: priests were arrested and churches closed, atheist propaganda was spread in newspapers and school lessons, and, of course, anybody known to be religious could expect no favours or promotion. All this did nothing to allay fears in other countries about what 'Bolshies' would do if ever they got the chance. Each side feared infection from the other.

The effort of government was too great for Lenin's strength. In 1918 he was shot by a would-be assassin, and never recovered full health. In 1923 he became almost paralysed and on 21 January 1924 he died. Lenin had been the acknowledged leader since the start of the Bolshevik revolution, and now he was honoured as the prophet and creator of the USSR. Petrograd was renamed Leningrad. His body was embalmed and enshrined in a mausoleum beside the wall of the Kremlin in Moscow. His writings and speeches were revered as perfect wisdom, a guide to all future decisions.

But who would take charge now?

There were two men who stood out as the most likely successors, Trotsky and Stalin. Neither, as it happened, was a pure Russian. The future of both the USSR and the world

The rivals for power

Trotsky was a Ukrainian Jew, born in 1879; his real name was Lev Davidovich Bronstein. He was a lively, brilliant speaker who had lived many years in foreign countries and had an international outlook. He wanted to push ahead with world revolution and thought that the Third International Workingmen's Association (founded in 1919 and often known as the Communist International or Comintern) could be used for this, stirring up strikes and revolts in all parts of the world, with support from Moscow.

Stalin (the name means 'Man of Steel') was a Georgian, born in 1879; his real name was Joseph Vissarionovich Djugashvili. He distrusted anyone and anything foreign. He was careful and efficient, and some thought him brutal. He believed that the world revolution could wait while the USSR concentrated on becoming strong – though of course the Comintern could be used to distract and weaken other countries.

Communist movement depended on the result of the duel between these two men.

Stalin had a great advantage. He was Secretary of the Russian Communist Party, and this key post gave him the power to use or suppress any of the information in the Party's records, to influence meetings and to twist the meaning of decisions. He was the man who managed the Party's business, so it is not surprising that he won. In 1929 Trotsky was expelled from the USSR. In 1940, while he was living in Mexico, he was murdered by one of Stalin's supporters.

Stalin and the Soviet Union

The resources of the USSR were enormous, but they were hardly being used. Stalin believed that an all-powerful government could plan economic development as a whole – mines, farms, factories, power-stations, canals, railways, roads – so that all the parts fitted properly together and all the stages were completed at the right time. He decided that it was most convenient to plan progress in five-year programs. The first Five Year Plan was launched on 1 October 1928.

The task was to turn the sprawling land with its extreme variations of terrain and climate into a modern industrialised state, better and stronger than any capitalist state. A population of peasants had to become engineers, technical and clerical workers, with desperately few people able to teach them. Almost inevitably there were many failures. Often the new factories were pushed so hard to produce the quantity of goods that the Plan required that they neglected quality, and many of their products were shoddy. Newspapers carried stories of how this or that had gone wrong – but always because some managers were stupid or corrupt, never because there was any defect in the Plan or Stalin's government. Newspapers, radio and films, and every form of art from poetry to painting were controlled by the state and urged the Soviet peoples on to greater efforts. Workers who achieved more than the Plan required were rewarded and honoured, but failure could mean loss of privileges, imprisonment in a labour camp or death; after all, since the Plan was right, failure must be the result of laziness or deliberate treachery. Clumsily and painfully the massive state-owned industries began to make more goods. Though there were still not nearly enough, and the quality was poor, nobody could deny that the Plans were bringing results.

A Soviet cartoon of 1933. At the top, a Western capitalist mocks the Five Year Plan of 1928; 'delicious dream Utopia' he sneers. But a few years later he is green with mortification at what the plan has produced. This sort of propaganda was intended to make Soviet citizens think that their shortages were nearly ended, and that they were beating their capitalist enemies.

What Stalin's critics argued was that equal or better results could have been achieved by allowing more freedom.

Agriculture had to be treated like any other industry. The state must organise it on a big modern scale. The peasant farmers had been reprieved by Lenin's NEP, but now they must go. The Party was particularly anxious to get rid of the *kulaks*, or 'fists'. These were the more prosperous peasants who had built up their holdings into fairly large farms and who were men of influence in their villages. So they were destroyed – 'liquidated', in the jargon of the time. They and their families were carried off to the labour camps, where many of them perished – the exact figure is not known. This cleared the way for dividing up the best part of the land in the Soviet Union into state farms *(sovkhoz)* and collective farms *(kolkhoz)*; the latter were formed by persuading all the peasants in a district to lump all their holdings together in one huge estate, where they would all work as their officials directed. According to the Plans, these big farms should be much more efficient than the little peasant holdings, but food production did not increase.

The USSR up to 1936
- -→ Population movements
■ Republic capital
0   500 miles
0   500   1000 km

It was Stalin, not Lenin, who really created the Soviet system, and to make these gigantic changes he used force and terror on an equally gigantic scale. There had been security police in Russia for many years before the revolution, and the Bolsheviks followed the example of the tsars. Under Lenin they were called the *Cheka* for short – the full title meant 'Extraordinary Commission for Combating Counter-Revolution, Sabotage and Speculation'. Now they were the *Ogpu* ('All-Union State Political Organisation') and grew into a large army, with almost unlimited powers. Anyone suspected of not supporting the Soviet system would disappear, most probably into a labour camp where the conditions killed mill-

ions of prisoners. Some selected scapegoats were publicly tried for treason or sabotage, as a warning to others. So the Soviet people learned to be loyal to the Communist regime.

Next Stalin made sure of the loyalty of the Party itself. In 1933 the 'purges' began. All Party members were examined, and about a third of them were judged not to be good enough , and were deprived of their membership; the rest took care to support Stalin's policies. By 1935 he felt strong enough to remove the men who might still have been able to check him. These were the 'old Bolsheviks', leaders of the revolution, heroes of the civil war, friends and assistants of Lenin himself, whose names were honoured among Communists. Their past

The purge of the Red Army, 1937–8

Political officials and officers:	Original number	Executed
Members of Supreme Military Soviet	80	75
Vice-Commissars of Defence	11	11
Army Commissars	17	17
Corps Commissars	28	25
Brigade Commissars	36	34
Military officers:		
Marshals	5	3
Army Commanders	16	14
Corps Commanders	67	60
Division Commanders	199	136
Brigade Commanders	397	221

Of the total of 35,000 officers of all ranks, about half were either shot or imprisoned.

Note: Precise figures were never produced. These figures are based on a Soviet estimate made many years later, after Stalin's death.

record did not save them. Hundreds of them were arrested and accused of being Trotskyites or of being in the pay of foreign capitalists. Many were put on trial in Moscow, and, to the astonishment of foreign journalists invited to these 'show trials', they humbly confessed their treason and accepted their death sentences. It was unthinkable that such men could ever have turned against the cause to which they had dedicated all their earlier lives, yet they did not give the impression of having been drugged or tortured. In 1937 it was the turn of the army and navy to be purged. Since the accused were usually dealt with by court martial, in private, it was hard to tell how many were killed, but later it became obvious that almost all the highest and most experienced officers had been liquidated.

In other countries, most of the newspapers denounced or mocked at what was going on in the USSR, but there were also the local Communist Parties and a good number of socialists who defended the Soviet Union. Some of them said that all the reports of Stalin's tyranny were lies, propaganda invented by the capitalists. Others admitted that Stalin might sometimes be a little hard, but only because it was necessary in order to achieve the happy new society of the future – 'You can't make an omelette without breaking eggs!' In fact, Stalin wielded more power than Ivan the Terrible or Peter the Great or any other tsar.

Mussolini and Fascist Italy

When Italy joined the Allies in 1915 they promised her great rewards after victory, but at the peace treaties they allowed her much less than they had offered. Italy had been cheated, but there was nothing that she could do about it. Some Italians, led by the poet Gabriele d'Annunzio, were so furious that they tried to take by force the Adriatic port of Fiume, which Yugoslavia also claimed; after holding it for over a year, they were forced to leave in January 1921. This was only one sign of the frustration that many Italians felt. Meanwhile the politicians merely talked.

Italy was a poor country and was at least as hard hit as Britain and France by the difficulties of finding jobs for her ex-soldiers. This added to the discontent, and caused many people to support either the Socialist or the Communist Party.

Benito Mussolini (see opposite) had socialistic ideas, but was against both of those parties. First and foremost he wanted to see Italy strong and respected by other nations. He thought the Communists, who preached internationalism instead of nationalism and seemed more devoted to Russia than Italy, were traitors. As for the Socialist Party in the Italian Parliament, he thought they were useless windbags. Parliamentary democracy had failed; what was needed was a strong national government that would get something done, instead of this endless arguing. He formed groups of men who shared these ideas of his and who would do whatever they could to oppose the Socialists and Communists. The groups were called *fasci*, after the bundles of rods that had been carried in ancient Rome by the lictors, the men who escorted magistrates and punished criminals. Officially Mussolini's party was the Voluntary Socialist National Movement (MVSN), but was usually called the *Fascists*.

The discontent in Italy seemed to be growing. There was rioting in the streets, in the parliament many Socialist representatives refused to take the oath of loyalty to the king, and the government seemed to be losing control. In street brawls the people who were always ready to fight the Reds were the Fascists. Indeed, they wanted violence. They believed that it was manly and noble. They wore a semi-military uniform with a black shirt and a dagger, and their marching song was 'Giovinezza', Youth. Some Italians saw the Fascists as the best hope of saving Italy from disorder and perhaps revolution, though others thought that it was the behaviour of the Fascists themselves that was causing most of the trouble.

It was clear that most Italians still supported parliamentary democracy. In the 1921 elections the Liberal Party won 275 seats, the Socialist Party 123 and the Catholic Party 107. The Communists won only 16, the Fascists 35. Yet these tiny parties caused so much disturbance that when bands of Fascists from all parts of Italy began to march towards Rome the Prime Minister thought that he could not govern the country by normal means, and asked the king to declare martial law, so that the government could use the army to enforce obedience. The king refused. The Prime Minister resigned. In this predicament the king decided to try the man who had been calling most loudly for firm government. He invited Mussolini, who arrived by train from Milan with some of his supporters, and was appointed Prime Minister on 30 October 1922. (Later the Fascists called this their 'March on Rome', which sounded much more dramatic and masterful.) In November parliament and the king agreed that, to give the new Prime Minister a good chance to get things running smoothly, he should have the powers of a dictator for a year.

The idea of dictatorship in ancient Rome was that it should be short, to deal with an emergency. But even if Mussolini were able to set things right within a year, was it likely that he would want to restore power to the parliamentary system that he had condemned as useless? The Fascists used that year to put their men into key positions, they altered the election rules, and they bribed and bullied. In the 1924 elections they won 375 seats, and with this overwhelming majority Mussolini was able to continue as dictator, claiming that the great mass of Italians was behind him.

Mussolini tried to turn Italy into what he called a *corporate state*; that is, one complete body with all the limbs and organs working in unison for the benefit of the whole. There must be no opposition, for that would cause illness or injury to the body. Therefore newspapers and the radio must only say what the government wanted, and troublesome critics were removed – often to special prisons on the Lipari Islands. There could be only one political party, of course, the MVSN. Thus united, the nation could use all its intelligence and strength to thrust forward. Mussolini wanted Italy to excel in science and technology, especially aviation. This ought to bring industrial prosperity and, above all, respect from other nations.

Benito Mussolini was born in 1883 near Forli. He went to work in Switzerland, 1902–4, to avoid service in the army; while there he learned about socialism. Back in Italy he joined the Socialist Party and became a journalist and speaker. In 1915 he broke with the Socialists because they were against Italy's entry into the Great War. He joined the army and was wounded in action. Afterwards he became editor of the Milan newspaper 'Il Popolo d'Italia'.

This photograph shows Mussolini in typical style after becoming dictator, projecting an image of dynamic leadership to his assembled followers. The microphone (placed at a safe distance from his powerful voice and gestures) carries the message of Il Duce (as he was called) to the Italian nation.

Fascist dagger. With its strong double-edged blade and plain wooden haft, shaped to give a good grip, it is meant for use rather than ornament. The steel sheath has the fasces symbol and the initials MVSN.

In many ways Fascist Italy was like Communist Russia – one political party, censorship, arrest of opponents, united effort for the common good. Both were dictatorships and both claimed to be supported by the whole people. But there were big differences. Communists saw the people of the world as being divided not into nations but into classes, and fought for the working class against the others. Fascists fought for the nation, and insisted that all classes should unite to make their country great. Communists persecuted religion, but Mussolini, though he had once been anti-Church, made a concordat with the Pope in 1929 that ended the long feud between the Vatican and the kingdom of Italy. Communists confiscated property, but Fascists protected the wealthy as long as they supported Mussolini. The Fascists were not revolutionaries. The king,

the nobility, the capitalists all went on as before – indeed, though they may have despised the Fascists as vulgar upstarts, many of them were glad enough to profit from contracts and business deals with Mussolini's men. The workers were organised in trade unions, but these were (like those in the USSR) meant not to fight the employers but to act as welfare societies. Finally, though the Fascists could sometimes ill-treat or kill their opponents, there was nothing in Italy to compare with the Soviet labour camps and the millions of deaths that took place inside them. Compared with Stalin's dictatorship, Mussolini's was mild and humane.

Did Fascism work? Certainly it kept Italy peaceful after the threat that law and order might break down. There was a great show of efficiency – one standing joke was that Mussolini had

National corporate states and international class war
How were people divided?

The Fascists believed in national unity, with rivalry and conflict between nations.

The Communists believed in the 'class war', between the workers of all nations and those who were 'exploiting' them.

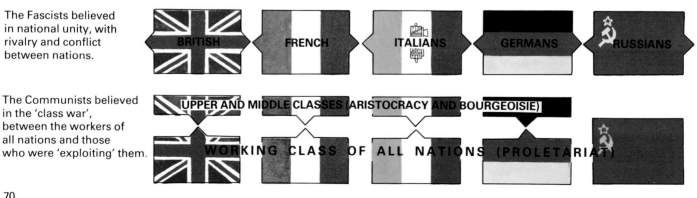

Exhibition of the Fascist Revolution, Rome 1933. It displays the massive Cubist style that many dictators favoured in their architecture – perhaps because of its suggestion of uncluttered efficiency and brute force. The columns above the entrance are giant modernistic fasces.

enough. In 1935 he used a frontier dispute as an excuse to invade Abyssinia and conquer it. Thus he displayed the strength of his forces, and avenged the defeat that the Abyssinians had inflicted on Italy forty years before at the battle of Adowa. The League of Nations condemned Italy for aggression, but Mussolini ignored the protests and showed that the League was powerless to stop him.

In other countries many people thought of Mussolini as an absurd braggart always making melodramatic speeches from his balcony. Some said that the Fascists were oppressive and corrupt, and inefficient too; their strength was all on the surface, and would crumble if they came up against an enemy better-armed than the Abyssinians.

On the other hand, Mussolini had his admirers in other countries, too. People who thought that parliamentary democracy was failing, for example, to deal with unemployment and depression, but who disliked Communism; people who felt that their countries were slipping into poverty and weakness, and that they needed a strong leader to appeal to the nation's patriotism and self-respect; people like these sometimes founded Fascist-style parties in their own countries. These parties did not belong to an international organisation, in the way that Communist Parties did. Most of them (the British Union of Fascists was an exception) did not have the word 'Fascist' in their names: for example, the Romanian Iron Guard, the *Croix de Feu* (Fiery Cross) in France and the *Falange Española* (Spanish Phalanx). There were also extreme nationalist movements that were much older than Fascism, like *Action Française*, founded in 1899 in the midst of the Dreyfus controversy (page 11), which had a good deal in common with some Fascist ideas. Fascism was not an international party, but it was an attitude that people in many countries shared.

Hitler and Nazi Germany

The new German republic that took over from the Kaiser in 1918 seemed surrounded by enemies. The Allies at Versailles inflicted harsh and humiliating terms. Many Germans despised the republic's leaders for having submitted to them. Some soldiers said that the German army had never really been beaten by the Allies, but had been 'stabbed in the back' by traitors and cowards in Germany. But inside Germany

at last got the trains to run on time. There was more work, too. Some of it was on such much-publicised projects as draining the marshes near Rome, and building the first road in the world for high-speed cars, the *autostrada* across the Lombard plain. Italian engineering gained a high reputation for fast cars, aircraft and ships. There were also more jobs in the armaments industry.

Mussolini wanted to impress the rest of the world with the strength and virility of the new Italy. Spectacular flights across the Atlantic or the North Pole by Italian airmen were not there was near-starvation because of the Allied blockade, and even after the Armistice the Allies had been very grudging about letting supplies in. There were outbreaks of revolution in some places; for a while Bavaria was ruled by a Communist government in Munich. Along Germany's new eastern borders there was still fighting as the new nations tried to claim territory which local Germans were trying to hold. In the midst of all this, private armies were formed, the *Freikorps*, ex-soldiers who were ready to go on fighting, either on the eastern borders or against Communists inside Germany.

Yet the new republic survived, perhaps because of all these enemies. The Freikorps helped to put down revolutionaries, but dared not try to overthrow the republic because of the Allied troops in the Rhineland. When the economy seemed about to collapse (page 49) the Allies stepped in to save it, for fear the collapse might spread to their own economies. Gradually Germany settled down and began to show signs of prosperity. In 1926 Germany was admitted to the League of Nations and recognised as one of its most important members.

There was a strong feeling in many countries that the Great War had been a ghastly blunder, and that all war was wrong. In an effort to get away from the military atmosphere of the Second Reich, the republicans met at Weimar to agree on the German constitution. Weimar was famous as the home of Germany's greatest poet, Goethe, and the makers of the Weimar Republic wanted to stress that it was the fame of Germans in literature, music, the arts and sciences that they were proud of, not war. Among the Allies many people recovered from their hysterical hatred of Germany and felt rather ashamed, especially when they learned that many of the stories of German war crimes had been pure invention. On both sides the main feeling came to be one of tragic waste; in Germany the novel *All Quiet on the Western Front* was published in 1929, and in Britain the play *Journey's End* was first performed in 1928. Also in 1928 Frank Kellogg, the American Secretary of State, made an agreement with the French Foreign Minister, Aristide Briand, that neither country would ever fight a war except in defence, and they invited other countries to sign; more than sixty did so. It was a hopeful time.

The Wall Street crash came at the end of 1929 and soon Germans felt and feared poverty again. As poverty and unemployment spread, the forces that the Weimar Republic had put down ten years before revived. More and more people felt

'Grey Day', painted by Georg Grosz, 1893–1959. Grosz produced many pictures revealing the misery and the greed, complacency and corruption that he saw in post-war Germany. Here a haggard, maimed ex-soldier makes his painful way down a bleak street, disregarded by the workman striding across the background and the well-dressed fat man (with an anti-republican badge in his coat) who stares, cross-eyed, out of the foreground. An enigmatic bespectacled man watches, half-hidden by a wall.

that parliamentary democracy had failed after all. Some of these turned to Communism, and others turned to the National Socialist German Workers' Party (NSDAP are the initials of its German name) or *Nazis*, led by Adolf Hitler.

The beliefs of the Nazis were all in Hitler's book *Mein Kampf*. They were written in such a rambling, exaggerated style that many people thought they were not intended to be taken as sober plans – even Hitler himself sometimes suggested that they were to be understood as the musings and imaginings of a man in prison; but they turned out to be a true reflection of Nazi feelings and intentions. The Germans, they said, were the greatest nation on earth, destined to be the leaders of all others; they were the *Herrenvolk* (master people). They had been betrayed in the Great War by greedy capitalists, who were interested only in making money, and by deluded revolutionaries; and these traitors were led by Jews. The Jews, they said, were a wicked race who hated and wished to destroy the Germans, and they must be driven out and destroyed themselves. There were other inferior races, too, especially the Slavs and coloured races; Germany would be justified in spreading eastwards and taking possession of the wide lands that the Slavs did not know how to use. Germans would lead the world.

This wild talk may have appealed to people who felt beaten and desperate. But the Nazis also argued that only a strong, determined government could save Germany from Communism and restart German industries and find work for everybody. Obviously the politicians of the Weimar Republic did not know how to do this. Also, they were letting Germany become decadent; the Nazis said that the modern art and literature that flourished in Germany during the twenties were mad and rotten, and were undermining the moral character of the Germans, just as the night-clubs and sex shows of Berlin were doing. Many Germans who took no notice of Hitler's racial fantasies were impressed by these arguments.

The Nazis also appealed to young men who liked dressing up in uniform and parading about, and to those who also liked fighting, frightening and hurting other people. They joined the SA (*Sturm Abteilungen* or Storm Troops), who wore brown military-style uniform, or the select SS (*Schutzstaffeln* or Security Squads) who acted as Hitler's bodyguard and wore a black uniform.

While things in Germany were going reasonably well, in the later 1920s, the Nazi Party remained small, though it got money and help from a few rich businessmen who thought it might turn out to be their best defence against Communism. When things went wrong after the Wall Street crash both the Nazis and the Communists suddenly gained new supporters. In the 1930 elections to the Reichstag they increased their seats from a handful to 77 Communists and 107 Nazis. Street fighting between Nazis and 'Reds' became more savage, and many were killed – one of them was Horst Wessel, who wrote the song named after him, which became the Nazi anthem. As the violence grew, more Germans – especially, it seems, lower middle class people – saw the Nazis as their protectors against

Adolf Hitler was born in 1889 in Braunau, Upper Austria. He fled to avoid military service in the Austrian army; after his return he tried to become an artist in Vienna but had little success. In 1914 he went to Bavaria and joined the German army, fought on the Western Front, was wounded and decorated. In 1919 he joined the tiny NSDAP in Munich and in 1920 became its leader. In 1923 the party tried to seize control of Munich by a putsch, or armed take-over; it failed and Hitler was imprisoned for a year. He spent his time in prison writing 'Mein Kampf' (My Struggle).

This is one of his best-known images. Nazi propaganda used pictures like this to reassure people – such a man could not possibly permit brutality. (The children shown in these pictures were always very 'Aryan'-looking.)

revolution, and in 1932 they won more seats than any other single party in the Reichstag.

The Nazis did not have more seats than all the other parties combined, and the President, old General Hindenburg, disliked them. But no other party leader was able to find enough support in the Reichstag to form a government, so at last he had to appoint Hitler Chancellor, or Prime Minister, on 30 January 1933.

Hitler wanted complete power, which only an overall majority in the Reichstag could give him, so he called a fresh election. Shortly before polling day, on the night of 27 February, the Reichstag building was gutted by fire. Hitler declared that this was part of a Communist plot, and persuaded Hindenburg to use his emergency powers to control the press and limit free speech. Probably the fire had been started by the Nazis themselves, and it certainly allowed them

Hitler addresses a crowd of 20,000 in the Berlin Sportspalast, 6 October 1938. He is inaugurating the annual Winter Relief campaign, appealing to his people to give generously to provide comforts for their fellow-Germans suffering hardship through old age or poor health. Lighting has been used to great effect. The rows of attentive faces gaze from the darkness towards the brilliant stage where their leader stands alone. Behind, the floodlit wall carries the bold, simple message: 'A People Helps Itself!'

to gag their opponents, but still they failed to get an overall majority when the election took place on 5 March. However, Hitler managed to get enough members of other parties to vote with the Nazis to pass the Enabling Act on 23 March. This act gave the Chancellor dictatorial powers for four years.

He kept his promise to put Germany back to work. The state organised ambitious projects – forestry, monumental public buildings, houses for workers, wide highways *(autobahnen)* criss-crossing Germany. He announced that Germany was no longer bound by the Treaty of Versailles, and gave orders to German shipyards and factories for warships, aircraft, tanks, guns, uniforms. Many thousands of young men were drafted into the army, navy and air force, and there were thousands more jobs for officials to organise all this activity.

Hindenburg died on 2 August 1934 and Hitler took his place as head of the German state. He did not use the title of President but *Führer* (leader). He announced that the Third Reich had begun, a new German empire that would last a thousand years, and the Nazi badge, the swastika, became part of the German national flag. The German people approved. Whenever he made a big change, Hitler held a plebiscite to ask his people for their support, and they always gave him what he wanted – a 'yes' vote of about 99%. This may have been partly because of what Hitler was doing for Germany, but there were other reasons.

Hitler's propaganda was directed by Dr Josef Goebbels, a brilliant and unscrupulous journalist who believed that people would accept any story as long as it was told loudly and often; the bigger and bolder the lie, the more likely it was to be swallowed. He made sure that all the newspapers, radio, books and films agreed with the story that Hitler was the greatest genius of all time. Führer-worship reached its height in the Party rallies, gigantic meetings where thousands of uniformed Nazis paraded with their banners before vast crowds. The spectators were worked into a state of near-hysteria by the sight, the music, and the rhythmic chanting; then at the right moment the Führer himself would appear and speak to his people. Even firm anti-Nazis who went out of curiosity to such meetings have admitted they could hardly resist being swept along in the tidal wave of mass adulation. It had all been very expertly managed.

There were other ways of encouraging loyalty. People tended to get better jobs if they were for the Party, and to suffer misfortunes if they were known to be against. People who were too 'unpatriotic' were taken away to special camps where they could be 're-educated' by brisk, healthy discipline. Over the gates of these camps was the inscription *Arbeit Macht Frei* (Work Makes You Free). But soon the rumour spread that these concentration camps were places of starvation, overwork, brutality, torture and murder; they were run by the SS who were interested only in breaking their prisoners' bodies, minds and spirits. So there was always a shadow of fear behind the cheering.

Anybody, even a close relative, might turn out to be a spy,

trying to earn favour by telling tales to the *Gestapo (Geheime Staatspolizei*, Secret State Police), who were linked to the SS. The clearest warning that nobody was safe came in June 1934. Hitler came to suspect that the chiefs of the SA had ideas of their own about how Germany should be governed, and that they criticised his actions. 'The Night of the Long Knives', 30 June, was the result. SS men arrested and killed almost all the leaders of the SA. For a time some Germans were foolish enough to believe that this was a good sign, that Hitler had taken the only possible way of getting rid of the thugs and bullies who had given the Nazis a bad reputation. In fact it

Building the new Reich. A propaganda photograph showing the coming generation of Germans, strong and enthusiastic, hard at work on one of Hitler's projects. These young men represent the Herrenvolk, *the superior nation, who will lead the world.*

Illustration from a children's book of the Third Reich. Clean, bright little Germans are looking at a notice-board for 'Der Stürmer' (The Stormer). This was a wildly anti-Jewish paper run by Julius Streicher; some of the headlines describe different aspects of the Jewish 'conspiracy', and there is an announcement of a meeting to be addressed by Streicher himself. On the left huddles a small group of Jews, comic but unpleasant, like the three birds beside them. Propaganda as crude as this may not seem likely to influence intelligent adults, but it was aimed at children; besides, Goebbels believed that anybody would come to accept any story, if it were repeated often and loudly.

meant that from now on the SS were to be in charge, and they were far worse. It is not surprising that ordinary Germans preferred to close their eyes to the horrifying side of Nazi rule, and got into the habit of believing what Goebbels told them and giving the Nazi salute and saying *'Heil Hitler!'* whenever they met anyone.

It was easier to excuse Hitler's oppression because he had not only removed the fear of unemployment and poverty, he had made Germany a great power again. He asserted that all people of German race had the right to be within the Reich, and set about extending his frontiers to include German-speaking areas that were at present under foreign rule. His first success was the Saar. This was a small but rich coalfield on the frontiers of France and Germany, and both countries wanted it. After the war it was administered temporarily by the League of Nations, until 1935. Then the Saarlanders had to vote on where they wanted to belong, and voted for Germany by a 90% majority. It was a proud moment, and Hitler made his next move in the same region. The last Allied troops had withdrawn from the Rhineland in 1930, but that part of Germany was to remain demilitarised, according to the Treaty of Versailles; that is, German troops must not be stationed in it. Hitler ordered them to occupy the Rhineland in March 1936. Britain and France protested, but took no action; it was not worth fighting over, and they had other worries. As for international opinion, Hitler had shown what he thought of that by taking Germany out of the League of Nations as early as October 1933.

The most obvious German-speaking land that was not part of the Reich was Austria. After the war, when Austria lost her empire and was left a small state, some Austrians suggested joining Germany – after all, Austria had been the leading member of the Germanic Confederation until 1866; but the Allies forbade it. The idea had not died, though. In 1934 some Austrian Nazis made a clumsy attempt to seize power, but all they succeeded in doing was killing the Austrian Chancellor, Dr Dollfuss. Hitler may not have had a hand in that attempt, but he made careful preparations for the next; born an Austrian himself, he could not admit that Austria was not German. After four years of propaganda, promises and threats the Austrian government gave in. In March 1938 German troops moved peacefully into Austria, greeted by cheering crowds. Next month there was a plebiscite to ask the Austrians if they

One of the Nazi posters that told the Austrians how to vote in the plebiscite on the Anschluss. Its message is: 'The whole people says Yes! on 10 April.'

wanted *Anschluss* (union) with the Reich, and 99.75% of the voters said 'Yes'.

With every success Hitler's hold on Germany grew more secure. Some had hoped that this would make him more reasonable and mild. But, though Goebbels' propaganda always emphasised what a good, kind man the Führer was, the Nazi tyranny grew worse. This was particularly obvious in the persecution of the Jews.

Jews had often been persecuted before, but usually because of their religion. This time it was because of their race. The Nazis had what they called scientific theories to show that people cannot do anything to alter their racial qualities, for good or ill, and that the Jewish race was utterly debased. So anyone born with Jewish blood – even one grandparent – was bound to be corrupt and evil. Propaganda kept on churning out the message that all Jews were vile creatures, and no good German should have anything to do with them. Nazis painted signs on Jewish businesses and stood outside to see if any non-Jew dared go in. They insulted and beat Jews in the street.

They banned great German music because it had been composed by Jews, and burned great German books because they had been written by Jews. The Nuremberg Laws of 15 September 1935 deprived Jews of all their rights as German citizens; henceforth they had no legal protection. It became a crime, punishable by death, for a German to marry a Jew. Any sign of resistance or protest, of course, meant condemnation to a concentration camp. Thousands of Jews, among them some of the best scientists, writers and musicians in Germany, fled abroad, many of them to the USA. At first the Nazis seemed glad to see Jews go, but then put difficulties in their path unless they were rich enough to buy their way out; most Jews would have to stay where the Nazis could do as they pleased with them.

It was probably the persecution of the Jews that showed other nations most clearly that there was a streak of madness in the Nazi dictatorship. Even Stalin, who was killing and imprisoning on a far larger scale than Hitler, could have claimed some sort of political reason behind his suspicions and cruelty. In Germany, though, hundreds of thousands of Germans were being cast out from society and treated as sub-humans, not for anything they might have done or believed, but simply because they had been born. There was no need to prove guilt before punishing any one of them, because every member of that race must be bad. In the past there had been many wars and massacres between people of different nationalities and races, but it was hard to think of anything like this; and it was going on within a country that had been for hundreds of years in the forefront of European civilisation.

Still the Reich seemed to prosper and grow stronger. But after a few years some economists started to wonder how long it could last. True, people were working; but were they producing goods that other people would buy? In fact most of the new employment was not solidly based on increased trade, but was being paid for by the government out of taxes, out of wealth seized from the Jews and other victims, and out of loans. Some of Hitler's economic advisers were uncomfortably aware that they were just managing to make their accounts balance by clever juggling with figures, that Germany was dangerously close to bankruptcy and that they could not keep up the appearance of success for much longer. But the financial crash they feared never came. Instead, Europe was plunged into another Great War.

The People's Radio. When they came to power the Nazis quickly produced a cheap, reliable receiver. By 1939 four times as many Germans owned radios as in 1933. This advertisement reads: 'The whole of Germany hears the Leader on the People's Receiver.'

The People's Car. This 1938 advertisement announces that any German, by paying only five marks a week, can eventually drive his own KdF car. (KdF stands for Kraft durch Freude, Strength through Joy; this was the organisation that arranged holidays and all sorts of leisure activities for citizens of the Third Reich.) Many thousands joined the scheme and subscribed a great deal of money, but before they got their cars war came, and the Volkswagen factory had to supply the army instead. After the war the VW 'Beetle' became the best-selling car in the world.

Comparing the dictators

The years of the dictators

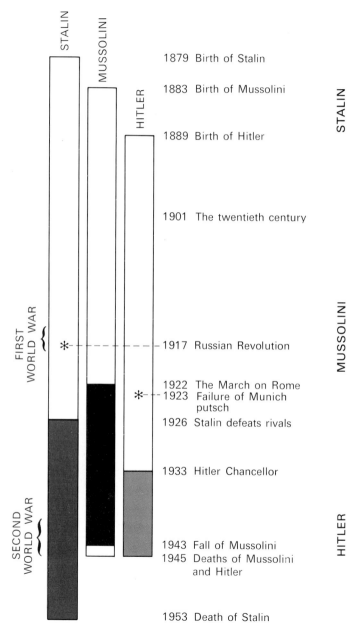

STALIN

MUSSOLINI

HITLER

1879 Birth of Stalin

1883 Birth of Mussolini

1889 Birth of Hitler

1901 The twentieth century

FIRST WORLD WAR

✳ –––––––––––––––– 1917 Russian Revolution

1922 The March on Rome
✳–– 1923 Failure of Munich putsch

1926 Stalin defeats rivals

1933 Hitler Chancellor

SECOND WORLD WAR

1943 Fall of Mussolini
1945 Deaths of Mussolini and Hitler

1953 Death of Stalin

What were their ideologies?

COMMUNISM   A form of socialism expounded by Karl Marx in *Das Kapital* (1867), as interpreted by Lenin. Main ideas were:

Human societies inevitably pass through stages of development. Industry and capitalism replaced rural feudalism and must in turn decay.

All history is a struggle for power between different economic classes, and now it is the turn of the workers to win. The class war is international, and nationalism is a device of capitalist rulers to turn workers against workers, instead of their real enemies.

Eventually, after world revolution, classes and states will wither away as everybody shares and co-operates freely. Meanwhile the state, on behalf of the workers, must seize all property and exercise dictatorial powers ('the dictatorship of the proletariat').

Religion, 'the opium of the people', must be discouraged and finally wiped out.

STALIN

FASCISM   *A combination of socialism (his first belief) with nationalism (aroused in war), made by Mussolini himself. Main ideas were:*

A man's first duty is to the greatness of his nation.

All members of the nation must work together, whatever their class, as one body ('the corporate state'). Obviously there can be no opposition to the leader of the nation.

Men show their finest qualities in action and violence, and must do so in serving the nation.

Though at first anti-clerical, Mussolini came to terms with the Church and accepted it as part of the tradition of Italian greatness; but ancient Rome was the most glorious inspiration.

MUSSOLINI

NAZISM   Similar to Fascism, but given special slants by Hitler in *Mein Kampf* (1925). Main ideas were:

The German nation is the finest part of the Teutonic, Aryan race, is superior to all others and should lead the world.

While the whole nation, including Germans at present under other governments, must be united under one all-powerful leader, non-Aryan elements (specifically Jews) must be excluded.

Communism is the great enemy not only because it is anti-national but because it is directed by Slavs and Jews, who have always tried to harm the Germans.

The true spirit of the Germans is represented not by the Christian religion but by the myths and legends of the Teutonic barbarians.

HITLER

How did they rise to power?

Joined an existing party (Bolsheviks) with a strong ideology and leader (Marxism and Lenin).

Did not lead revolution and civil war, but played a prominent part.

Gained key appointment of Secretary of the Party.

At Lenin's death was one of the most obvious candidates for leadership, and his position gave him the advantage over his rival Trotsky.

Gained experience as journalist and socialist speaker.

After leaving army was able to spread influence as newspaper editor.

Took advantage of wartime nationalism, disappointment with peace treaties, post-war depression and fear of Bolshevism. Claimed to be able to stop disorder (which he had partly created) and was asked by king to form government when previous Prime Minister proved incapable. Appointment was therefore legal, and confirmed by parliament soon afterwards.

Overwhelming victory at next general election (though dishonest means were used) provided parliamentary majority which supported dictatorship.

Joined tiny German Workers' Party (DAP); very quickly became leader. Took advantage of wartime nationalism, bitter resentment at peace treaty, post-war depression and fear of Bolshevism. Supported by some army officers. Party organised on semi-military lines.

Fiasco of Munich *putsch*, 1923.

Resumed after release from prison; supported by some wealthy businessmen as a defence against Communism. Further depression after 1929 – more support for extreme parties, both Nazis and Communists; after street violence Nazis gained general support and many more seats in *Reichstag* (parliament). Nazis largest single party, Hitler invited by president to form government. Appointment was therefore legal.

At next general election still failed to win overall majority, but persuaded Reichstag to vote him dictatorial powers.

How did they hold on to power?

The Party already controlled USSR; Stalin strengthened hold on Party through purges.

Force applied chiefly through *Ogpu* (under Beria). Huge numbers of people disappeared – none dared criticise.

Propaganda in two parts:

1 Communism the one true faith, and Lenin the great founder. Everything from works of art to scientific ideas must express Marxist principles, and conform to whatever policy the Party thought expedient ('the Party line').

2 Stalin, the successor of Lenin, always portrayed as the wise, good and strong guardian of Communism, never wrong.

The Party *became the only one permitted. No one could hold public office unless pro-Facist. Fascists and their friends got favours.*

Force *used against opponents (beatings, dosing with castor oil, imprisonment); but lacked the camps and pervasive fear of the other dictatorships. Uniforms and parades suggested strength.*

Propaganda *mainly control of press and radio to ensure favourable accounts of 'Il Duce' and Italian achievements under his orders.*

The Party expanded rapidly, covered the country with an administration that duplicated the ordinary machinery of government. Hitler wiped out leadership of SA, suspecting disloyalty, and relied entirely on SS (under Himmler), which grew enormously until almost 'a state within a state'. Prominent (and ambitious) people put under pressure to join Party, sometimes SS too.

Force applied through SS and *Gestapo* (secret police), with spies and informers – beatings and concentration camps. Persecution of Jews added to atmosphere of terror. Uniforms and mammoth rallies suggested massive, irresistible strength.

Propaganda, directed by Goebbels, thorough and all-pervasive – even to daily greeting of '*Heil Hitler*'. Press, radio and rallies used mainly to represent Hitler as the greatest genius of all time, and to stir up hatred of his enemies.

What did they achieve in their own countries?

STALIN

Kept order, suppressed everything non-Communist.

With Five Year Plans made USSR a totally Communist society, which Lenin had not done; hence sometimes credited with the real Communist Revolution.

Agriculture: independent peasant farmers destroyed (liquidation of *kulaks*), almost all organised in collective or state farms (*kolkhoz* and *sovkhoz*) with tractors and machinery. But food production did not increase.

Industry: rapid expansion of heavy manufacture, mines etc., much of it in Siberia and using forced labour. But shortages continued and quality was often very poor.

Defence: large forces and armaments industry. But efficiency reduced by purges of officers and unreliability of much equipment.

Education: vast increase in literacy, technical and university qualifications. But everything had to be understood as fitting in with Marxist ideology and Party policy.

Minority populations: in theory had their own republics and could secede from USSR if they wished. In practice had to obey central government in Moscow, and Russian settlement (e.g. in Central Asia) increased.

MUSSOLINI

Kept order, suppressed criticism.

No economic reorganisation (though trade unions became part of the state organisation). 'Prestige' efforts in e.g. aviation, ships, roads gave Italian engineering a high reputation for a time.

No social changes.

The feud between the Italian state and the Catholic Church (since 1870) was ended.

HITLER

Kept order, suppressed everything but support for *Der Führer*.

Society was not transformed, as in the USSR, but a Nazi hierarchy was created alongside, and to some extent in opposition to the old order, which many Nazis despised.

Industry remained in private hands, and prospered, largely from government orders for military equipment and uniforms, aircraft and ships. Many thousands were also employed on large government projects, e.g. building, forestry.

Defence: large and rapid expansion of all forces.

How did they deal with other countries?

Continued policy of isolation, but had normal contacts at diplomatic level; joined League of Nations, 1934.

Through Comintern controlled Communist Parties in other countries. Encouraged alliances of Communists with other 'Left' parties in Popular Fronts, so as to gain influence, during 1930s.

Supported Republicans in Spanish Civil War, 1936–9, but tried to gain control and destroy other Left parties.

Offered to join France and Britain in opposing Hitler over Czechoslovakia, 1938, but was distrusted and kept out.

Made agreement with the arch-enemy, Hitler, in August 1939 to divide Poland.

*Continued to distrust 1914–18 Allies, and to **want everything** they had promised; also resented French possession of Savoy, Nice, Tunis.*

At first suspicious of Hitler, and protected Austria against him. Then changed policy completely, formed Rome-Berlin Axis 1936.

Conquest of Abyssinia, 1935–6, exposed powerlessness of League.

Sent much aid to Nationalists in Spanish Civil War, 1936–9.

Resigned from League, 1937.

Seized Albania, 1939.

Determined to overturn Versailles settlement, bring under German rule all territories where the people spoke German, make Germany the greatest power in Europe, expand eastwards and destroy Communism.

Resigned from League, 1933. Extended rule over German areas: Saar 1935 (plebiscite), Rhineland 1936 (remilitarised), Austria 1938 (occupied and plebiscite), Sudetenland 1938 (Munich agreement), Memel 1939 (ceded by Lithuania).

Supported Mussolini (Axis 1936) and Japan (Anti-Comintern Pact 1936). Aided Nationalists in Spain, 1936–9.

Continued expansion into non-German territory: occupied Bohemia, Moravia and Slovakia as protectorates 1939. Claim to Polish Corridor (mixed population) followed by invasion of Poland and start of Second World War.

How did they affect the Second World War?

Guaranteed the speedy destruction of Poland, annexed the eastern part, 1939.

Took advantage of the other powers' being engaged elsewhere to seize territory from Finland and Romania and to force the Baltic republics (Estonia, Latvia, Lithuania) to become part of the USSR, 1939–40.

Despite warnings, completely surprised by Hitler's attack, 1941. Early Russian disasters partly the result of this, partly of his purge of experienced officers.

Tight security system, Russian patriotism and propaganda enabled him to survive his mistakes and claim credit for the later victories, to which his movement of industry to Siberia had certainly contributed.

In 'Summit Conferences' with Roosevelt and Churchill secured aid and agreement that eastern Europe should be occupied by Soviet forces.

Entered war in 1940 by attacking France when German victory was already certain.

Attacks on Greece and on British in Egypt and Somaliland, 1940, were failures; lost Abyssinia, 1941, and was rescued by Germans in other areas. Henceforward a mere client of Hitler. Italian defeats the result of poor training, inadequate equipment, lack of enthusiasm for Fascism – all the fault of Mussolini.

After Allied invasion of Sicily and Italy, 1943, dismissed by king and imprisoned. Rescued by German paratroops and set up a Fascist republic in northern Italy. At end of war caught and shot by Italian anti-Fascists.

Conquered almost all mainland Europe in swift campaigns, 1939–41. Claimed credit as great military genius. His position stronger than ever. But made Nazi tyranny wider and worse in Europe, and aroused bitter opposition and resistance movements.

His interference with military plans partly responsible for disaster in Russia and turn of war against Germany, 1943. Survived bomb plot, 1944, tightened hold of SS on Germany, put trust in V-weapons for ultimate victory.

Remained in Berlin as Soviet forces arrived; finally convinced of total defeat, committed suicide.

What were their legacies?

Remained master of USSR until he died, 1953. During this time established USSR as one of the two world superpowers, and began the 'Cold War' relationship with the West.

Some reaction after his death: Beria dismissed and shot 1953; Stalin's tyranny denounced by Khrushchev 1956; slight relaxation of controls over expression of opinions.

In general, Soviet policy continued as it had been under Stalin, and the USSR held the position in the world that it had gained under his dictatorship.

He was toppled so easily that it seems very few Italians believed in him then, and possibly most of them never had – they had merely put up with him.

After his fall Italy changed sides in the war, and therefore did not share the utter ruin that befell Germany.

In the new Italian Republic (founded 1946) moderate parties took control; the Communists were strong, but usually worked within the parliamentary system; and neo-Fascist groups were very small.

Germany fought to the end under Hitler, and ended the war in ruins and occupied by her enemies. The occupying powers tried to create in their zones methods of government which they themselves preferred. The Western powers set up the Federal Republic and the USSR the Democratic Republic in 1949.

Prosecution and punishment of former Nazis for war crimes (e.g. in concentration camps) were taken over by German courts and went on for many years; few signs of any attempt to justify Nazi crimes, though many attempts to explain how it happened.

Enormous effort of both Germanies to rebuild; within about twenty years they became economically the most successful countries in their respective halves of Europe.

Germany remained in the front line of the Cold War, split by the 'Iron Curtain'.

Hitler and his regime left at first a reputation for insane and cruel tyranny without equal in the history of civilised peoples, and this remained the usual judgment. Yet the prowess of his armies and the pageantry of his parades fascinated many people even in the countries that had suffered under his yoke, and they studied the Third Reich and collected its relics.

5 The Second World War, 1939–45

The failure of the League

During the 1920s it seemed that the League of Nations was succeeding, on the whole, in keeping peace in the world, and the international atmosphere was hopeful enough to encourage the Kellogg-Briand Pact (page 72). But perhaps this was because during the twenties there was no serious threat of war involving one of the big powers. During the thirties a few strong countries chose to reject the authority of the League, and revealed that the League was powerless.

Japan was the first of these countries. The land of Japan was quite small, but the population was large and growing; the government felt that they must get possession of fresh resources. They must seize more territory on the mainland of

The Japanese never recognised it as a war, but their army conquered a great part of China from 1937 onwards. Here we see a column of Japanese infantry marching into the Chinese capital, Beijing (Peking).

Asia. Warfare did not seem bad to them. Many of the leaders of Japan were steeped in the traditions of the *samurai*, the warrior class who had been masters of Japan until the country 'modernised' itself in the later nineteenth century. In fact members of this class continued to fill the most important positions under the emperor, and some of them still believed that the most noble thing in life was to fight and conquer, or die heroically. Men inspired by modern economic greed and old-fashioned love of battle were the dominating personalities in the Japanese government in the 1930s.

Japan had held Korea since the Russo-Japanese War of 1904–5, and this had also given her a 'sphere of influence' in Manchuria. As we have seen (page 59), the first step was to seize Manchuria and turn it into a puppet state called Manchukuo in 1932. The League of Nations protested, and the only two countries that eventually recognised the new state were Italy and Germany. But nobody interfered, and Japan quickly developed very useful industries in Manchukuo. This was such a success that in 1937 Japan invaded the Republic of China, and began a war that was still going on in 1941 when it became part of the Second World War.

Why did the League let Japan 'get away with it' in 1932? The main reason is that the only member countries that might have been strong enough to take action, Britain and France, were a long way away and had the depression sapping their strength. Besides, technically Manchukuo was independent – Japan had only helped the Manchurians (who were in fact different from other Chinese) to free themselves from China. Japan eventually resigned from the League in 1938. By then the League had become so weak that there is no point in asking why it did nothing about the 'China Incident' of 1937.

The event that really showed how feeble the League was took place in 1935 – the Italian attack on Abyssinia (page 71). This time the League applied economic sanctions; that is, its members were forbidden to trade with Italy. The idea was that what amounted to a world-wide blockade would soon bring the delinquent country to its senses, but in fact so many exceptions were allowed, and so many countries turned a blind eye to profitable smuggling that sanctions were a farce from the start. In May 1936 Italy completed the conquest of Abyssinia and declared it part of the Italian Empire, so in July the League ended its sanctions. Italy resigned from the League at the end of 1937.

By the middle 1930s it was becoming clear that three important countries, Japan, Italy and Germany, believed that they were entitled to do whatever they thought was best for themselves, whether or not it meant using force; they cared nothing for the words of others. Many people in Europe began to see Fascism, Nazism and similar movements as one huge alliance of tyrants who intended to attack their neighbours and put an end to democracy wherever they could. They saw Europe as the arena where a great struggle between Fascism and freedom was about to take place. It was the Spanish Civil War that seemed to bring this conflict into the open and challenge everyone to take sides.

In fact there was nothing simple and straightforward about the Spanish Civil War. For well over a century Spain had been continually disturbed. There were all sorts of political groups, including some who wanted self-government for their own bits of Spain, some who either loved or hated the Catholic Church, a much bigger Anarchist Party than elsewhere in Europe, and the normal range of parties that included everything from royalism to Communism – and often there were rival versions of each of these. There had been many riots and risings. In 1931 the King of Spain left the country, though he did not abdicate. A republican form of government was set up, and disputes became more violent still. Many Spaniards hoped that at last Spain would get a democratic government that would curb the power of the Church and the upper classes, and do something to cure the grinding poverty in which millions of Spaniards lived and died. But many, on the other hand, feared that the country was about to fall into revolution, chaos and bloodshed. One minister after another tried to keep order and balance the different parties, but this only made the more extreme groups on either side think that the government was treacherous or weak.

The senior officers of the Spanish army believed that it was the duty of the army always to protect Spain, and that meant

Civil wars are especially full of tragedy. In July 1936 rebel Colonel Moscardó defended the Alcázar of Toledo against the government forces in the town. Their commander telephoned him: he had Moscardó's son, and would shoot him unless the Alcázar surrendered. Moscardó asked to speak to his son, and said goodbye. The young man died, the Alcázar held. This is the room, restored after the war, where the colonel made his agonising choice.

saving the country from self-destruction as well as from foreign attack. Besides, most of them had never cared much for the republic, and sympathised with the Church and the more conservative groups. In July 1936 some of them decided that they could wait no longer. They had prepared for a long time, and now they tried suddenly to get the army to take control everywhere in Spain and her colonies. In the colonies and about half of Spain the plot worked, but in the more densely populated parts of Spain the take-over failed and the republican government remained in charge. What had been intended as a quick, smooth emergency operation turned into a messy, long civil war.

On the side of the rebel generals were all the groups and parties that are loosely called 'Right-wing', from old-fashioned monarchists and aristocrats to the Falange, very similar to the Fascists in Italy, who wanted to organise an efficient corporate state in Spain and had little respect for upper-class conservatives. The Right was a very mixed alliance, but their enemies called them all by the one name – Fascists. Just as inaccurately, the rebels called the government side Reds, though it included all shades of 'Left-wing' opinion from moderate liberals and socialists to Communists, both Stalinists and Trotskyites; there were also Catalan and Basque nationalists, who thought that the republicans were much more likely to give them home rule than the rebel generals, who believed in a strong and united Spain. Outside Spain most people did not know or did not care about the complications. They saw it not as the latest tragic episode in Spain's tangled story, but as a 'show-down' between the Right and the Left in European politics. Italy and Germany sent weapons, airplanes and 'volunteers' to help the rebel generals. The USSR did the same for the republican government, though it was more difficult from so great a distance; so rather than send their own soldiers they backed International Brigades organised mainly by the Communist Parties of other nations. Britain and France and the smaller parliamentary democracies of Europe symphathised, on the whole, with the government side, but they tried to prevent the war from becoming international. They got the other countries to agree to what was called a policy of non-intervention, and set up naval patrols to intercept gun-runners. But this attempt to leave the war to the Spaniards proved as much a farce as sanctions against Italy had been. Even France unofficially allowed supplies and men to cross into republican Spain. Thus the war became a trial of strength between Right and Left from all parts of Europe.

There was cruelty and heroism on both sides, but the rebels had an advantage from the start; they began with more trained soldiers. Taking the name of Nationalists, they all accepted General Francisco Franco as *caudillo,* leader. The republicans, on the other hand, were torn by feuds; the Communists tried to get control, and succeeded in breaking the Anarchists and Trotskyites and shooting hundreds of them. Yet the aid from the USSR to the republicans never matched the aid the Nationalists received from Italy and Germany. In March 1939 Franco overcame the last remnants of the republican forces and became dictator of all Spain.

It looked as though the 'Fascist' powers were going from strength to strength, and they were working together. In October 1936 Mussolini and Hitler agreed to co-operate (Mussolini called this 'the Rome-Berlin Axis' and the name stuck) and next month Germany signed the Anti-Comintern Pact with Japan, to oppose Communism everywhere; Italy signed a year later. With things going so well, Hitler began to put pressure on his neighbours.

Hitler's steps to war

It may be that Hitler intended war. He had certainly made preparations, and had used Spain to test some of his men, machines and methods. But it is equally possible that he hoped to get what he wanted without having to fight a big war. He had the same argument every time he demanded more territory – he was only asking for what was rightfully German, for lands where the people spoke German. It was a strong argument, for the Allies had accepted the principle of national unity and freedom of choice in Wilson's Fourteen Points (page 32) and the peace settlements.

He began with Czechoslovakia. It stuck like a wedge between Austria and the rest of the Reich, and round the western end there were mountains which formed a strong natural defence. In this frontier region, though, the people spoke German, not Czech. They were known as the Sudeten Germans, and Hitler said that the Sudetenland should be part of Germany. He sent agents into the Sudetenland to stir up the people to make the same demand and to complain that the Czechs had been oppressing them for years. This the Czechs denied, and they said that the mountains were essential to their own safety. They would not yield the Sudetenland to Germany, and appealed for help to France and Britain, the Allies who had done so much to create Czechoslovakia in 1918. Hitler was confident of the support of Mussolini and prepared to use force. It was the autumn of 1938 and the danger of war in central Europe seemed very real.

All over Europe people remembered 1914. The Prime

One of the best-known and most controversial scenes of the century, Chamberlain's return from Munich, 30 September 1938. This shows him after landing at Heston Airport, telling a relieved crowd that he had brought back honourable 'peace in our time'. The paper in his hand, which everybody assumed to be the agreement with Hitler, was later said to be another document, and some people have seen this small incident as symbolic of the misunderstandings and deceptions of Munich.

but the Czechs, Chamberlain predicted 'Peace in our time'. Even as he spoke some people thought him wrong, and because of what happened later the policy of appeasement has come to mean something weak and foolish. But then the British and French Prime Ministers had little choice, and most of their people were glad to escape war. Just in case Hitler broke his word, they speeded up improvements to their armed forces. Many of their critics, however, who were already embittered at what was happening in Spain, thought that the USSR was the only country that could be trusted to stand up against Fascism. About this time a great number of highly talented young men at universities, from poets to scientists, became members of the Communist Party.

It took Hitler less than half a year to show that he was not to be trusted. In March 1939 German troops marched into what was left of Czechoslovakia; most of it became the Protectorates of Bohemia and Moravia, under the Reich, while Hungary annexed Ruthenia. This time Hitler's excuse was that Slovak leaders had invited him to protect them against the Czechs, who were still trying to dominate them. It was the first time the Third Reich had swallowed non-Germans. Rapidly

Ministers of Britain and France, Neville Chamberlain and Edouard Daladier, were in a dilemma. They were in honour bound to protect Czechoslovakia, but Hitler did have a case. Anyway, their troops could not reach Czechoslovakia, and after years of trying to keep armaments small they were in no condition to fight a serious war. True, Stalin offered to help; but they did not trust him – letting the USSR get a foothold in central Europe would be more dangerous than giving Hitler what he wanted. So they were in a mood to listen when Hitler swore that he had no designs on the rest of Czechoslovakia, or anywhere else; in fact, he would be willing to protect Czechoslovakia. In September Chamberlain and Daladier flew to talk with Hitler and Mussolini at Munich. They decided to trust Hitler. The Sudetenland became part of the Reich. At the same time Poland and Hungary were given small areas of Czechoslovakia that they had claimed for some years, and the Slovaks and Ruthenians were given self-government inside Czechoslovakia, as it was said that the Czechs had been dominating them.

After satisfying – or appeasing, as it was called – everybody

Germany in the late 1930s

- Boundaries, 1937
- Expansion, 1938
- Germany, 1937
- Expansion, Mar 1939

0 — 300 miles
0 — 500 km

Mussolini followed suit. On Good Friday, 7 April, Italian troops crossed the Adriatic and landed in Albania. Five days later Mussolini got an Albanian assembly to declare that the King of Italy was King of Albania too.

Was there now any way of stopping the two dictators? Which would be the next small nation to go under? France and Britain tried to form an 'anti-aggression front'. They sent envoys to seek the help of the USSR, which they had refused at Munich; they signed a treaty with Turkey; most important, they pledged themselves to protect the territories of Greece, Romania and Poland.

Hitler was not deterred. His next objectives were on the Baltic. When Poland had been restored as an independent country in 1918, there was no seacoast with a purely Polish population; so she had been given the so-called Corridor, which had a mixed German-Polish population, even though this cut off East Prussia from the rest of Germany. At the same time Danzig, a port where the population was almost entirely German, was made an international port under the League of Nations, though Poland was given some control over it. The port of Memel was taken by the new republic of Lithuania. Hitler wanted them all back.

Lithuania did not argue; Memel became part of the Reich in March 1939. It was easy for the Nazis to persuade the people of Danzig to demand reunion with Germany, and sooner or later the League of Nations was bound to give in. But Poland refused to consider yielding an inch of her territory, and prepared to fight.

At this point Hitler achieved his master-stroke. On 23 August he signed an agreement with Stalin to divide Poland between the Reich and the USSR. The arch-enemies were now confederates, and Poland's position was hopeless.

On 1 September German armies invaded Poland, and on 3 September Britain and France declared war on Germany.

The years of Axis conquests

Hitler's armies smashed the Poles by using a new method of warfare – *blitzkrieg,* lightning war. It depended on two weapons that had been new in the 1914–18 war, the tank and the airplane; both had developed into much swifter and stronger machines during the past twenty years. The German army used its tanks by massing them together in *panzer* (ar-

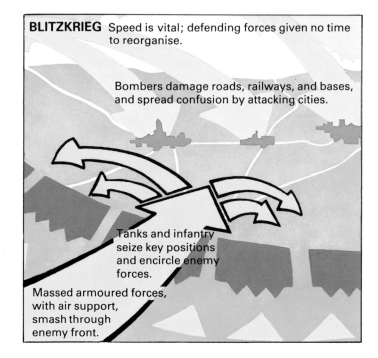

BLITZKRIEG Speed is vital; defending forces given no time to reorganise.

Bombers damage roads, railways, and bases, and spread confusion by attacking cities.

Tanks and infantry seize key positions and encircle enemy forces.

Massed armoured forces, with air support, smash through enemy front.

moured) divisions that could smash a hole in the enemy front, rush through and then spread out, surrounding enemy troops and making havoc among the enemy supply lines. Aircraft worked closely with the tanks. They bombed and machine-gunned enemy strongpoints that were holding up the panzers and they struck far in the enemy's rear, destroying bridges and railways, battering cities to cause terror and confusion. Behind the tanks came the infantry, some motorised, to overwhelm the enemy forces before they could reorganise, and so to occupy the country.

The Poles fought with their traditional bravery, but it was all over in a month. Western Poland became part of Germany, eastern Poland part of the USSR, and the central part, around Warsaw, became the General Government of Poland, administered by Germany.

Britain and France watched helplessly. Ever since 1918 France had been planning for the next war with Germany, and had constructed a wonderfully elaborate fortification along the frontier, called the Maginot Line after the minister responsible for it. It was a magnificent defence, but it needed

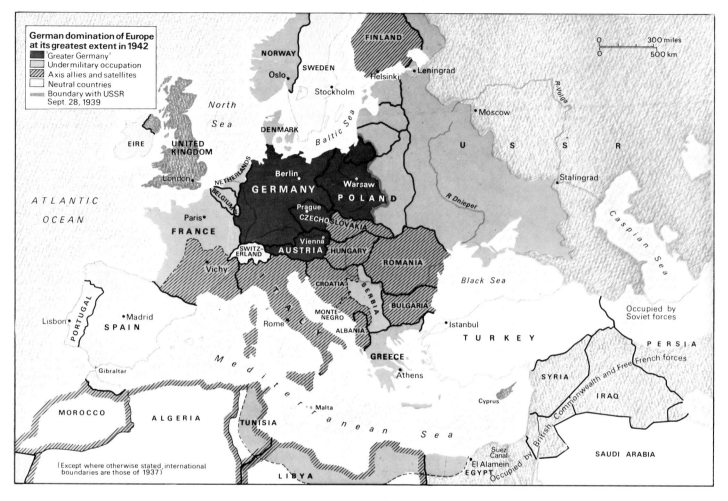

(Except where otherwise stated, international boundaries are those of 1937)

so many soldiers to man it that the French army was hardly capable of any other major task. The Germans too had their defences, known to the Allies as the Siegfried Line, not as powerful as the Maginot Line but too strong to be broken without a big effort. The French and the British Expeditionary Force which soon joined them needed time to prepare an attack. So Allied and German armies sat in their fortifications and quietly watched each other through the autumn, winter and spring of 1939–40; this was nicknamed 'the phoney war'.

During that winter Stalin demanded territory from Finland, and when the Finns refused the Red Army attacked them. At first the Red Army did very badly against its tiny adversary,

possibly for lack of the experienced leaders whom Stalin had purged, but soon their sheer weight told; Finland had to surrender the territory Stalin wanted. The Allies were sympathetic to the Finns, but unable to send them help. The League of Nations expelled the USSR, which had no effect. Meanwhile Communists in Britain and France described the war against Nazi Germany as being no more than a quarrel of capitalists, and did what they could to persuade their fellow-countrymen not to fight Hitler.

The Allies, however, felt quite confident. They held the sea, and began a blockade as in the 1914–18 war. Behind the sea and the Maginot Line they could build up their strength.

All the members of the British Commonwealth joined the Allies. President Roosevelt was sympathetic, and would probably try to help the Allies as much as he dared, short of getting the USA involved in the war. On 4 April Chamberlain told Parliament: 'Hitler has missed the bus.' Within a few days he was proved terribly wrong.

On 9 April German forces struck suddenly into Denmark and Norway, and overran them within a few days. Allied help was sent to the Norwegians trying to hold out in the far north, but failed. Now Hitler had a long coastline from which U-boats and surface raiders could operate, and the Allied navies were going to have a much harder task to protect their merchant ships.

On 10 May the blitzkrieg smashed into the Netherlands, Belgium and Luxemburg. It was like the Schlieffen Plan again, but with tanks and aircraft and radio messages that allowed the generals to keep a better grip on what their armies were doing. This time it worked perfectly. The little neutral countries were quickly overrun, the panzers swept round the northern end of the Maginot Line, Paris fell on 14 June and France signed an armistice on the 22nd. Most of the British Expeditionary Force escaped across the Channel from Dunkirk, but badly battered and without its equipment.

Mussolini declared war on the Allies on 10 June, just in time to join in Hitler's triumph. Stalin took this opportunity to force the three small Baltic republics of Estonia, Latvia and Lithuania to become members of the USSR, and to take Bessarabia and the mouth of the Danube from Romania.

Hitler's victory was swifter and more complete than any Napoleon had ever won, but Britain again continued the war alone, depending on the Royal Navy to hold the seas even though the whole opposite coast was in enemy hands. In the autumn of 1940 Hitler tried to subdue Britain by using air power alone in what became known as the Battle of Britain, but his *Luftwaffe* (air force) failed to destroy the Royal Air Force or to paralyse British cities by bombs. He decided that without supremacy in the air it would not be wise to risk sending an invasion force in small boats to get past the British warships, and anyway Britain could not interfere with his great plans for Europe. He left it to his U-boats to strangle Britain. (The 'wolf packs' nearly succeeded; after a long, costly struggle, it was only new methods of detecting submarines below the surface, many extra aircraft and help from the USA that enabled the Royal Navy to win the Battle of the Atlantic.)

It was time for Hitler to turn eastwards again, but first Italy needed help. In the autumn of 1940 Mussolini's forces in Albania invaded Greece, and those in Libya and Abyssinia attacked the British troops stationed in Egypt and Somaliland. It all went wrong. The Greek army resisted stubbornly in the mountains, the British defeated and captured large Italian forces in the North African desert, the Royal Navy compelled the Italian fleet to shelter in harbour, and in April 1941 British troops entered Addis Ababa and ended Mussolini's empire in Abyssinia.

Hitler's response was to strike into the Balkans. His armies swept over Yugoslavia and Greece. When the British tried to hold Crete, using their naval superiority, the Germans used another new form of warfare and captured the island with airborne troops. Meanwhile a small German force, the *Afrika Korps*, slipped across to Libya, rallied the Italian army there and pushed the British back to Egypt.

By the summer of 1941 Hitler was master of all Europe. He had no need to interfere with neutral Sweden, Switzerland or Portugal, and to everyone's surprise General Franco managed to persuade him that Spain, exhausted as she was after the civil war, would be more useful as a friendly neutral than if she came into the war. But before he could organise the Nazi 'New Order' properly, Europe must rid itself, once and for all, of the evil monster of Communism.

On 22 June 1941 he attacked the Soviet Union. Stalin was taken completely by surprise. Soviet armies were broken and surrounded, hundreds of thousands of their soldiers were killed or captured, the blitzkrieg drove hundreds of miles deep into Russia. Any country less gigantic must have collapsed under such losses. What was more, as the invaders advanced they were often met by cheering crowds; Lithuanians, Latvians and Estonians, Ukrainians and Cossacks, even Russians who had suffered under Stalin's tyranny greeted the Germans as liberators. Many of them joined Hitler's armies. Hungary, Romania and Bulgaria became Hitler's allies, and contingents came from most of the countries he had conquered. As his armies settled down to endure the Russian winter of 1941–2 Hitler could claim to have launched a great all-European crusade.

On the other side of the world the Japanese government thought that the time was ripe for them to try to become mas-

above: *The US battleships* West Virginia *and* Tennessee *after the Japanese air raid on Pearl Harbor. The photograph shows vividly not only the destruction of the ships, but also how they had been moored close together in the harbour, virtually helpless, a perfect target.*

ters of South-East Asia. Only one country might be able to stop them, the USA. Japan and the USA had seen each other as naval rivals in the Pacific for the past twenty years, and while none of the European powers was now capable of finding ships and men to fight Japan, the USA was not likely to let Japan gain a huge new empire without resisting. In the summer of 1941, when Japan sent troops to occupy French Indochina (the French, under German control, had to agree), the USA responded by cutting off its trade with Japan. This affected oil supplies that were vital to Japan but, rather than give way, the Japanese decided that their best chance was a surprise attack. On the morning of Sunday 7 December 1941 Japanese naval aircraft bombed the US base at Pearl Harbor, Hawaii. Surprise was complete. There had been no declaration of war – Japan had planned to make the declaration immediately before the attack, but it was accidentally delayed. The US Pacific fleet suffered such losses that it could be

A Japanese propaganda leaflet, probably 1943. Prostrate across a map of India, a scrawny Indian is being bled by a British officer, while the bloated Churchill feasts. But retribution is on its way. The message is: 'Teach the wicked a lesson with a stick and save India!' The Japanese set up a 'Government of Free India' but failed to persuade many Indians to help them.

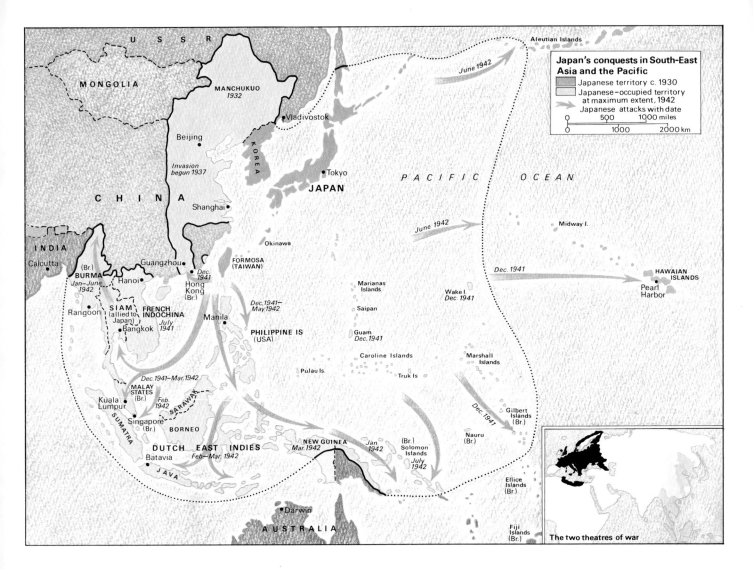

Japan's conquests in South-East Asia and the Pacific

Japanese territory c. 1930
Japanese-occupied territory at maximum extent, 1942
Japanese attacks with date

0   500   1000 miles
0   1000   2000 km

The two theatres of war

ignored as a serious fighting force for a long time to come.

Swiftly Japanese expeditions struck across the eastern seas at the lands held by Western powers. Within a couple of months they had taken Hong Kong, the Philippines, Malaya and the Dutch East Indies – Singapore, Britain's vaunted 'Gibraltar of the East', surrendered with hardly a struggle on 15 February 1942. Next they invaded Burma, on the way to India, and New Guinea, threatening Australia. They announced that they had come to liberate the peoples of Asia

from the European imperialists, and promised a great new era of peace and prosperity under their leadership, much as Hitler was promising in Europe.

By mid-1942 this really was a world war. The main powers on each side were: Axis – Germany, Italy, Japan; Allies – Britain and the Commonwealth, the USSR, the USA, China. The Allies far outnumbered the Axis, but the Axis were victorious everywhere.

Hitler's 'New Order'

Any army of occupation is likely to be resented, no matter how hard it tries to win the good-will of the people it is holding down. If a war is still going on, it is even more likely that there will be ill-feeling between the soldiers and the people whom they suspect of being on the side of their enemies. But this was not the reason why millions of people in Europe hated the Germans. The reason was the Nazi tyranny.

It was not the army, but the SS and Gestapo that created the terror and loathing. They spread their spies and agents wherever the German army conquered, looking for people who might still be working for the enemy. They tortured suspects almost as a matter of course – something that Europeans had regarded as barbarous for centuries. They sent thousands to the concentration camps, and the fear of these camps haunted all Europe. There were many more of them now, and the things that went on inside them were far worse than before 1939. Prisoners died by the thousand; there were plenty of them, and the Nazis were winning, so why not? Some prisoners were injected with diseases or mutilated, as experiments, by Nazi doctors; the prisoners were sub-human criminals who deserved to die anyway, so why not make them serve a useful purpose? To the SS guards, the suffering of such people was of no importance; and some enjoyed what they were doing. They treated all prisoners cruelly, but worst of all the 'inferior races'– Poles, Russians, gypsies and, of course, Jews.

As the war spread, Nazi racial theories became even more violent and their hatred of Jews even more insane. They decided on the 'final solution' to the Jewish problem: destroy them all. They built special extermination camps, mostly in Poland, rounded up all the Jews they could catch and sent them by the trainload to the camps from every part of Europe. They said that the Jews were merely going to be resettled in eastern Europe, and perhaps some Jews believed the story until they were in the gas chamber. It is impossible to know how many people altogether died in Nazi camps, but one moderate estimate is about twelve million, half of them Jews.

Even those who kept clear of the Gestapo might still be carried off to Germany. As the war grew bigger, so did the need for weapons and munitions, and at the same time Hitler needed Germans in the army, not in factories. So people were sent from other countries to labour in German industries, often in conditions that amounted to slavery.

There seemed to be no escape from Nazi tyranny, yet there was still hope as long as some of the Allies, at least, remained unconquered. Some men escaped to Britain to join forces like the Free French, led by General Charles de Gaulle. Others formed resistance groups, receiving encouragement and instructions by radio from Britain, and supplies of arms and equipment dropped by parachute. The Nazi reply was to punish more savagely; if a railway were sabotaged or a soldier murdered, they would take hostages and shoot them, sometimes even whole villages.

In every country, though, there were people who preferred to be on good terms with the Germans, to 'collaborate' as it was called. Some of them genuinely believed in the struggle against Communism and in the new Europe that Hitler would build, and thought that the stories about the concentration camps were exaggerations and lies invented by Hitler's enemies. (After all, atrocity stories of 1914–18 had turned out to be false.) Perhaps some were seizing this opportunity to settle old scores, or simply wanted to be on the winning side. Conditions varied greatly from country to country. In France, after the collapse in 1940, a government was formed with its capital at Vichy, so friendly to Hitler that it was allowed to rule part of France, while the northern and western seacoasts and their hinterlands were occupied by the German forces. In Yugoslavia there was ferocious resistance, led by Josip Broz (known as Tito), a Communist, in the Serbian mountains; but the Croats in the north, who had resented the way the Serbs had dominated Yugoslavia ever since its foundation in 1918, were glad to set up their own state and help the Germans and Italians. Hitler's Europe was no 'New Order', but all confusion and conflict, held down by force.

The destruction of the Third Reich

Once again it was the strength of the USA that turned the tide, and this time the Americans used it with a speed that astonished both friends and enemies. As they began to make ships, airplanes, guns and every sort of warlike equipment in quantities that had seemed impossible, Germany faced the problem of 1918 all over again: either a quick victory or the certainty of being overwelmed.

The scales tipped against Hitler's armies on two far distant fronts at almost the same time. The first was North Africa. In October 1942 the Afrika Korps was driven back from Egypt at the battle of El Alamein, and just as it was retreating a British and American force landed behind it, in Algeria. The Axis forces held out as long as they could in Tunisia, but had to surrender on 12 May 1943. Meanwhile a much more serious disaster befell Germany on the Russian front. Here a German army thrust forward in the summer of 1942 towards the Volga; if it could get control of that vital river, it might split the USSR. The Red Army saw the danger, and at Stalingrad on the Volga the Soviet soldiers held on desperately, no matter what the cost. They held on while autumn became winter, and fresh Soviet forces were organised, and then the German army at Stalingrad found itself cut off. It surrendered on 31 January 1943.

Now the war swung steadily against the Axis. From North Africa the British and Americans invaded Sicily in July 1943 and Italy in September. The King of Italy dismissed Mussolini and the new Italian government ceased resisting the Allies and declared war against Germany, though German troops held most of Italy. Then the Allies began to fight their way up Italy from south to north, slowly, against determined and skilful German forces. But this struggle was small compared with that on the vast Russian front, where there were gigantic battles as the Red Army, freshly supplied and strengthened from what seemed to be the limitless manpower of the Soviet Union, threw its whole weight into the attack. Slowly, with immense losses on both sides, Hitler's armies were forced back westwards. Then, on 6 June 1944, ('D-Day', in the military jargon of the time) American and British armies landed on the coast of Normandy and began a new Western Front.

Many highly placed Germans had detested Hitler for years, but had not dared to attack him while he was victorious. In July 1944 a group that included important generals decided that the time had come. One of them, an officer on the general staff, Count von Stauffenberg, succeeded in exploding a bomb during a conference at the Führer's headquarters, but Hitler received only minor injuries. After this, the SS and Gestapo grip was made tighter than ever.

Hitler knew that he could not make peace. The Allies had announced their policy of 'unconditional surrender', which meant that Germany would have no rights and would be entirely at the mercy of people who had good reason to hate the Reich, and its leaders especially. He had no choice but to fight on, and there was still a hope of victory: new weapons. There was the V1, a small pilotless aircraft packed with explosive, a flying bomb; and the V2, a giant rocket with an explosive head. (V stood for *Vergeltung*, repayment, because during the past years British and American bombers had devastated German cities, and these weapons were directed on London.) Next there was to be a new explosive, more terrible than anyone had imagined possible; Hitler's scientists were on the point of discovering how to split the atom (page 20).

It all failed. The V weapons hurt London, but no worse than the raids of 1940–1, and the atom was not split – it was later claimed that some of the scientists deliberately worked slowly. The Allied armies surged forward and their aircraft reduced more and more cities to rubble. Defeat was certain, but the Germans went on fighting. Some may have thought that 'unconditional surrender' meant that the Allies intended to destroy Germany altogether, so it was better to fight to the last. Others believed that as the eastern and western Allies discussed what to do with their victory they would fall out, and that at the eleventh hour Britain and the USA would ask Germany

The destruction of the Third Reich

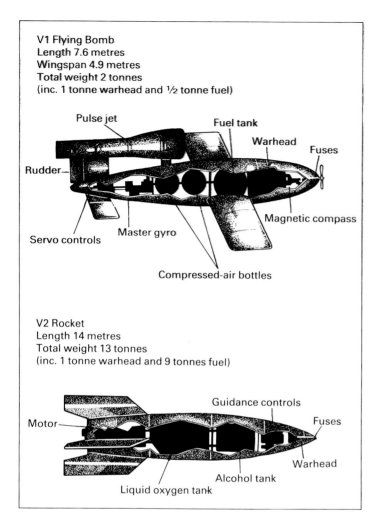

V1 Flying Bomb
Length 7.6 metres
Wingspan 4.9 metres
Total weight 2 tonnes
(inc. 1 tonne warhead and ½ tonne fuel)

Pulse jet
Fuel tank
Warhead
Fuses
Rudder
Magnetic compass
Servo controls
Master gyro
Compressed-air bottles

V2 Rocket
Length 14 metres
Total weight 13 tonnes
(inc. 1 tonne warhead and 9 tonnes fuel)

Guidance controls
Motor
Fuses
Warhead
Alcohol tank
Liquid oxygen tank

to help them against the USSR. By April 1945 the Allied armies were inside Germany, moving steadily forward to meet in the middle. The Red Army entered Berlin. In his 'bunker' in Berlin Hitler was refusing to believe the truth, trying to send orders for new counterattacks to armies that did not exist; when at last he understood that there was no hope, he killed himself, on 30 April 1945. (Two days earlier Mussolini had been caught by Italian resistance fighters while trying to escape to Switzerland, and shot.) During the next week the surviving German forces laid down their arms and on 8 May the Allies celebrated VE Day – Victory in Europe.

Germany was divided into four zones, to be occupied respectively by Soviet, American, British and French troops. Berlin, though it was well inside the Soviet Zone, was similarly divided. Austria was separated from Germany, and divided in similar fashion. A German state no longer existed.

The surrender of Japan

In Asia the war turned in the same way. After their amazing conquests the Japanese found that they had stretched their strength too far. They faltered, failed to push forward any farther, and then were forced relentlessly back by the Allies.

In March 1944 Japanese troops had advanced all through Burma and were poised to invade India. They proclaimed that they had come to liberate India from British rule, and hoped that Indians would rise and help them. A few did, but very few. The Indian army remained faithful to its leaders, and British and Indian troops together stopped the Japanese advance in two grim long struggles at Kohima and Imphal. The Japanese had strained themselves to the limit, and, as they recoiled and the British and Indians pursued, they lacked the strength to make a stand. By the end of 1944 the Japanese had lost all northern Burma and were still going back.

Saving India was important, but Burma was a very long way from Japan. It was from the Pacific that Japan was most exposed to a counter-attack. Here the turning-point of the war came surprisingly early, on 4 June 1942, though few people realised it at the time. Near Midway Island a force of Japanese aircraft carriers planned to surprise and destroy the American aircraft carriers which, by pure luck, had not been at Pearl Harbor when the rest of the US fleet was put out of action. But the Americans had discovered the code that the Japanese used for their naval signals, heard the Japanese radio messages and were ready for the attack. The Japanese lost all four of their carriers, the Americans only one of their three. As it turned out, aircraft carriers, not battleships, were to prove the most powerful warships in the Pacific war, and Japan's shipyards could not build at anything like the rate that the USA was achieving.

The Pacific war now became a succession of fights for groups of islands scattered across the vast sea. It moved gradually closer to Japan as American superiority in ships and aircraft increased. The Japanese fought fanatically. They believed that a

Allied and Axis deaths during World War II

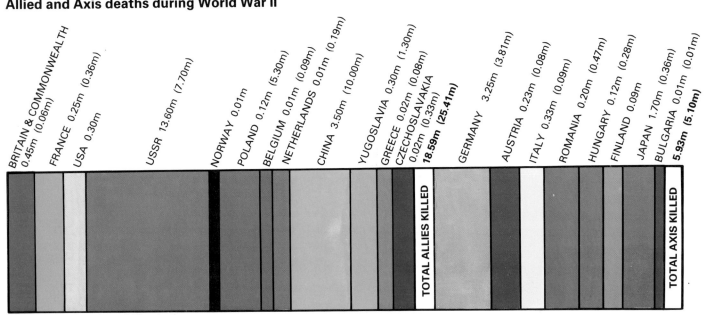

| BRITAIN & COMMONWEALTH 0.45m (0.06m) | FRANCE 0.25m (0.36m) | USA 0.30m | USSR 13.60m (7.70m) | NORWAY 0.01m | POLAND 0.12m (5.30m) | BELGIUM 0.01m (0.09m) | NETHERLANDS 0.01m (0.19m) | CHINA 3.50m (10.00m) | YUGOSLAVIA 0.30m (1.30m) | GREECE 0.02m (0.08m) | CZECHOSLOVAKIA 0.02m (0.33m) | **18.59m (25.41m)** TOTAL ALLIES KILLED | GERMANY 3.25m (3.81m) | AUSTRIA 0.23m (0.08m) | ITALY 0.33m (0.09m) | ROMANIA 0.20m (0.47m) | HUNGARY 0.12m (0.28m) | FINLAND 0.09m | JAPAN 1.70m (0.36m) | BULGARIA 0.01m (0.01m) | **5.93m (5.10m)** TOTAL AXIS KILLED |

Figures in brackets show civilian deaths

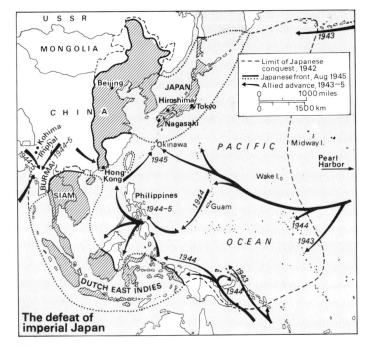

The defeat of imperial Japan

- — — Limit of Japanese conquest, 1942
- ········ Japanese front, Aug 1945
- ⟶ Allied advance, 1943–5

0   1000 miles
0   1500 km

warrior should accept death, never captivity. A soldier who surrendered lost all honour and respect – this was one reason why Allied prisoners of war were often treated as slaves by the Japanese, though it is worth remembering that they often used just as harshly the Asian people they had come to 'liberate'. Some of the Japanese airmen went to certain death. These were the *kamikaze* (divine wind) pilots who crashed their bomb-laden planes into US ships, stabbing themselves in traditional *samurai* fashion just before they crashed. They took their name from the storm that had destroyed an invasion fleet approaching Japan more than six centuries before. They inflicted heavy losses on the Americans, but could not stop them. At last the Americans were close enough to Japan to prepare a full-scale invasion.

It was the summer of 1945 and the war in Europe was over. The Japanese should have seen that now they could not win, but they went on fighting as hard as ever. The Americans knew what it had cost them to take small islands against soldiers who fought to the death, and could guess at the slaughter when such men had to defend Japan itself. But as they braced themselves for the last and worst bloodshed of the war, their

By August 1945 American incendiary bombing raids had largely destroyed more than fifty Japanese cities – many of the buildings had been wooden – killed 200,000 civilians and injured 500,000 more; eight million townspeople were now refugees in villages. Still Japan refused to give in, and so the atom bomb was used. This photograph shows what only one atom bomb did to the city of Hiroshima.

scientists found an alternative. Like the Germans, Allied scientists had been working for some years on the idea of an atomic explosive, and at last they had something that they thought would work. On 17 July 1945 they tried it, in a desert in New Mexico. There was a flash 'brighter than a thousand suns' and a blast of astounding power. Some scientists exulted in their success, others were already fearful of what they had created.

There were arguments in the American government, and people have argued ever since. Rightly or wrongly, President Harry S. Truman (Roosevelt had died on 12 April, after a stroke) decided to use it. On 6 August an American bomber dropped an atomic device over the Japanese city of Hiroshima. The whole city was laid waste by that single bomb; 100,000 people were killed and as many more injured – some by radiation which would kill them slowly over the next years. There had never been anything like this in the entire history of warfare. The Japanese government hesitated. On 9 August the same thing happened to Nagasaki. They gave in. On 14 August the Japanese government decided to capitulate and the formal ceremony of surrender took place on 2 September aboard the battleship USS *Missouri,* anchored in Tokyo Bay.

This had been a world war far more truly than 1914–18. The first remained essentially a European conflict with minor campaigns elsewhere. In the second a European war became linked to an equally big Asian war, and for the first time in history it was the Pacific rather than the Atlantic where the battle-fleets struggled for supremacy. The war machines that were just being developed in the first war dominated the second – the airplane, the tank and the submarine. Both sides had gas but never used it; it was too inaccurate and uncertain. But in some ways the second was a more merciless war than the first, civilians were killed just as ruthlessly as soldiers, and now the phrase 'total war' meant exactly that. The second war too saw its new technical developments. Radio could steer machines at great distances, and radar could detect obstacles or enemies in darkness or fog. The first practical jet planes flew before the war ended, and the first giant rockets. Most terrifying of all, at the very end of the war scientists had released nuclear power, and politicians and soldiers had used it.

The League of Nations

Founded 1919 by the Allies at Versailles Peace Conference; based on President Wilson's ideas as expressed in the Fourteen Points. Official beginning 10 January 1920.

Aims stated in League of Nations Charter (26 articles): to safeguard peace by
submitting international disputes to arbitration,
reducing armaments,
promising not to attack fellow-members,
supporting fellow-members against aggressors,
applying economic or military sanctions against aggressors.

Structure

COUNCIL: 8 members – 4 permanent (Britain, France, Italy, Japan) and 4 elected by Assembly.
Four meetings per year originally, later three.

ASSEMBLY: all member states represented equally, no matter how large or small.
One session per year. Decisions were binding only if they were unanimous.

SECRETARIAT: an international 'civil service' carrying on the day-to-day administrative work; in fact responsible for many of the League's activities, especially when Council and Assembly were not available for consultation.

Membership originally the Allies. Extended in 1920s and 1930s to include most of the world's independent states (colonies were not represented separately). But there were serious gaps:
The USA never joined.
Germany withdrew in 1933, Italy in 1937, Japan in 1938.
The USSR did not join until 1934 and was expelled in 1939.
This meant that in practice the leading members were Britain and France.

Special Committees were set up to deal with
armament reduction,
health and dangerous drugs,
international finance,
mandates,
minority populations,
refugees.

The League also supported
International Labour Office (ILO), founded 1919, and
Permanent Court of International Justice, founded at The Hague 1920.

Headquarters built in Geneva.

The Palace of the Nations, headquarters of the League. A dignified building in neo-classical style, it stands in a park overlooking the beautiful lake at Geneva, Switzerland. The site chosen for the League's home was in the heart of Europe, the dominant continent, but also in a small country famous for its policy of neutrality. The building was not completed until 1936, when the League was already in decline.

What the League achieved is usually judged by its record in dealing with international disputes, because this was its main objective.

Successes

In the years after the war it settled several disputes that seemed likely to end in fighting, but these mainly were between smaller countries, e.g.
1921 Sweden – Finland
1921 Yugoslavia – Albania
1923 Greece – Italy
      Poland – Lithuania
1925 Greece – Bulgaria

1923 Locarno Treaties
      and
1928 Kellogg Pact
      were both very much in the spirit of the League's Covenant.

Failures

During the same period it could not stop Poland seizing Vilna from Lithuania, nor Estonia seizing Memel from Germany.
It did not interfere with big powers, e.g. French occupation of the Ruhr 1923.

1932 China appealed against Japan; the League's Lytton Commission proved vague and ineffective.

1933–4 No results from World Disarmament and Economic Conferences.

1935–6 Fiasco of sanctions against Italy over Abyssinia.

1936–9 League was virtually ignored over Spain 1936; China 1937; Austria 1938; Czechoslovakia 1938–9; Memel, Danzig, Poland 1939.

Useful routine work went on meanwhile in the special committees and agencies: e.g. aiding refugees, reducing drug smuggling, collecting health and labour statistics so as to show where conditions most needed to be improved.

> The League dissolved itself in 1946, handing on its buildings, its duties and some of its special subsidiaries to the United Nations.

Was the League bound to fail?

Advantages

1 It began when all the most powerful nations were exhausted and sickened by war, and wanted peace above all things.

2 The peace that the League was trying to preserve was guaranteed by the winners of the war, who were also leaders of the League.

Disadvantages

1 War-weariness gradually disappeared, and several nations were aggrieved at the result of the war.

2 Even from the start one of the chief Allies, whose President had done most to inspire the creation of the League, refused to join.

3 The League had no clearly agreed means to coerce a country that broke the peace; most important, it could not raise an armed force.

What caused World War II?

In the First World War most of the great powers were fighting from the start, August 1914. In the Second, fighting spread gradually and the biggest powers came in late. So we must ask both why it started and why it grew.

Where and when did it begin?

Poland, September 1939, is the usual answer. But a great war, which became part of the Second World War, had already been raging in Asia for two years. It is best to think of two beginnings, one in Asia and one in Europe.

ASIA: *Japan* invaded *China*, 7 July 1937

Why?

– Japan claimed to need more space, resources and markets for her increasing population.
– The men governing Japan wanted to revive the warrior code of the *samurai*, which, they thought, made people noble.
– China had been the victim of Western imperial powers for a century, and Japan had followed their example since the 1890s. Now, by setting up a pro-Japanese government in China, Japan would be able to push out the Westerners and make both China and Japan more prosperous.
– China was still divided and weak, but showing signs of gaining strength; it was therefore wiser to attack without delay.
– The Manchukuo experiment in 1932 had shown that there really were economic advantages in this sort of expansion; and that the League of Nations and other powers might disapprove but would not interfere. It was profitable and safe to go ahead.

'*The China incident*' was war on a big scale, but no other countries were involved. Most of the world's leading powers were preoccupied with the crises in Europe during the later 1930s.

EUROPE: *Germany* invaded *Poland*, 1 September 1939

Why?

– Germany claimed the Corridor because many (Germany said 'most') of the population were German-speakers; this was in accord with the principle of national self-determination, recognised in Wilson's Fourteen Points and the peace settlements after 1918.
– Similar German claims, all contrary to the terms of the Treaty of Versailles, had succeeded without fighting: Rhineland 1936, Austria 1938, Sudetenland 1938, Memel 1939.
– Poland could not possibly resist successfully. Not only was Germany too strong, but the USSR agreed (23 August 1939) to press its own claims to eastern Poland.

Yet Poland did resist. **Why?**

– Poland claimed to need the Corridor as her only access to the sea; which was why she had been given it in 1919.
– Poland had a long tradition of fighting Germans and Russians. Even when conquered and partitioned, the Poles had never lost their national spirit, and were ready to face any odds. As recently as 1920 they had beaten an apparently overwhelming Russian attack.
– Britain and France had guaranteed that they would stand by Poland.

Within a month Poland was completely occupied by German and Soviet forces. This war was over. Need it have led to a great European war?

How did the war in Europe spread?

Britain and *France* declared war on Germany, 3 September 1939

Why?

– They had guaranteed Poland against a German attack.
– They believed that Germany intended to dominate all Europe by force, and must be stopped before she grew any stronger.

- They had come to this conclusion in March 1939 when Germany occupied the non-German parts of Czechoslovakia. This showed that their previous policy of 'appeasement' had failed; it might even have encouraged Germany to demand more, and not to heed their warnings.

But it seemed an empty declaration because Britain and France could not find a way of transporting troops to Poland, and were not ready to attack Germany's western frontier. After conquering Poland, Germany offered peace in October 1939 to Britain and France. They refused.

Why?

- It would show that their promise to Poland had been worthless, and they would lose the respect and trust of all other nations.
- They were beginning to see this not as an 'old-fashioned' war about territory, but as a sort of crusade against Hitler and Nazism. Thus they could not make peace until Germany got rid of her government – which was not likely while they were victorious.

So the war continued. But, except at sea, there was virtually no fighting. Meanwhile Britain and France hoped to grow stronger, with aid from their dominions and colonies around the world.

Denmark and *Norway*, 9 April 1940
Netherlands, *Belgium* and *Luxemburg*, 10 May 1940
were invaded by Germany

Why?

- 'Military Necessity' was the German excuse for attacking neutrals; it was intended to bring quick victory and so avoid the deaths and destruction of a long war.

But this was not the result. Though the small countries and France were conquered, Britain held out; the war was not over yet.

Italy declared war on Britain and France, 10 June 1940

Why?

- Mussolini was a close ally of Hitler, and wished to share in the victories.
- Italy claimed territories that France had gained in the nineteenth century: Savoy, Nice, Tunis.

Hungary, *Romania* and *Bulgaria* became allies of Germany and Italy, Autumn 1940 – Spring 1941

Why?

- They had little choice. Germany wanted to make sure of south-eastern Europe before turning against the USSR, and they dared not resist.
- They either had gained or expected to gain from Germany's friendship. Hungary had received Ruthenia when Germany broke up Czechoslovakia in 1939. Romania had lost Bessarabia to the USSR in 1940, and wanted it back. Bulgaria had an old quarrel with Greece over Macedonia.

Greece and *Yugoslavia* were invaded by Italy and Germany, Autumn 1940 – Spring 1941

Why?

- Greece stood in the way of Italy's plans to control the eastern Mediterranean area.
- Yugoslavia at first agreed to help the Axis, but there was a sudden change of government and the rejection of German proposals.

In contrast to 1914–18, the blitzkrieg campaigns of 1939–41 were quickly over. By early summer 1941 the Axis controlled almost all mainland Europe. The war was ended, except for:
a. sea and air action against Britain,
b. fighting in North Africa, where both Italy and Britain had colonial interests.
Yet within a few months this situation had been transformed into a world-wide conflict, involving more great powers.

How did the Asian and European wars become one world war?

'Operation Barbarossa' – USSR invaded by Germany, 22 June 1941

Why?

- Despite his agreement with the USSR over Poland, Hitler had never changed his purpose to destroy Communism and subjugate the Slavs.
- Germany could expect wide support. Finland and Romania wanted to regain territory, Estonia, Latvia and Lithuania their independence from the USSR. Many 'minority' peoples inside the USSR might also rise (e.g. Ukrainians, Cossacks, Kazaks, Uzbeks), and even Russians who had suffered under Stalin's rule. After Communist attempts to weaken the British war effort, and Soviet aggressions in eastern Europe, not even Britain could have much sympathy for the USSR.
- The USSR was badly prepared. Stalin's purges had removed most of the best officers, and the Red Army had appeared incompetent when invading Finland in 1939.

'Barbarossa' changed the war completely. The USSR proved too big to be knocked out quickly, and a gigantic struggle began on the Russian front. Britain immediately offered help to the USSR, so that Germany now had to deal with determined enemies on both sides.

The USSR stretched from Europe to the Far East, and was on bad terms with Japan – in 1938 and 1939 border disputes in Manchukuo had resulted in months of heavy fighting between their troops. But at this time neither country thought it would be wise to fight the other, so the USSR did not become the link between the Asian and European wars.

Pearl Harbor – USA attacked by Japan, 7 December 1941

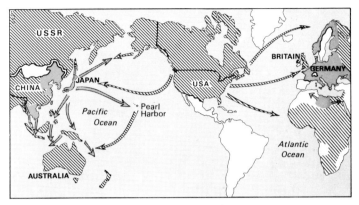

Why?

- Long-standing competition for trade in the Far East had led to naval rivalry between Japan and the USA. Many people in both countries thought that only war could settle the contest.
- Though officially neutral, the USA was aiding Germany's enemies, and seemed to be extending this hostility to Japan. Unofficially, American airmen were helping China. When Japan occupied parts of French Indochina in July 1941, with French consent, the USA joined Britain in stopping oil supplies to Japan. So the USA was behaving like an enemy that was just waiting to declare war.
- The USA had vast resources, but was not yet ready for war. A sudden attack by Japan might seize enough resources to make her even stronger than the USA could become.

The Japanese attack was two-fold:
a. into the Pacific, to prevent the USA from interfering in the conflict;
b. across South-East Asia to gain control of its resources and set up the Greater East Asia Co-Prosperity Sphere under Japanese leadership.

This linked the Asian and European wars:
a. the USA faced both, across the Pacific and Atlantic respectively, and when forced to fight on one side decided that she was so closely committed to Britain already that she could no longer try to be a neutral on the other;
b. Japan over-ran the colonies of European countries at war with Germany (Britain, Netherlands) and advanced towards India and Australia.

Now the war encircled the northern hemisphere; the three Axis powers (Germany, Italy, Japan) against the four Allies (Britain and Dominions, China, USA, USSR) with smaller countries assisting, willingly or unwillingly, on both sides. Generally all the main powers on one side were at war with all the main powers on the other; but Japan and the USSR were not at war, nor China and Italy.

Who was to blame?

The rights and wrongs of international conflicts are usually complicated and difficult to judge; it is particularly so with the Second World War. Because of the way it began and spread, many countries have been blamed, to a greater or lesser degree, for having caused, extended or prolonged it.

JAPAN
– began the whole thing by attacking China;
– turned it into a real world war by attacking USA and S-E Asia;
– and did all this because of deep-rooted martial traditions and the ambition to dominate Asia.

GERMANY
– began the European war by attacking Poland;
– spread the war over all Europe, attacking many countries and forcing others to help;
– and did all this because of theories of racial superiority, and the ambition to dominate Europe, possibly the world.

POLAND
– provoked war by refusing to consider the German case;
– and this was typical of Polish nationalism, as shown in earlier disputes with e.g. Lithuania, Czechoslovakia.

BRITAIN AND FRANCE
– provoked war by irresponsibly encouraging Poland, which they knew they could not protect;
– did this not because of any direct threat from Germany but to maintain their own superior position in Europe and the world;
– previously had encouraged Germany by the policy of 'appeasement' instead of insisting on keeping to the Versailles terms;
– did this (the British more than the French) because of bad conscience over their harshness at Versailles.
– Even if Germany was most to blame in 1939, her leaders were men who gained power because of the bitterness and desperation to which the Germans had been reduced by Versailles.
– Finally, Britain and France could have ended the war after a month, but chose to turn it into an all-or-nothing 'holy war'.

ITALY
– set the example of flouting international opinion by attacking Abyssinia;
– supported Germany's demands invariably;
– extended the war to the Mediterranean and North Africa;
– did all this from nationalistic feelings of self-glorification and the ambition to dominate the Mediterranean.

USSR
– ensured that the European war would begin by agreeing with Germany to divide Poland;
– increased tension and war-mindedness by seizing territory from smaller neighbours, 1939–40;
– did all this as part of a double plan: to extend the Soviet empire; and to foment Communist revolution in other countries after they had been exhausted by war.

USA
– kept the European war alive by encouraging and supplying Britain, 1940–41;
– was at least as much to blame as Japan for the commercial and naval rivalry between the two countries;
– did all this to promote 'dollar imperialism' – wanted economic rivals (including Britain) to weaken themselves in war, while the USA remained safe and profited, and so gained more influence in the world.

BRITAIN, USSR, USA
– jointly kept the European war going and ensured that it would be fought desperately to the end, by their policy of 'Unconditional surrender' and refusal to support anti-Nazi Germans.

All the statements above are merely accusations. Each one may be true or false – or partly true. Even if all are true, they may not be equally important.

Even if it is possible to decide which countries were more or less to blame than others, another problem arises. The names 'Germany' or 'Britain', for example, are simply a short and convenient way of referring to the people who ruled those countries. And if we go on to try to share out the blame among those people, we must try to understand the conditions and pressures under which they took their decisions.

6   The United Nations and the divided world

UNO: the quest for security and human rights

After the Great War they had said, 'It must never happen again', but only twenty years later men who had lived through that disaster led their countries into another. How could the victors of 1945 take wiser precautions than those of 1918? They decided that the League of Nations had been right, in principle, but that it had failed in practice because it had lacked the strength to make its wishes respected. So the Allies set up a new body called the United Nations Organisation (UNO) and tried to make sure that the decisions it took would have the backing of the most powerful states in the world.

This is how they did it. Every country that was a member would send a representative to sit in the General Assembly.

This Assembly would discuss and vote, rather like a parliament, but the 'government' of the UNO would be the Security Council. This Council would have only fifteen members; ten would be elected by the General Assembly, and would change regularly, but the other five would be permanent. These were the five biggest Allies – the USA, the USSR, Britain, China and France (treated once more as an equal partner by the others after her liberation in 1944). Thus the Security Council would have overwhelming strength; it would include the only countries that might be powerful enough to stand out against the rest, if they chose. It was important to ensure that all these five would support any decisions the Council made, so each was given the right of veto. This meant that any one of the five could forbid all further discussion of a proposal it did not like.

The Nuremberg trial which opened on 20 November 1945. The accused are seated in two rows, guarded by American military police. Facing them, high up, are their judges, with Allied flags behind them. Lower down sit court officials, with lawyers opposite, in front of the accused. Most of the courtroom is filled by reporters from all over the world.

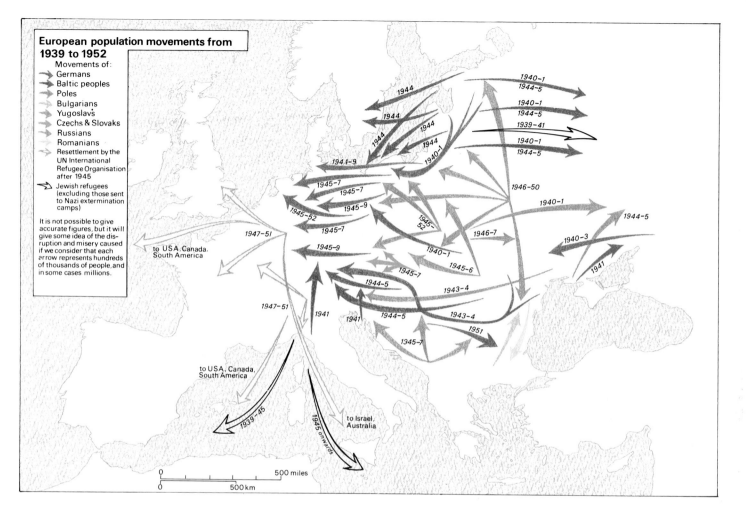

European population movements from 1939 to 1952

Movements of:
- Germans
- Baltic peoples
- Poles
- Bulgarians
- Yugoslavs
- Czechs & Slovaks
- Russians
- Romanians
- Resettlement by the UN International Refugee Organisation after 1945
- Jewish refugees (excluding those sent to Nazi extermination camps)

It is not possible to give accurate figures, but it will give some idea of the disruption and misery caused if we consider that each arrow represents hundreds of thousands of people, and in some cases millions.

1940-1
1944-5
1940-1
1944-5
1939-41
1940-1
1944-5
1944
1944
1944
1944
1944
1944
1940-1
1941-9
1946-50
1945-7
1945-7
1940-1
1944-5
1945-9
1945-7
1945-9
1945-52
1945-52
1945-7
1946-7
1940-3
1941
to USA, Canada, South America
1947-51
1940-1
1945-6
1944-5
1945-7
1943-4
1940-1
1947-51
1941
1941
1944-5
1943-4
1345-7
1951

to USA, Canada, South America

to Israel, Australia

1939-45
1945 onwards

0   500 miles
0   500 km

Obviously this carried a danger that if serious disagreement arose among the five, nothing could be decided. But it seemed better to risk this than a repetition of the pathetic performance of the League. Besides, optimists hoped, the Allies ought to have learned enough by now to work together.

The war had proved how small the world had become. There was a strong feeling that all nations were neighbours now, and the only way of getting along with one another was for all nations to be free and equal. The nations must treat each other as fellow-citizens of the world community, just like law-abiding individuals within one country. It made no difference whether they were big or small, strong or weak, rich or poor, black, white, brown or yellow. Every sane person in the world could understand the basic rules of right and wrong, and that all human beings should be treated accordingly: these were natural human rights.

Germany and Japan had broken this natural law, and the people responsible must be punished. The leaders of both countries and many of their followers were put on trial by the Allies, accused of war crimes: torture, murder, massacre. The biggest of the trials was held at Nuremberg, where the court heard a vast amount of evidence about the horrors that the Nazis had inflicted; there could be no doubt about the facts. But many of the accused tried to defend themselves with the

103

argument that they had only been doing what they had been ordered, and that if they had disobeyed they would themselves have been killed. The judges rejected these pleas. They said that even a soldier in wartime must not obey an order which offends against the law of humanity. So not only were the leaders given sentences of death or long imprisonment, but so were those who had actually committed the crimes.

This was a very important ruling. Perhaps it might have sounded even more convincing if all the judges had not belonged to the victorious nations, or if they had tried some of their own people who had ordered or committed unnecessary slaughter and destruction. But that did not lessen the case against the accused. It might also have been objected that the laws of humanity had never been written down so people could know exactly where they stood. This was soon remedied.

In 1948 UNO drew up its Declaration of Human Rights. These rights were mainly the sort of freedom and protection that were already part of the law in parliamentary democracies, and in many other states also (though the law may not always have been scrupulously observed). So it was that most, though not all, the member states of the United Nations accepted the Declaration, and agreed that these were essential human rights that belonged to every living person.

The victors: exhaustion, ambition and suspicion

It was urgent to start repairing the ruin and bring some order to Europe, and only the victorious powers were in a position to attempt it. Cities, industries and communications had been smashed to rubble and twisted metal by battle or bombing. Hundreds of thousands of people who had fled to escape the fighting, or had been carried off as forced workers, were stranded in what had been the Third Reich. Many of them were herded into Displaced Persons camps where the Allies tried to feed them and find somewhere to send them. DPs could not simply return to their old homes; often, especially in eastern Europe, frontiers and governments had been changed so much in the last stages of the war that these people would be treated as strangers or enemies if they went back; many Soviet citizens who returned from Nazi captivity to the USSR were accused of being traitors, and either killed or sent to slower death in the labour camps. Finding new homes for these un-

Germany, Year Zero. Near the ruined Reichstag building. Berliners dig potatoes. The photograph may have been deliberately taken to point a moral about the once-proud Reich, but it was only too true that Germany, like other parts of central and eastern Europe, was a devastated land where people had to seek food and shelter wherever they could.

lucky people was one of the most serious and painful problems in the rebuilding of Europe.

The victors themselves had suffered heavy loss, and both of the western European powers were exhausted. France had been crushingly defeated in 1940 and then forced to obey Hitler for four years. Those years divided French people deeply. Some had collaborated in the New Order, some had just got on with their own jobs more or less philosophically, and some had been active in the resistance. After the liberation in 1944 a new republic – the Fourth Republic – was set up. It faced a hard enough task in trying to restore industry and trade, and rebuild what the fighting had laid waste; but this was made worse because the old divisions between French political groups (page 11) had been deepened and complicated by the divisions of 1940–44.

Britain had escaped that sort of misfortune, but she was the only country that had fought Germany for the whole war. Now the strain was telling. British losses in deaths and damage, bad though they were, did not seem serious compared with some other countries', but in less obvious ways Britain was crippled. Her industries had concentrated on making things for war, not trade, so Britain's share of overseas markets had withered. Materials bought in those overseas countries had to be paid for, nevertheless, and British investments and businesses overseas had to be sold in order to do it. Under 'Lend-Lease' agreements the US government had allowed Britain to borrow huge amounts, and in 1945 cancelled the debt. This was a great help to Britain, but it did not restore the British assets that had been sold, or the lost markets. Few of the British people really understood how much poorer their country had become. Many of them still thought of their country as being 'the workshop of the world' and had no idea of what winning the war had cost Britain economically.

What the British wanted, and thought they deserved, was a time of peace better than the twenties and thirties. They wanted something better than the unemployment and poverty that had followed the first war and the Wall Street crash. During the 1939–45 war the main political parties had joined together to form a coalition government, under Winston Churchill, who was a member of the Conservative Party. He had a strong and picturesque personality and was a great orator; many people thought that it was his determination and leadership that had rallied the British to struggle through the darkest part of the war. The Conservative Party felt that, with Churchill at their head, they were bound to sweep to victory in the general election that was held when the war in Europe was over, in July 1945. Instead the Labour Party, under the much less colourful Clement Attlee, won a large majority. The reason, probably, was that the Conservatives seemed to have little idea of what to do except to let Churchill lead in peace as he had in war, while Labour promised to turn Britain into a 'welfare state'.

The Labour plan was to set up a national health service to provide medical treatment, free, for everyone who needed it; to give to the old and the poor, as their right and not as charity, enough money to let them live in reasonable comfort; to ensure that the British working population had 'full employment'; and to guard against any more depressions that might be caused by the ups and downs of the stock market (like the Wall Street crash). They tried to achieve these last two aims by taking over some key industries and managing them for the benefit of the whole nation. This was termed 'nationalisation', and the Labour government of 1945–51 nationalised (among other industries) the railways, coal and steel.

They also thought that it was wrong to hold in the British Empire peoples who wanted to be independent, particularly the Indians. Britain, it seemed, was weary of power and glory. Many British assumed that the rest of the world would still treat them with respect, out of admiration and gratitude, but in fact Britain was ceasing to be a first-class power.

This left only two powers strong enough to provide help and leadership to Europe: the USA and the USSR. Both were giants, but while the USA had been safe from any serious threat to her home territory the USSR had endured appalling devastation and death. It was easy for the Soviet people to feel that they alone had borne the full savagery of Hitler's war, and Stalin's propaganda taught them that the British and American capitalists had held back to give the Nazis a chance to wipe out Communism. It was no thanks to their so-called western Allies that the Soviet people had won. Suspicious as they always had been of capitalist countries, the Soviet leaders grasped at every opportunity to strengthen their own position against plots and attacks from the western powers.

The first thing to do was to extend the frontiers of the USSR as far westwards as possible. When the Red Army advanced during the last year of the war, the USSR regained the three Baltic republics, annexed East Prussia and seized a wide slice of eastern Poland which the Russians had always regarded as theirs. Poland was compensated by being given Silesia and other parts of eastern Germany.

The next important thing was to be able to influence neighbouring countries, so that they would act as a cushion against any new attacks. So, as the Red Army drove the Germans out of eastern Europe, in one country after another it helped local Communists, or parties that were prepared to work with the Communists, to form the government; soon the non-Communist members of such governments were squeezed out, and every state in eastern Europe became a member of what was known as the Communist *bloc*. In every way these countries supported the USSR; they traded and sent aid to make good Soviet war damage, even though they were sometimes in great need themselves, and they stood by the USSR in any international dispute. Like the USSR, they guarded their frontiers jealously, so that Westerners could not enter without strict surveillance and their own citizens could not leave. In March 1946 Churchill described the situation in a phrase that was instantly adopted in English-speaking coun-

A 1952 cartoon from the Soviet satirical magazine 'Krokodil'. The British lion, a dashing cavalier in the seventeenth century, has now become a weary old soldier, drooping with the weight of his armament. The title is: 'The evolution of English fashion'.

part of Communist teaching, and that Communist Parties in other countries had often been accused of taking their orders from Moscow; in Britain, for instance, the Communists who had opposed the war while the USSR remained at peace with Germany (page 87) had suddenly become violently dedicated to the crusade against Nazism when Hitler invaded the Soviet Union. In countries occupied by the Germans it had often happened that the Communists were the best-organised and most successful resistance fighters. This earned them popularity, and after the war they tried to use that popularity to build up big parties. In France and Italy they did it very well; remaining within the law, they got many members elected to parliament and won control of many local councils. In Greece they tried force, but lost in a short, savage civil war. All this activity made anti-Communists believe that all Communism was being organised from the Kremlin as part of a new Russian imperialism, far more dangerous than that of the tsars.

After 1918 the USA had backed out of any reponsibility in the affairs of the rest of the world. It was very different after 1945. Now the American leaders understood that the world was too small and the USA too big to try to hide in its old policy of isolation. The USA stood for a very different approach to life from Communism: her capitalist ideas meant that people

tries: 'from Stettin in the Baltic to Trieste in the Adriatic, an iron curtain has descended across the Continent'.

It may have been no more than a defensive attitude on the part of the Soviet Union, but it looked menacing to others. Many remembered that world revolution had always been

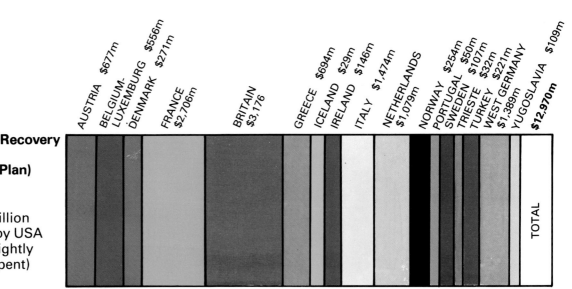

AUSTRIA $677m
BELGIUM-LUXEMBURG $556m
DENMARK $271m
FRANCE $2,706m
BRITAIN $3,176
GREECE $694m
ICELAND $29m
IRELAND $146m
ITALY $1,474m
NETHERLANDS $1,079m
NORWAY $254m
PORTUGAL $50m
SWEDEN $107m
TRIESTE $32m
TURKEY $221m
WEST GERMANY $1,389m
YUGOSLAVIA $109m
$12,970m

European Recovery Program (Marshall Plan) 1948-52

$13,150 million allocated by USA (though slightly less was spent)

TOTAL

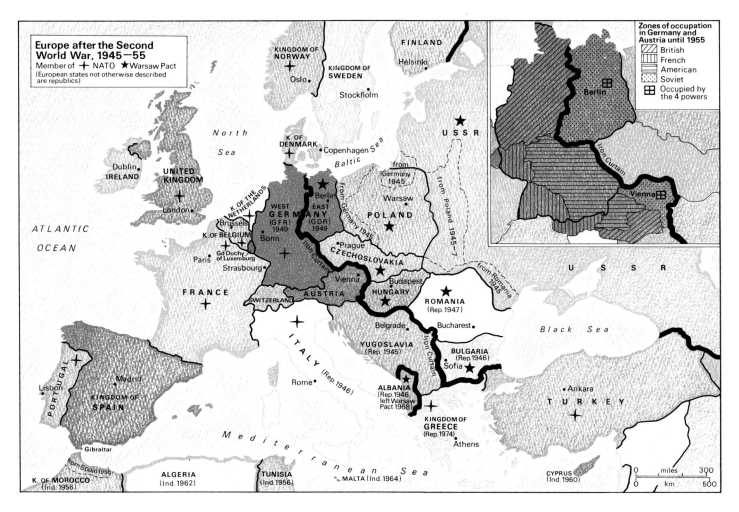

Europe after the Second World War, 1945—55
Member of ✚ NATO ★ Warsaw Pact
(European states not otherwise described are republics)

Zones of occupation in Germany and Austria until 1955
British
French
American
Soviet
⊞ Occupied by the 4 powers

should have freedom to compete in the struggle to become rich, that everyone was responsible for looking after himself without being cared for by the state, and that there must be free speech and free elections. It was true that Roosevelt and his New Deal had earned a lot of gratitude (page 52), but now America was prospering again and the traditional beliefs were as strong as ever – perhaps stronger because freedom seemed to be threatened by a world-wide Communist conspiracy.

The American government realised, however, that when people were so poor and miserable that they felt they had nothing to lose, then they would listen to Communist ideas about the need for revolution and a new system of sharing

wealth. The western European nations must not be allowed to sink under their post-war difficulties and become desperate enough for that to happen. Instead, they must be helped to re-build their cities and industries, and appreciate the good things of capitalist democracy. In 1947 the US Secretary of State, General George Marshall, suggested the scheme which began the following year as the European Recovery Program (ERP), more commonly called the Marshall Plan; Western European countries formed the Organisation for European Economic Co-operation (OEEC) to administer it. (Eastern European countries were invited, but the USSR would not allow them to accept.) It was a great help for Britain and

France; and at the same time those countries and the USA helped the people in their zones of Germany (page 93) to rebuild, and to begin a new way of life in the parliamentary democratic fashion that the Weimar Republic had tried to establish (page 72). The western Allies hoped that Germany would emerge as a republic with institutions like their own. In eastern Germany, though, the Soviet authorities organised their zone as a Communist state. Two different Germanies were being created, and what had been a united nation was being pulled in two different directions, dictatorial Communism and democratic capitalism.

The Cold War: the Iron Curtain and the Berlin blockade

The east–west disagreement came to a head over Berlin. Those quarters of the city occupied by the three western Allies were being treated as part of western Germany, where a federal republic was being fostered. But Berlin stood well within eastern Germany, so the Soviet authorities saw this as a challenge to the system they were setting up. They decided to force the USA, Britain and France to accept Soviet proposals for the future of Germany by using Berlin as a hostage. On 24

June 1948 they closed the road that ran through their zone of Germany, linking Berlin to the west. Without the supplies that normally streamed along that road, West Berlin would soon be starved into submission and the western Allies would have to admit defeat and appear weak in the eyes of the rest of the world.

Instead, it was the USSR that had to give in. The western Allies met the challenge with aircraft. During the war the number of big, long-range planes had increased hugely, and they had often been used for supplying troops who were otherwise cut off. There had never been an attempt to supply so many people as this; it would demand great expense, effort and organisation, and it would have to be kept up for as long as the road remained closed. But unless they did it, the western Allies would have either to submit or to use force and risk starting a war. As it turned out, the Berlin 'airlift' was a

Berlin, 17 August 1948. At the British-controlled Gatow air base Germans – and VW 'Beetle' cars – help to unload an American Globemaster, while a Dakota comes in with more supplies. This sort of non-stop activity with the biggest available planes – the Globemaster, the biggest of all, could carry twenty tons of flour – had to continue in all weathers for more than a year, but it succeeded in keeping a great city alive.

triumph for the skill and determination of the West. Even through the worst of the winter the big transport planes kept arriving every few minutes in Berlin, to be unloaded immediately and flown back for more supplies. Occasionally there was a crash and airmen died, but the endless procession of aircraft went on. The USSR quietly reopened the road on 12 May 1949, but the airlift was not completely ended until September; by then it had carried 277,264 plane-loads of supplies into West Berlin.

At about the same time the USSR suffered another setback. At the end of the war Yugoslavia had become a Communist republic under Tito (page 91), a dedicated Communist who had been trained in Moscow. Stalin thought this meant that he could use Yugoslavia as a puppet state, but Tito was not like some other leaders of eastern European states. He refused to do anything that was not likely to benefit Yugoslavia, no matter what advantage it might bring to the Soviet Union. Stalin decided to bring Tito to his senses. The international association of Communist countries (now called the Cominform, not the Comintern, since it was officially said to be no more than a center for exchanging information) had a meeting just about the time the Berlin airlift was beginning, and expelled Yugoslavia. But instead of asking to be forgiven, Tito tightened his grip on the Yugoslav government and opened his frontiers to Western trade and tourists – though the country remained Communist. It made the Iron Curtain look rather less solid.

By 1949 there was no more pretence of friendship between the USSR and the western Allies, led by the USA. The phrase 'Cold War' was invented to express the feeling of deep hostility which stopped just short of shooting. In 1949 most of the countries of western Europe joined the USA in forming the North Atlantic Treaty Organisation, which soon set up a NATO military alliance for defence against eastern Europe. In 1955 the USSR and her supporters announced the formation of the Warsaw Pact for defence against western Europe. In 1949 the two parts of Germany were organised as separate republics; the US, British and French zones became the German Federal Republic; while the Soviet zone became the German Democratic Republic – which Westerners considered to be a misuse of the word 'democratic'. In 1955 the two German republics became members of NATO and the Warsaw Pact respectively, so that the front line in the Cold War ran through the middle of Germany. Ten years after the Second World War, Europe was a continent divided between two suspicious, heavily armed alliances, each led by one of the world's two superpowers.

The Cold War: Communist China and the Korean War

Because of their size and position, the USA and USSR face each other across the Pacific as well as across the Atlantic. In Europe, where the Cold War first seemed most tense and dangerous, the advantage seemed to rest with the USA. It was different in Asia.

The Japanese attack on China had interrupted the war between the Guomindang, or Nationalists, and the Communists (page 59), but it had not made them friends. Chiang Kai-shek and the Guomindang government got American money, arms and advisers to help them to resist the Japanese, and when Japan surrendered to the USA the Guomindang naturally took over. Chiang was victorious, the ruler of most of China, and would have little difficulty now in putting down the Communists – or so it seemed. In fact, the opposite happened. The Guomindang crumpled up, and by the summer of 1949 Chiang had to abandon the mainland of China altogether and ferry what was left of his forces to the island of Taiwan (Formosa), where the US fleet could protect them. Mao Zedong led the Communists into Beijing and there, on 1 October 1949, proclaimed the People's Republic of China.

The reason for this amazing overturn was really quite simple. Chiang's followers were tired, inefficient and, above all, corrupt; Guomindang officials looked after themselves and their friends and anybody who could bribe them, and it was the old story that the Chinese knew so well – the rich and the landlords being favoured at the expense of the peasants. But the Communists earned the reputation of being exactly the opposite – honest, hardworking, living as simply as the peasants themselves. They dispossessed the landlords and organised the villagers to hold the land as common property and to share out the work and the rewards communally. The Communists apparently wanted nothing extra for themselves, they practised what they preached; so the millions of Chinese turned from the Guomindang towards them, and they became masters of the biggest nation on earth.

The Korean War, 1950–3

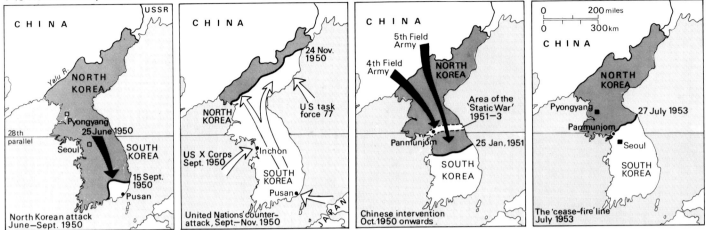

Mao's government faced the enormous task of changing the ancient civilisation of China into a twentieth-century Communist society. This was bound to take most of their energies, and they tended to turn their backs on the outside world (which was something that China had done very often over the past two thousand years). But they could not avoid a Cold War argument in the United Nations. Chiang Kai-shek and his Nationalists still claimed to be the rightful government of China although the only Chinese territory they held was Taiwan; and they still held the Chinese seat among the permanent five members of the Security Council (page 102). The Communist government in Beijing repeatedly claimed the seat, and was supported by the USSR. But the USA always supported the Nationalists, and they won the votes and kept the seat.

The next confrontation was in a war. After the surrender in 1945 Japan was occupied by US forces and began to work as a capitalist parliamentary democracy, though the emperor remained as the head of state. Japan had held Korea for forty years, but now Korea was 'liberated'; this meant that the country was divided into two, with Soviet troops occupying the north and American the south. It was rather like the situation in Germany, for here too a Communist state was set up in one part, a parliamentary state in the other. Almost all the Soviet and American troops were withdrawn, and the Koreans were left to run their own affairs. Suddenly, on 25 June 1950,

the North Korean army invaded the South. Within three days they held the South's capital, Seoul, and the South seemed on the point of total collapse. Hurriedly the US government ordered troops from its forces in Japan to go to prop up South Korea, and in the UN Security Council demanded that the United Nations should take action against North Korea.

The Communist countries argued that it was the South that had attacked the North, but few others believed that. Most of the Security Council agreed with the USA. But each permanent member had the right of veto. This meant that the USSR could forbid any UN action over Korea, and the USSR had already shown on previous occasions that she would not hesitate to say 'No!' But the USSR made an amazing miscalculation. The Soviet representative on the Security Council had been showing disapproval by boycotting meetings, and he was not present when the vote on Korea was taken. That was how the UN was able to do something that the League had never even attempted; it invited members to send troops to Korea to fight as a United Nations army against the North Korean invaders. This was the first time in history that a worldwide international peace-keeping organisation had used force to stop an aggressor.

The Korean War was also the first time the two sides in the Cold War came seriously to blows. The fighting swung violently to and fro. At first it seemed that North Korea was advancing so quickly that there would be nothing left of the

The increasing power of nuclear weapons

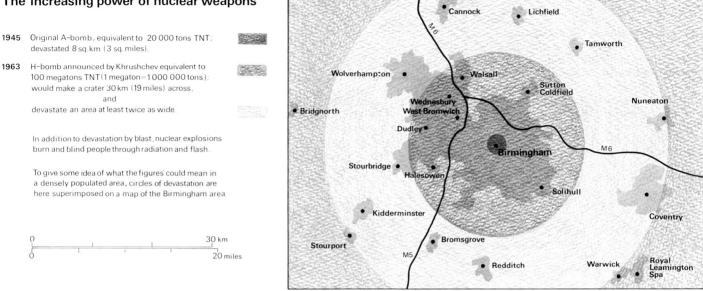

1945 Original A-bomb, equivalent to 20 000 tons TNT; devastated 8 sq.km (3 sq. miles).

1963 H-bomb announced by Khrushchev equivalent to 100 megatons TNT (1 megaton = 1 000 000 tons); would make a crater 30 km (19 miles) across,
and
devastate an area at least twice as wide.

In addition to devastation by blast, nuclear explosions burn and blind people through radiation and flash.

To give some idea of what the figures could mean in a densely populated area, circles of devastation are here superimposed on a map of the Birmingham area.

South to rescue, but US and UN forces arrived just in time to hold the southernmost tip of the country. When their strength increased they drove the North Koreans back to their own country and then through it to the Chinese frontier. At this point the Chinese Communists decided that the North must be saved, and sent in a great army of 'volunteers' who pushed back the UN army. By the summer of 1953 the front was roughly along the 1950 border between North and South Korea, each side recognised that the other would not give in, and they did not want this to grow into a big war. On 27 July they agreed an armistice that left things as they had been before the war began.

The Cold War: nuclear missiles and the Cuban confrontation

Korea had shown that it was possible to use force in the Cold War – up to a point. But it would be very dangerous for the main powers to get involved officially in the fighting. In Korea the Americans never fought Soviet troops, and officially, anyway, they were not fighting as US but as UN soldiers. Officially, too, China did not take part in the war – the government merely 'permitted' men to go as 'volunteers'. So it be-

came understood that the Cold War could be waged by any means short of outright fighting between the main combatants; propaganda, spying, sabotage, stirring up rebellions, backing small nations in small wars were all possible, but there must be no major war.

The reason for this caution was the atom bomb. In 1945 only the USA and Britain knew the secret of how to make such weapons. If a war had broken out then, they could have crushed the USSR in a few days. But by 1949 the USSR also knew the secret, partly because a few British scientists had thought it right to share their knowledge with the great Communist power. This meant that each superpower was now able to inflict – on the other, if necessary – death and devastation on a scale never known before.

The weapons themselves were growing more dangerous. On each side scientists strove to produce even bigger explosions and they also took up Hitler's idea of using rockets. Soon, with the help of German scientists, they developed missiles with atomic warheads that could hit targets thousands of miles away, and the range, accuracy and killing power constantly increased as each side tried to gain a decisive advantage. They tried to develop defences, too. During the war scientists familiar with radio and electricity had explored a

MISSILE ERECTOR

5 TRUCKS UNDER CAMOUFLAGE NETTING

CABLE

THEODOLITE STATION

5 TRUCKS UNDER CAMOUFLAGE NETTIN

MISSILE SHELTER TENTS

whole new field of science and technology which became known as electronics. They could guide and detect aircraft and ships by radar, and now they used similar devices to navigate or to intercept rockets. Their machines came to work with a speed and accuracy that was truly superhuman, far beyond the most brilliant pilots and mathematicians. But since the same skill and the same sort of gadgets were used in both attack and defence, nobody could doubt that some missiles were going to get through defences, and even a few could wreak the most dreadful destruction.

It became more usual to call these missiles nuclear, not atomic, as new methods of releasing intense power were discovered. At each step forward, fears grew that any country that took part in a nuclear war would be wiped out; and it was

Taken from a US spy plane in 1962, this is one of the photographs that revealed what sort of weapons were being installed in Cuba. This site was near the western end of Cuba; from it missiles might be launched towards the mouth of the Mississippi or any other targets on the south coast of the USA.

also possible that the blast and radiation from a full-scale war with nuclear weapons might produce uncontrollable effects that would destroy civilisation, perhaps the whole human race, even all life on earth. The idea became accepted that if each side knew that, even if it destroyed the other, it would certainly be destroyed itself, it would not dare to start a war. This was the theory of Mutual Assured Destruction, MAD for

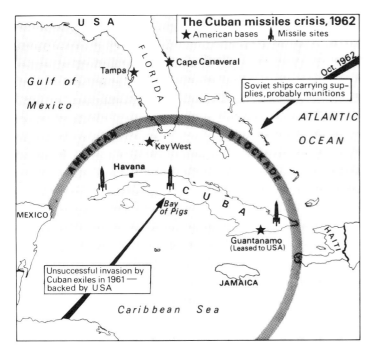

The Cuban missiles crisis, 1962
★ American bases ⚬ Missile sites

USA

FLORIDA

Cape Canaveral

Tampa

Gulf of Mexico

Oct. 1962

Soviet ships carrying supplies, probably munitions

ATLANTIC OCEAN

Key West

AMERICAN BLOCKADE

Havana

MEXICO

C U B A

Bay of Pigs

Guantanamo (Leased to USA)

HAITI

Unsuccessful invasion by Cuban exiles in 1961 — backed by USA

JAMAICA

Caribbean Sea

short. Since no sane government could fail to be deterred from attacking a country capable of hitting back with nuclear weapons, it was also called the Nuclear Deterrent. The hope was that men had now produced a weapon so devastating that all-out war was suicidal. All the same, the two superpowers were not content with what they already had. Both went on piling up more and deadlier weapons, while some other countries decided that they would not be safe, and would not have any influence in the world, unless they too could deliver a nuclear attack.

While the scientists tried to build better bombs, their political leaders tried to gain advantages by other means. The USA made arrangements with countries near the USSR to allow American rockets to be sited there, aimed at Soviet cities. America was so far away that the Soviet government had problems in finding sites for its rockets within range, and its best hope was to encourage revolts in all parts of the world, to get Communist or, at least, anti-American governments installed in those countries. Stalin died in March 1953. His death caused considerable changes within the USSR, but not in the diplomatic struggle. Sometimes the threats and bluffs seemed

so dangerous that the word 'brinkmanship' was invented to describe the game of outmaneuvering your opponent by getting closer to the brink of war than he dared, without falling in.

They came very close to the brink in the Cuban missiles crisis of October 1962. Four years before there had been a revolution in Cuba, and its leader, the new ruler of the country, soon showed himself to be a Communist; his name was Fidel Castro. The US government were alarmed at the thought of a friend of the USSR so close to American shores, so they helped Castro's enemies to try to recapture Cuba. Their efforts failed dismally, and the main result was to make Castro ask the USSR for more help. Among the weapons they sent him were rockets capable of hitting US cities.

Among the many spying devices used in the Cold War were airplanes that could fly extremely high and fast, and at the same time take accurate photographs of the ground far below. One of these American spy planes flying over Cuba took pictures that showed launching sites for rockets, pointing towards the USA. The President of the USA, John F. Kennedy, decided that, at almost any price, the threat must be removed. He demanded that the sites should be dismantled, and ordered the US navy to blockade Cuba and prevent any Soviet ships from bringing weapons. The Soviet navy was much too small to do anything against the US navy, so the Soviet leader, Nikita Khrushchev, had this choice: either agree to the removal of the rocket sites or fight, knowing that the fight must become a nuclear war. For a few days the whole world waited in fear. Then Khrushchev consented to withdraw the missiles in return for a promise by Kennedy never again to interfere in Cuban affairs.

Both sides claimed to have got what they wanted, but both – and everybody else – had had a bad fright. For a while they tried not to challenge each other directly. There was talk of 'peaceful co-existence', the idea that the world was big enough for Communism and capitalism to go on side by side, and some people even thought that the Cold War was ending. But the USSR set about building a large navy so that the USA could never again 'rule the waves' unchallenged, and both sides went on quietly stockpiling and improving their weapons. As their ICBMs (inter-continental ballistic missiles) improved, the USA and the USSR became able to hit each other from their own territories, and there was no longer such need for launching sites in other countries.

113

7 The rise of the Third World

The new states of Asia

Either superpower could have dominated the world, if it had not been for the other. As it was, the world seemed split into two opposing camps. But were they quarrelling about the things that mattered most to the majority of the people of the world?

It was still very much a white man's world. The two rival giants and their creeds were products of European civilisation. However, both claimed that they treated all nations as free and equal, no matter what their size, wealth or colour might be. This was the attitude of the UN, too, and there would be no support for European nations that tried to hold on to their colonies. Meanwhile the demands for independence among colonial peoples were growing more vigorous than they had been in the 1920s and 1930s. So, while the Soviet and American governments fought the Cold War from Berlin to Korea to Cuba, other changes were happening in Asia and then in Africa, which might prove just as important for the future.

India set the example. Even before the war Britain had been almost ready to grant self-government to India (page 54), and during the war had made a definite promise, in return for the loyal support Indians were giving on many fronts. Now, though Churchill and a few others grumbled about feebly abandoning the empire, the British government was determined to keep the promise and to leave India to the Indians, without any fighting.

There was one great difficulty – the deep dislike and distrust between the Hindus, who dominated the Indian National Congress Party, and the Muslim League. Congress wanted to keep India as the British had made it, one united enormous country. But the Muslim League feared that in such a country the Hindus would use their large majority of voters to keep power for themselves and keep Muslims down. Therefore they demanded that areas where most of the people were Muslim should be formed into a separate country, to be called Pakistan. When Congress objected, the Muslims threatened to fight. It was no idle threat – already there had been bloody riots between Hindus and Muslims. It would be impossible to

In addition to Hindu–Muslim violence, the government of the newly independent republic of India had to cope with political disturbances. This photograph, dated January 1948, shows members of the Communist-led All India Students' Federation, after breaking through a police cordon, rushing into the Workers' Field, Bombay, to hold a meeting that the authorities had banned.

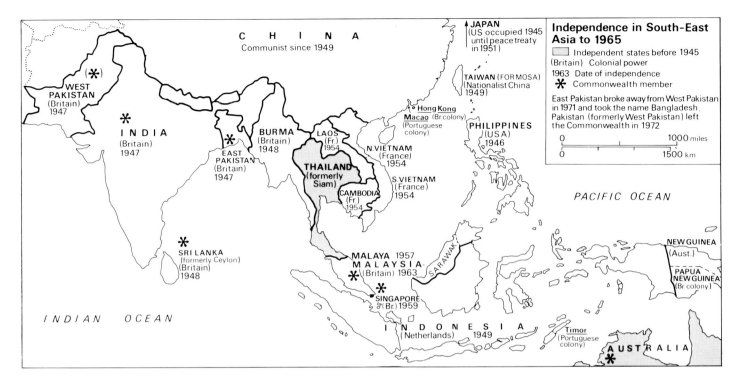

Independence in South-East Asia to 1965

- ▨ Independent states before 1945
- (Britain) Colonial power
- 1963 Date of independence
- ✳ Commonwealth member

East Pakistan broke away from West Pakistan in 1971 and took the name Bangladesh. Pakistan (formerly West Pakistan) left the Commonwealth in 1972

0 ————— 1000 miles
0 ————— 1500 km

establish the new India in the midst of a full-scale civil war so, very unwillingly, Congress agreed.

On 15 August 1947 the British Empire in India officially ended and the two new republics of India and Pakistan came into being. But despite the agreement between their leaders, the hatred between Hindus and Muslims burst out more violently than ever in riot, pillage and massacre. Hindus living in what was now Pakistan, and Muslims in India, were murdered in thousands, and multitudes more fled as refugees across the new frontiers, spreading tales of terror and vengeance. Mahatma Gandhi (page 53), now an old man, did all he could to stop the slaughter; he saved the lives of many Muslims, so a Hindu fanatic killed him. Eventually the new governments of India and Pakistan managed to quell the violence, but there remained a legacy of suspicion between the two countries.

Britain granted independence to her other Asian colonies at the same time. On 4 January 1948 Burma was proclaimed an independent republic, and on 4 February Ceylon became independent, later taking the name of Sri Lanka. Like India and Pakistan, Sri Lanka remained a member of the Common-

wealth, and this was what most former British colonies decided to do as they became independent. The British remained a few years more in Malaya, mainly because Communists were fighting a guerrilla war in the jungle. This war might have been very dangerous and have spread to other countries of Indochina if the guerrillas had been able to get shelter and help from the local people; but the Communists were mostly Chinese, who were disliked by the Malay villagers, and they were eventually wiped out. In 1963 the Malay States joined with Singapore and North Borneo to form the Malaysian Federation.

The British were wise to give independence so readily. By now the peoples of South-East Asia had learned a great deal about the white man's methods, and thought that they could do just as well themselves. And the Japanese conquests in 1942 made it impossible for Europeans ever again to assume their old air of confident superiority.

When the Dutch returned to the East Indies they did not fully understand how things had changed. They thought, quite rightly, that the people would be glad to get rid of the

Japanese but they underestimated the strength of the local leaders who were now demanding independence. Before the Dutch had taken charge, the different peoples of these islands had been divided, at odds with one another, a prey to bandits and pirates; they were still of several different nationalities and religions. It was Dutch rule that had created peace and one united government, and without the Dutch it would all fall apart – or so the Dutch believed. But the Indonesians, as they called themselves, could and did stand together, and after a couple of years' fighting the Dutch were sensible enough to recognise that they had been mistaken. On 27 December 1949 they officially handed over their powers to the independent government of the United States of Indonesia.

The French regained control of their colonies in Indochina determined to hold them firmly. There was an independence movement in Vietnam which soon began a guerrilla war; but the French knew that the guerrillas were Communists, and therefore believed that they did not represent a truly national revolt, and that the Vietnam people, both Buddhists and Catholics, were too religious to support an 'anti-God' movement. But this was not Malaya; these rebels were among their own people, where they could hide, and get food and information. The guerrilla bands grew into a large, well-disciplined army. In 1954 the French allowed one of their forces to be surrounded at Dien Bien Phu, hoping that in a hard-fought siege the rebels would prove no match for the tough professionals of the French army and Foreign Legion. It turned out otherwise, and in May, after a long and desperate fight, the French force surrendered. Two months later the French left Indochina. They left the three independent states of Laos, Cambodia and Vietnam, but Vietnam was divided. Rather like Korea, North Vietnam became Communist while the South became a republic in the style – or so it was hoped – of the Western democracies.

Ten years after the Second World War there were only a few fragments left of the European empires in Asia. Portugal had given up nothing, but her colonies were small and there were no powerful independence movements in them. Britain kept Hong Kong; it was tiny, and part was technically still Chinese property held by Britain on a long lease. Both China and Britain found it very useful as an unoffical market when the two governments were officially on bad terms. The USA, after driving out the Japanese at the end of the war, gave the Philippines their independence, as they had earlier promised.

The USA, however, remained a great power in South-East Asia. There was a strong American occupation force in Japan, and there was valuable trade to be protected. The US government were well aware that two great Communist countries, the USSR and China, were facing them directly across the North Pacific. The countries of South-East Asia found that their independence did not save them from becoming battlegrounds in the Cold War.

The new states of Africa

Now that the colonial powers had given independence in Asia, could they refuse to do the same in Africa? Some argued that the case was different. The Asian peoples were civilised, with great cities, splendid architecture and art, profound and subtle religions, philosophies and literatures. They said that except

A French armoured column – the footslogging infantry, though, are Vietnamese – operating against rebels about 60 km (40 miles) from Hanoi, October 1953. The original press report that accompanied the photograph described the operation as a success. But the following May Dien Bien Phu fell to the comparatively ill-equipped rebels and in July France withdrew altogether from Indochina.

where Islam had become established, north of the Sahara, it was hard to see anything in Africa similar to Asia. Only the coming of the Europeans had brought most of the African continent into contact with the modern world, and there had not yet been time for the black tribesmen to learn to run their countries successfully in twentieth-century conditions. Against this was the argument that already there were large numbers of well-educated Africans, lawyers, doctors, clergymen, civil servants, engineers and businessmen, who were perfectly capable of running their countries. Furthermore, many of these men were becoming politicians and demanding independence, because they felt that the whites were holding them down, keeping the best jobs for themselves while most of the blacks remained poor and under-educated.

Most of the colonial powers saw that sooner or later they would have to give way to these demands, so it would be better to do so in a peaceful, friendly way–even if some of them had misgivings. They began to employ more Africans in important jobs, training them to take over, eventually. But the process seemed too slow to many Africans, and they suspected that the whites had no real intention of ever giving up their privileged position. In some places violence broke out, and what happened in Kenya in the early 1950s showed the tensions and uncertainties at their worst. Here a secret society called the *Mau Mau* spread among the Kikuyu people. They murdered whites by hacking them with jungle knives, and did the same or worse to blacks who refused to join them. They made their recruits swear loyalty in ceremonies that were deliberately designed to fill them with horror and fear. After two or three years the British authorities managed to stamp out the Mau Mau, but were left with an anxious dilemma: could people like this be trusted to govern a country? The authorities decided that the Mau Mau was the work of a small mad minority, and that the best way of preventing such outbursts was to hand over power to the responsible and reasonable Africans. Most colonial governments came to the same conclusion, and inside twenty years they gave independence to their African colonies.

The liberation of black Africa began in August 1956, when the Gold Coast Assembly voted for independence, and Britain granted it next month, to take effect in March 1957. The new country took the name of an old West African kingdom, Ghana, to show the world that Africans had proud traditions

Two African leaders of independence movements

Kwame Nkrumah of Ghana, 1909–72, born and educated (degree 1930) in British colony of Gold Coast. Wrote and spoke for independence in 1940s, founded Convention People's Party 1949. Elected Prime Minister of colony 1954, negotiated independence 1956–7, became President 1960; name of country changed to Ghana. Declared Ghana a one-party state 1964. Deposed by army 1966.

Jomo Kenyatta of Kenya, 1891–1978, Kikuyu tribesman. Studied in London. Returned to Kenya 1946, became president of Kenya African Union 1947. Convicted of organising Mau Mau terror campaign (which he always denied) and detained 1953–9. Led Kenyan negotiations for independence 1962, became Prime Minister 1963, and the country's first President 1964. Remained in office until his death and retained parliamentary system.

of their own. As they became independent, other African countries such as Mali did the same, though others such as Niger and Chad preferred the names of rivers or lakes. The only colonial power that refused to give independence was the oldest, Portugal, and for many years Portuguese troops fought a wearisome war against guerrillas who demanded independence for Angola and Mozambique. The war went on until 1974, when there was a peaceful revolution in Portugal, and the new government granted independence to Portugal's colonies in Africa.

The only part of Africa where the whites refused to give up their mastery was the south. This was where whites had settled in large numbers, and some of them, the Boers or Afrikaners, had been there for three hundred years. This was their homeland, and they were not going to hand over the government to people they considered to be their inferiors. The Union of South Africa was a self-governing member of the Commonwealth, so there was nothing that the British or any other members could do when the South African government enforced a policy it called *apartheid*, separateness. The idea was that it was best for both blacks and whites to be allowed to develop their own cultures separately, and for the blacks not to be forced to adapt too rapidly to the needs of a white industrialised way of life. There was no doubt that black communities had often been demoralised and destroyed by 'progress', so apartheid might have been a wise and humane policy. It did not work that way. The blacks got a few poor areas as 'homelands', while the biggest and best part of South Africa remained white. Here the blacks, and other coloured people, were treated as an inferior race – with unskilled jobs, poor pay, shanty towns to live in, and no mixing with whites even on public transport or at sports grounds. The police stamped hard on any sign of disobedience. In March 1960 a big crowd of Africans demonstrated at Sharpeville to protest against the 'pass laws' that forced all blacks to carry identity cards, and the police shot 72 of them. It was the 'Sharpeville Massacre' that triggered off condemnation of apartheid all round the world. The UN voted against it, and there was so much criticism in the Commonwealth that South Africa declared herself an independent republic and left the Commonwealth.

Despite all the disapproval, other countries were unwilling or unable to take action that would really hurt the South African government. All the same, the South Africans did not enjoy the constant feeling of hostility, and over the years claimed to be doing all they could to improve conditions for blacks and gradually reduce apartheid. But this was not enough, and South Africa was eventually the only white-ruled country in the continent, distrusted and often hated by the others.

For some years one of South Africa's neighbours also tried to maintain white supremacy. This was Southern Rhodesia. In the early 1960s, while still subject to Britain, the white Rhodesians began to fear that the British government was going to give more power to the blacks, so in 1965 they declared themselves independent without British agreement – their Unilateral Declaration of Independence or UDI. Britain, the Commonwealth and the United Nations were all against it, though all they did was to impose economic sanctions – the device that had failed against Italy in 1936 (page 83). Meanwhile South Africa did what she could to support the white Rhodesians who went on prospering. This could have continued indefinitely, but a guerrilla war began among the black Rhodesians, and the guerrillas steadily became stronger despite the great numbers that the whites' forces killed; the neighbouring black states sheltered and supplied the guerril-

las, and Communist countries sent them weapons. At last the whites were forced to recognise that they could never win and live in peace, so they submitted once more to Britain. In 1980, therefore, Britain held elections in Rhodesia, and for the first time blacks could vote on the same terms as whites. The result was an overwhelming victory for the former guerrilla leaders, and Rhodesia became the republic of Zimbabwe.

The black governments that now ruled almost all of Africa faced two serious problems. The first was that their states were often the creations of the whites. They might include many very different peoples, sometimes old enemies, who were together now because they had been conquered by the same white nation, and for no other reason. These states were not nation-states, nor were they federal unions that had been formed freely and naturally. The other problem was poverty. The climate and the nature of the land in many African countries were not well suited to modern mechanised farming, and the people could not afford the machines or maintain them anyway; they still farmed or herded in their old ways, producing enough to live on (except in drought years) but no surplus for sale. Some countries were rich in certain minerals or even particular crops, but they had to ship them off to factories in Europe or America, because the former colonial rulers had never thought it worth while to start big industries in Africa.

These problems caused strains that frequently led to war inside the new states. In Sudan, for example, fighting dragged on for many years between the black peoples of the equatorial south and the Arabic-speaking Muslims of the northern plains and deserts who thought of themselves as the rulers. That was mainly a conflict between different races, with some religious antagonism as well. In the two wars that attracted most international interest the causes were partly economic. In 1960 the province of Katanga, rich in minerals, tried to break away from the rest of the Congo – with, it was suspected, encouragement from some European mining firms. It was only subdued after the UN sent a force there. In 1967 the Ibo people tried to break away from Nigeria and form a new state called Biafra; enterprising and hardworking, they thought that they would be more prosperous on their own. It took the Nigerian army three years of desperate fighting to defeat them. These were the best-known civil wars, but there were disturbances in very many states.

One result was that parliamentary democracy did not seem

MADEIRA

CANARY IS.

MOROCCO
(France)
1956

TUNISIA
(France)
1956

ALGERIA
(France)
1962

(Spain) 1976

(Italy until 1947)
(Br. admin. 1947)
LIBYA
(Fr. admin.
1947)
1951

EGYPT

MAURITANIA
(France)
1960

MALI
(France)
1960

NIGER
(France)
1960

CHAD
(France)
1960

SUDAN
(Britain/Egypt)
1960

ERITREA

Red Sea

SENEGAL
(France)
1960

GAMBIA
(Br.) 1965

GUINEA-
BISSAU
(Portugal) 1974

GUINEA
(Fr.) 1958

UPP. VOLTA
(Fr.)
1960

NIGERIA
Britain 1960

1960

CENTRAL AFRICAN
REPUBLIC

DJIBOUTI (Fr.)
1977

(Britain)

ETHIOPIA
(formerly Abyssinia)

SOMALI REP. (Italy)
1960

SIERRA LEONE
(Britain) 1961

IVORY
COAST
(Fr.)
1960

GHANA

(Br.)
1957

LIBERIA

TOGO
(Fr.) 1960
BENIN (Fr.) 1960

1960

CAMEROON
(French
mandate)

GABON
(France)
1960

1960 (France)

CONGO (France)

ZAIRE

1960

(formerly
Congo)
(Belgium)

RWANDA
1962

BURUNDI
1962

UGANDA
(Br.)
1962

KENYA
(Britain)
1963

EQUATORIAL
GUINEA
(Spain) 1968

TANZANIA
(British mandate)
1961

INDIAN

OCEAN

ATLANTIC

OCEAN

ANGOLA
(Portugal)
1975

ZAMBIA
(Britain)
1964

MALAWI
(Britain) 1964

COMOROS
REPUBLIC
(France)
1975

NAMIBIA
(South-west
Africa)

(Under
South
African
admin.)

BOTSWANA
(Britain)
1966

ZIMBABWE
(Britain)
1980

MOZAMBIQUE
(Portugal) 1975

MALAGASY REP.
(formerly Madagascar)
(France) 1960

SOUTH
AFRICA

SWAZILAND
(Britain) 1968

LESOTHO
(Britain) 1968

**Independence in Africa
up to 1980**

Independent states before 1945

(Britain) Colonial power

1960 Date of independence

✱ Commonwealth member

0 _____ 1000 miles

0 _____ 1500 km

Two African military rulers

Mobutu Sese Seko of Zaire, b. 1930, Joseph Désiré Mobutu. Clerk in Belgian Congo army 1949. Later became newspaper editor, joined independence movement, was appointed Chief of Staff in Congo army at independence 1960. Supported President during civil wars then seized power for himself by military coup 1965. Kept firm control, suppressing rebellions sometimes with outside help. Africanised his own name and restored to the country the old river name, Zaire.

Idi Amin Dada of Uganda, b. 1925, Muslim tribesman. Joined British colonial army 1946, rose to highest non-commissioned rank. After independence, 1962, was rapidly promoted; Commander-in-Chief 1964. Made himself president by military coup 1971. Expelled Ugandan Asians, and many whites. Suppressed protests brutally. Quarrelled with neighbour states. Tanzanian invasion, 1979, restored previous president. Amin fled.

to work smoothly in Africa. Either the army would step in to restore order, and set up a military dictatorship, or a political leader would declare a one-party state with his party as the only one and himself as head of state. Another result was that outsiders sometimes were tempted to intervene.

The great powers and the Third World

The old great colonial powers understood by now that they must give independence to any colony that asked for it, and most of them did. All round the world new independent nations were appearing. Sometimes they were very small – an island or a group of islands, perhaps, in the Caribbean or the Pacific or the Indian Ocean. Every new nation could join the UN and vote equally with the others in the General Assembly. This was obviously going to make a difference to the character of the United Nations.

The former colonial powers were in some ways better off. They no longer had the expense of administering and guarding their colonies, though they usually kept their trading links

with them. Indeed, most former British or French colonies thought that it was useful to keep in touch with the other members of what had been the British and French empires; they became members of the Commonwealth (the name 'British' was dropped) or of the French Union. These were rather loose associations of nations, without strong rules, but the members believed that it was helpful for them all to discuss their problems; and, as in the United Nations, it came to be accepted that it was the duty of the rich or 'developed' members to aid the poor or 'undeveloped'.

Still, it was hard for some British and French to accept that they no longer ruled world empires, and their feelings of resentment sometimes boiled over. This caused two serious conflicts, both in North Africa. In 1956 President Nasser of Egypt was trying to raise money to build a huge dam on the Nile to irrigate wide areas of barren land, and was disappointed when the USA changed its mind about offering a loan. To get some money, he declared that the Suez Canal was the property of the Egyptian nation, and seized it from the company that operated it. The company was under British and French control. Britain and France were furious, and decided to act firmly. But instead of going openly to seize the canal back again, they made a secret agreement with Egypt's enemy, Israel. The plot was that Israel should attack Egypt and advance towards the canal, and that Britain and France would then intervene as 'policemen' and occupy the canal to prevent damage, leaving Israel with all the land to the east of the canal. Nobody was deceived. The UN condemned, the USA disapproved, the USSR threatened. Britain and France had no choice but to withdraw their forces, angry and humiliated, and to try to learn the lesson.

Meanwhile France was trying to deal with a very awkward situation in Algeria. Officially Algeria was not a colony, but part of France. The Arabic Algerians, however, were not treated as equal to the white settlers, so they naturally demanded what the colonial peoples were getting, independence. There began a guerrilla war that was even more cruel than most, for both sides were fighting for their native land. French governments failed to win the war, and fell. The leader of the Free French in the Second World War, General Charles de Gaulle, was elected Prime Minister in 1958, promising to keep Algeria French. He gave himself extra powers under a new constitution, the Fifth Republic, becoming President in

1959. But he too failed to suppress the Algerian revolt, and in 1962 he recognized Algeria as an independent republic.

Many Frenchmen, especially those whose homes had been in Algeria, felt that they had lost everything; there were plots to kill de Gaulle, 'the traitor'. But most of the French faced the fact that their empire was gone, and that if they wanted to assert French greatness, which de Gaulle, was constantly proclaiming, they must find some other way of doing it.

While the former great powers were being made to understand that they dominated the world no longer, there were others eager to take their place. Wherever in the world rebellions broke out or revolutions were planned, there would be Communists trying to take the lead. Often they were sincerely trying to do their best for their own people, and knew that they were likely to meet only hardship and death. But behind them the Soviet Union was always ready to offer advice, training and weapons. And if the USSR tried to spread its influence by helping revolutionaries, the USA thought it wise to help any government threatened by Communists.

Wherever there was severe poverty or harsh government there was material to start a revolution, and these conditions were fairly common in South America, Africa and Asia. South America had a long tradition of violent politics, and it was easy to find revolutionary movements in every country. There were many guerrilla groups, sometimes based in the mountains and forests which were the usual areas where guerrillas could hide, and sometimes in the big cities, where the so-called urban guerrillas were able to merge with the rest of the population. Most of them failed, perhaps because the governments were used to dealing with revolutionary activities. Cuba (page 113) was an exception. In Chile a socialist with Communist support, Salvador Allende, managed to get elected legally as President in 1970, but after three years he was overthrown and killed by the army, and a military dictator took his place.

In Africa the Communists and their sympathisers had more success than in South America. When white rulers were slow to leave, guerillas increased and came to rely more and more on Communists for leadership and weapons; thus, when at last the Portuguese withdrew from Angola and Mozambique in 1975, the black governments that took over belonged to Marxist or extreme socialist parties, friendly to the USSR. But this was not the only way Communists could get control. In Abyssinia,

now officially known as Ethiopia, the emperor was dethroned in 1974 by army officers; they set up their own military dictatorship which soon became Marxist. For a time it seemed that the whole of that part of the world was becoming Soviet-influenced, because both Somalia and South Yemen, across the entrance to the Red Sea, were Marxist too; but a frontier war between Somalia and Ethiopia showed that their desire for land was more important than any comradeship they might have felt from sharing the same political beliefs.

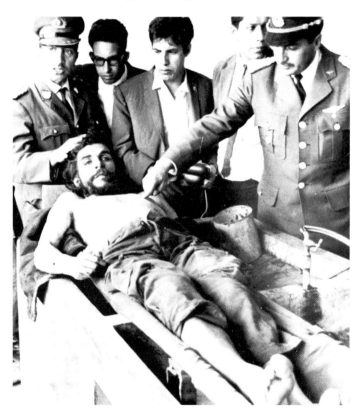

The end of a guerrilla legend. Ernesto 'Che' Guevara was an Argentinian who became one of Castro's best-known lieutenants in the Cuban revolution, wrote on guerrilla warfare and got a reputation as a hero among Left-wing young people all over the world. When he was reported killed in a skirmish with Bolivian troops on 8 October 1967, many did not believe it. This photograph was taken at Vallegrande two days later. It shows Bolivian officers displaying Guevara's corpse, in an attempt to convince the doubters.

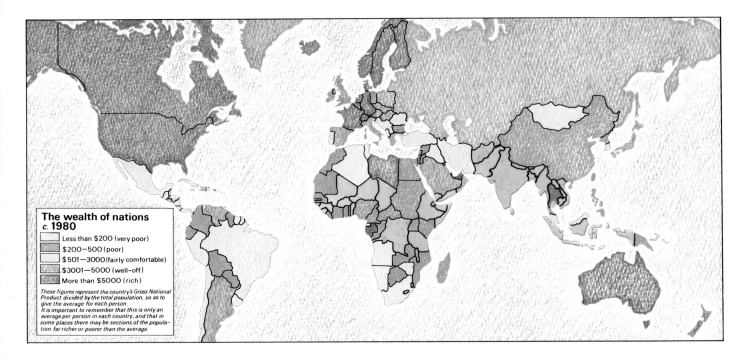

The wealth of nations
c. **1980**

- ☐ Less than $200 (very poor)
- ▨ $200−500 (poor)
- ☐ $501−3000 (fairly comfortable)
- ▨ $3001−5000 (well-off)
- ▨ More than $5000 (rich)

These figures represent the country's Gross National Product divided by the total population, so as to give the average for each person.
It is important to remember that this is only an average per person in each country, and that in some places there may be sections of the population far richer or poorer than the average.

In Asia we have already seen (pages 109–10, 116) how Communists came to rule China, North Korea and North Vietnam. With all this activity over the continents, it seemed to many people, especially in the USA, that there was a world-wide attempt at Communist domination, organised by the USSR.

Against this threat, the USA and her allies tended to believe that any people, given the choice, would choose parliamentary democracy and freedom rather than Communism and state control – which, in American eyes, was the same as dictatorship and tyranny. The USA was particularly anxious to prevent any Latin American states from falling into the hands of Communists – this seemed to them to be merely continuing the Monroe Doctrine of 1823, which stated that the USA would oppose any attempt by non-Americans to interfere in the affairs of the American continent, North or South. They failed in Cuba, but quiet US intervention may have been one of the reasons why revolts failed in other countries, and why Allende was overthrown in Chile. In other continents, too, American help went to any government that claimed to be 'free' and to believe in democracy, even though sometimes

those governments put down their opponents just as harshly as the Communists did. Their critics alleged that what the Americans meant by freedom was freedom for their big businesses to make money all over the world. It was certainly true that businesses were growing even bigger than before; a corporation might employ hundreds of thousands of people, directly and indirectly. Many of the most powerful were now 'multi-national', which meant that though their original headquarters might have been in one country, they also had factories and investments in several other countries, so that if necessary they could switch work from one to another. Firms like this could affect the prosperity of whole nations, and were richer than many governments. So while the USA feared international Communism, the USSR saw the USA as trying to help international capitalism to take over the whole world.

Thus the Cold War between the two superpowers and their allies quickly spread into the newly independent nations and what became known as the Third World. This term was sometimes taken to mean the nations that did not belong to either the Soviet or American camp. More often it was taken to mean nations that were neither great powers nor reasonably

Multinational companies

In 1976 the thirty largest multinationals (each with annual sales worth eight billion dollars or over) had their headquarters in these countries: USA (15); West Germany (6); Britain (3); Netherlands (3); France (2); Japan (1).

The extent of a multinational's business interests can be shown by the example of the **Royal Dutch/Shell Group**.

The group operates, either under its own name or through other companies in which it has a strong interest (e.g. Adria-Wien Pipeline in Austria, or Abu Dhabi Gas Industries in United Arab Emirates) in the following countries:

Australia, Austria, Argentina, Belgium, Britain, Botswana, Brunei, Borneo, Bangladesh, Bahamas, Bermuda, Belize, Brazil, Columbia, Cyprus, Comoro, Costa Rica, Cayman Islands, Cape Verde Islands, Canada, Central African Republic, Chad, Chile, Denmark, Djibouti, Dominican Republic, Ecuador, Finland, Fiji, France, Guatemala, Greece, Guinea, Gabon, Ghana, Hong Kong, Honduras, Ireland, Indonesia, Italy, Isle of Man, Iran, Ivory Coast, India, Iceland, Japan, Jamaica, Kenya, Kuwait, Liberia, Laos, Luxembourg, Lesotho, Libya, Malawi, Mali, Mexico, Malaysia, Morocco, Mauritius, Malta, Netherlands, New Zealand, Netherlands Antilles, Nigeria, Nicaragua, Norway, New Caledonia, Oman, Pakistan, Panama, Puerto Rico, Philippines, Peru, Papua-New Guinea, Portugal, Qatar, Reunion, Senegal, South Africa, Switzerland, Surinam, Salvador, South Korea, Sri Lanka, Sudan, Singapore, Swaziland, Sierra Leone, Sweden, Togo, South Yemen, Turkey, Thailand, Tunisia, Tanzania, Trinidad, USA, Upper Volta, Uganda, United Arab Emirates, Venezuela, West Germany, Zaire, Zimbabwe, Zambia.

In Britain alone the group controls many companies dealing in different products, including:
Bees (seeds, nurseries); Billeton UK (metals); Birtley Engineering; British Bitumen; British Methane; Bush and Johnson; Candles; Colborn (laboratories, veterinary products, etc.); Farm Seeds; ICB; Lion Emulsions; London and National Property; Lubricants Producers; Metal Scrap and By-products; Nickerson Seeds; Non-ferrous and Stainless Steel; Osma Plastics; R. E. Roberts; Rothwell Plant Breeders; Shell and BP Petrol; Shell-Mex and BP Petrol; Shell Coal Enterprises; Shell Gases; Shell Chemicals; Shell Composites; Shell Aircraft; Shell International Marine; Shell Deep Water Drilling; Shell Exploration (Libya); Shell Finance; Ward Blenkinsop (packaging, electronics); Webbs Farm Seeds.

prosperous industrial states, but countries where most of the population lived on the land and were miserably poor. It was a vague term, but it included most of the population of the world.

The USSR and China, the USA and Vietnam

When the rulers of the Soviet Union treated the countries of eastern Europe as if they ruled them too, there was sometimes trouble. Yugoslavia broke away (page 109) and later there were risings in East Germany, Hungary and Czechoslovakia that had to be crushed by Soviet tanks (page 142). There could be no such remedy when China objected to the policies of the USSR.

Mao Zedong thought of Communism in terms of a world-wide revolution that would never cease; it would always be changing, renewing itself, never settling down into a fixed accepted system. He was nearer in his ideas to Trotsky than to Stalin, and he suspected that the Soviet leaders were only interested in spreading Communism when it made the USSR stronger. During the 1950s Mao's disagreements with what he saw as the interference of Soviet advisers in China became sharper. Then the USSR withdrew aid and advisers just when they were most needed. By 1960 there was little chance of reconciliation; the Soviet Communist Party officially condemned Mao's ideas as being a perversion of true Communism. Then there were clashes between frontier troops about exactly where the Chinese-Soviet border ran.

This could have split the whole Communist world, but it did not. China merely closed even more firmly in on herself, and almost all the other Communist Parties in the world sided with the USSR. All the same, the USSR had turned a country with a quarter of the world's population from being a friend to being an enemy.

The USA soon suffered an equally serious set-back in Asia. In Vietnam, Communist guerrilla bands supported from the North began to spread through the South. The Southern government found it difficult to catch and destroy them, and asked for American help. The USA sent a few expert advisers. It was not enough. The guerrillas increased as North Vietnam sent in more supplies and men, so the USA sent in more advisers, then fighting troops. To use a word coined at the time, the war 'escalated' until there were half a million American troops in Vietnam by the end of the 1960s.

The harder they tried, the more obvious it became that the Americans could not win. Their enemies could conceal themselves in the jungle, could pretend to be ordinary villagers, or could retreat to the safety of North Vietnam. The US forces used staggering quantities of ammunition, burned or defoliated with chemicals wide tracts of jungle, emptied villages and herded the people into protected settlements, out still the enemy kept on reappearing, apparently as active and dangerous as ever. Meanwhile the government of South Vietnam was losing the loyalty of its own people; it could not protect them against guerrilla raids, its own troops often ill-treated villagers

Helicopters were one of the most important modern devices that the US forces employed in Vietnam. They dropped chemical defoliants and the dreaded napalm, or acted as 'gun-ships'; most often they were transports taking soldiers or supplies to inaccessible places. In this 1966 photograph, men of the 1st Cavalry are climbing down to search difficult country near Tuy Hoa.

they suspected of helping guerrillas – in fact, the villagers found themselves terrorised by both sides – and the members of the government enjoyed wealth and luxury while their people suffered misery and death. The American troops, many of them young men who had been conscripted and who were unwilling soldiers at the best of times, hated this war where they could never tell for certain their friends from their enemies; sometimes the strain was too much, some of them behaved very badly and the Communist propaganda was able to paint them as brutal, debauched, corrupt invaders. Of course the USA could have ended the war very quickly by using all her massive strength to smash North Vietnam. But this would have escalated the war so much that the USSR, which had so far only been sending weapons and supplies, would have felt bound to come in, and there would have been another world war.

The US government was in a dilemma. If they were to withdraw, they would lose prestige badly. Their allies might begin to think that they were not dependable. The Communists would almost certainly take the whole of Vietnam and would then topple other non-Communist states in Indochina, one after another (like dominoes, it was said). So they just went on, hoping perhaps that the enemy would tire and agree to a compromise as they had in Korea. But the American people were turning against the war. They were losing their young men, thousands upon thousands of them – for what? For an obscure little far-off country where the people did not want to be helped, anyway? Young men fled abroad to escape being drafted into the army, demonstrations swelled into huge processions, journalists who had supported the war now criticised it. With what seemed to be the majority of the nation demanding an end to the war, the US government gave in. The American army left Vietnam in 1973, after the government of the North promised not to invade the South.

Nobody was surprised, however, when, two years later, North Vietnam did indeed invade and overrun the South, and the two parts of the country were unified. Also in 1975 the next 'domino' fell when Communist rebels captured the neighbouring state of Cambodia – now renamed Kampuchea.

But if it was a severe defeat for the USA, it was not complete success for the USSR. The Vietnam Communists were Soviet-style, but the Kampucheans followed the ideas of Mao Zedong. In 1979 Vietnamese forces invaded Kampuchea to set up their own form of Communism, and Chinese attacks along the northern frontier of Vietnam failed to divert them. The unhappy peoples of Indochina were not only the victims of the Cold War now, but also of the equally bitter feud between the two sorts of Communism.

A new force in world affairs?

During the quarter-century after the Second World War the world grew rich as never before. Production of goods in the major industrialised countries had been increasing between the World Wars at a rate of 1% per year, but now the rate was 5%, and some countries, such as Japan, were doing better still. In these countries average people enjoyed a standard of living that their grandparents would have thought luxurious. It was not like that in the Third World.

In the non-industrialised countries the production figures were also rising, sometimes even more than in the industrialised countries. But these percentages meant very little, because the starting figure was so poor. In fact the gap between rich and poor nations became wider, because with better medical treatment and better food supplies the population of many Third World countries increased at such a great rate that soon their proportion of people to wealth became even worse than it had been. It seemed to many leaders of Third World countries that the really important division of the world was not East–West, between Communist and capitalist, but North–South, between rich and poor. Was there anything they could do to get a bigger share of the world's wealth for themselves?

An organisation of 'non-aligned' states, which might hold the balance between the two superpowers and their supporters, was suggested by (among other people) Tito of Yugoslavia. The idea sounded good, but in fact several of the states that joined were anything but non-aligned. For example, when the organisation met in 1980 in Cuba, Castro tried to use his position as host to get them to pass resolutions favouring the USSR and condemning the USA. This organisation proved far too divided to have any effect.

In the UN, by the 1970s, the Third World nations were numerous enough to outvote all the others, but mere voting power did not seem enough. Certainly the UN approved schemes to help the 'underdeveloped' parts of the world to improve their food production, for instance, and asked the richer countries to pay, which they agreed to do. But, even when they worked properly, such schemes only helped a few places, while the rich countries felt that they had now done their duty and could get on with their own problems.

Perhaps the answer really was to have smaller groups of Third World states that shared something in common. In 1948 the Organisation of American States was set up, and undoubtedly it enabled the members to co-operate in communications and obtaining aid from its rich member, the USA; but its critics said that this was merely helping the USA to control Central and South America. The Organisation of African Unity, founded in 1963, did not include any such rich and powerful nation from outside the Third World. It spent most of its time trying to resolve disputes between members, and in condemning South Africa without much effect.

However, in 1973 one group of Third World states suddenly became a force to be reckoned with. OPEC, the Organisation of Petroleum Exporting Countries, had been founded in 1960

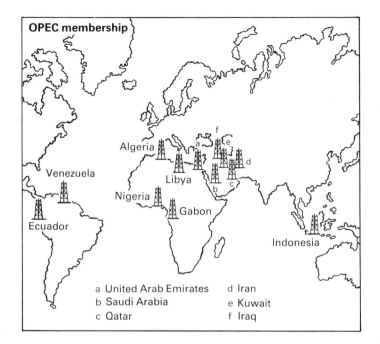

OPEC membership

a United Arab Emirates
b Saudi Arabia
c Qatar
d Iran
e Kuwait
f Iraq

but, although its members controlled three quarters of all the oil exported throughout the world, they had gone on accepting the low prices that the oil companies of the industrialised countries had always paid. Some of the main oil producing countries were Arab, though, and in 1973 they became so annoyed by the attitude of Western countries to the war that year between Israel and her Arab neighbours that they pushed up the price of oil and briefly cut off some supplies. With a shock, industrialised countries realised that they were at the mercy of this group of Third World countries, because their whole society had come to rely on burning oil in vast quantities. They paid up, and went on paying. Some of the poorest little countries in the world became the richest – for as long as the oil should last and no better form of fuel should be discovered.

There were other producer organisations among Third World countries, for such things as copper, tin, rubber, coffee, cocoa. None of these had the power of the oil producers, but they were able to influence prices for the benefit of their own countries. In ways like this, rather than by votes and appeals, Third World countries began to show that they could not be ignored.

Where was decolonisation delayed?

ALGERIA Large, well-established white population. Not a colony, yet Arabs treated as inferior. FLN (National Liberation Front) rebellion, 1954. Bitter war. President De Gaulle realised impossibility of victory, gave Algeria independence, 1962, despite settlers' fury.

ZIMBABWE Britain gave Northern Rhodesia independence as Zambia, 1964, and black majority took control. In Southern Rhodesia the whites feared the same would happen. Led by Ian Smith they announced UDI (Unilateral Declaration of Independence),

1965. Helped by South Africa, they prospered despite British and UN condemnation and economic sanctions. But black guerilla attacks, mainly from bases in Zambia and Mozambique, grew so strong that in 1979 the whites were forced to end UDI. Britain held elections, which the former guerilla groups won, and in 1980 the country became independent Zimbabwe.

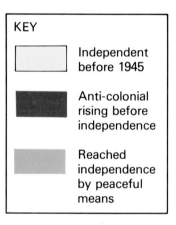

KEY

Independent before 1945

Anti-colonial rising before independence

Reached independence by peaceful means

ANGOLA Portugal oldest colonial power. Guerilla attacks began, 1961; leading group Marxist MPLA (Popular Movement for Liberation of Angola). Portuguese right-wing dictatorship resisted stubbornly, but was replaced by socialist government, 1974, which soon granted independence.

MOZAMBIQUE As in Angola, Portuguese rule resisted by nationalists, led by Marxist Frelimo. Socialist government gave independence in 1975.

NAMIBIA Former German colony. From 1920 South Africa held it as mandate, delayed independence to ensure white rule. UN objected, recognised SWAPO (South-West Africa People's Organisation) which waged guerilla war from bases in Angola against S. African forces.

SOUTH AFRICA From 1910 a self-governing dominion of British Empire, controlled by large white population. From 1948 dominated by Boer-led Nationalist Party, enforcing *apartheid* (separate racial development). Opposed by ANC (African National Congress) and condemned by UN and Commonwealth. 1961, South Africa left Commonwealth as republic. After 1980 the only white-ruled country in Africa; rich and powerful, but opposed by most other African states.

The decolonisation of Africa

How did it happen so rapidly?

After the 1939–45 war, independence movements spread quickly (e.g. Gold Coast, Convention People's Party, founded by Kwame Nkrumah, 1949; Tanganyika, African National Union, founded by Julius Nyerere, 1954).

Why?

- *Educated Africans,* becoming numerous, felt entitled to the well-paid, powerful jobs that Europeans mostly kept for themselves; these Africans had also learned European political ideas and methods.
- *African soldiers* had seen other parts of the world; they had also seen white powers divided and sometimes beaten.
- *Wartime economic development* in a few places had taught some Africans the skills needed in modern industries.
- *The UN* declared all nations had the right to govern themselves, and member states, including the colonial powers, accepted this; *both superpowers,* for different reasons, condemned colonial empires.
- *South Asian independence* was an exciting example.

Faced by demands for independence, the colonial powers usually gave way easily.

Why?

- *Britain and France,* the main colonial powers, were weakened by war; and some of their strongest political parties (including the British Labour government 1945–51) believed that it was wrong to force unwilling people to remain in their empires.
- *The UN* was responsible for former League mandates and Italian colonies; it soon made some independent and intended to do the same for the rest as quickly as possible.
- Colonial powers did not want to *offend the USA,* their chief protector, or provide *opportunities for the USSR* to stir up revolutions.
- *Ex-colonies would remain* friends and trading partners usually, as British experience was showing.

THEREFORE colonial powers peacefully handed authority to native governments in most parts of Africa. The exceptions are explained on the map opposite.

Why was there trouble after independence?

Built-in problems of many former colonies:

- *Divided populations*: some ex-colonies included peoples divided by tribe, nation or race (e.g. Arab/Negro), by religion (e.g. pagan/Christian/Muslim), by occupation (e.g. pastoral/agricultural/urban commercial).
- *Economic weakness*: imbalance between rich resources (e.g. oil, copper) in some areas, and poverty of much of land (e.g. deserts, forests) where many people lived. Lack of modern industries, communications and money to develop them. Many people left countryside in search of city jobs, often in government service; caused heavier taxes on others, and shanty towns around cities.

Outside interference:

- *Economic*: foreign companies from former colonial powers still owned mines, factories, plantations etc., and often wanted to control more of Africa's raw materials (e.g. uranium found in Namibia). Some used their wealth to back political leaders who would favour them, and defeat those who might tax or nationalise their property.
- *Political*: quarrelling African leaders often appealed for aid to one side or another in the Cold War. The USA, the USSR, China and their allies often responded with economic and military aid.

Confusion

All these problems frequently became entangled, as different political parties might represent different principles, different tribes, different economic interests, different foreign supporters – or all of these at once.

Political inexperience added to the difficulties, for the change to self-government had been so fast that few Africans had much experience of democratic government, with its negotiations and compromises. Men suddenly given power in government or army were tempted to 'save their country' by forceful means.

THEREFORE many countries became one-party states or military dictatorships, and violence easily broke out, as shown on the map on page 128.

Where there was post-colonial violence

CHAD Long, confused wars in very poor country, caused by tribal differences, north v. south; army coups, 1975 and 1979; personal quarrels of leaders; and Libyan intervention, 1980–81.

MOROCCO In former Spanish Sahara, from 1976 part of Morocco, Polisario revolt of Arab nomads, demanding independence, backed by Algeria.

NIGERIA Much divided by tribal and religious differences. The Ibo, an industrious and prosperous people, declared independent republic of Biafra, 1967. Crushed by Nigerian army after bitter war, 1970.

CONGO Belgium withdrew, 1960, leaving many conflicts between central government under Patrice Lumumba and tribal parties. Katanga Province, rich in minerals, seceded, backed by western industrialists. Lumumba was murdered, but the UN intervened and forcibly ended secession. Civil wars in several provinces continued until army leader Mobutu brought country under firm control in 1969. Changed its name to Zaire, 1971.

SUDAN Southern black peoples, mainly Christian or pagan, rose, 1963, against northern Arab Muslim government. In 1972 government gave very favourable terms to end war.

ANGOLA Fighting between rival liberation movements after independence, 1975. MPLA, helped by Cubans, won; but Unita continued fighting in its 'home' tribal area, with South African help.

THE HORN OF AFRICA 1942, Haile Selassie restored as Emperor of Ethiopia, with former Italian colony of Eritrea added as sea outlet. Eritrean revolt began, 1961. Somalia, independent 1960, began long conflict with Ethiopia over Somali nomads of Ogaden region. Army revolt in Ethiopia overthrew Haile Selassie, 1974, later set up Marxist regime. USSR helped Ethiopia in Eritrean and Ogaden wars, 1979 on. Somalia, though also Marxist, sought US aid.

UGANDA Tribal and party conflict. Milton Obote overthrew Buganda people and king from dominant position, 1966. Army leader Idi Amin, Muslim from a northern tribe, overthrew Obote, 1971. Disorder, brutality, poverty made Amin widely unpopular. Driven out by invasion from Tanzania, 1979. Obote restored in impoverished, disordered country.

KEY

Countries suffering from post-colonial wars

⊗ Centres of violent civil disturbance

✳ Wars

8   The challenge of the technological revolution

Greater promise, faster progress

Everything that happened after the Second World War was conditioned by the rapid changes that science and technology were making to the way people lived. This was a new Industrial Revolution, likely to transform the world even more than the old one. But while that had relied on coal, iron and steel, this one depended on oil and nuclear power, on chemically manufactured fibers and plastics, and on electronic equipment that could work infinitely faster than the human brain. Inventors, scientists and technologists were offering mankind powers and opportunities that would have seemed magic in any earlier century, and mere science fiction only a few years before.

The world was shrinking more rapidly than ever. The war had made aircraft not only bigger and faster, but commonplace; hundreds of thousands of people learned how to fly and maintain them, and to think of air transport as something quite normal. During the twenty years after the war, air lines and airports grew quickly all round the world, often financed by governments who thought that their prestige, prosperity and their ability to maintain a strong air force depended on having a good national air line. At the same time, air travel changed from being the expensive and glamorous transport of the rich and fashionable – the 'jet set' – to being the usual way businessmen and holiday-makers went on long journeys. Now that people could fly across a continent or an ocean in a few hours, there were fewer passengers for long-distance trains and the great liners died out. Messages travelled even faster, and now it was possible to see as well as to hear instantly what was going on thousands of miles away. Television, which was rare and wonderful in 1950, was part of the ordinary home by 1970, and almost a necessity of life to millions of people.

Now it was possible to transmit and record words and figures electronically, while machines were more powerful, accurate and reliable. So machines could be constructed that would be switched on and off, guided and controlled by electronic devices, and these could be set to do much of the mechanical and hard work in factories. The electronic devices

Seventy years after Blériot (page 5) the revolution in air travel had grown to this. Heathrow near London, the busiest international airport in the world, with about 24 million passengers a year. Across the top of the picture is the main landing run-way, nearly 4 km (2.5 miles) long; the tiny white speck at the east (right) end is a small airplane about to land. The big run-way across the bottom is for take-off, and a line of aircraft can be seen waiting their turn on the taxi-way leading to the run-way's east end from the central complex. This complex contains three terminals (for short, medium and long-haul flights), control and service buildings and local transport facilities of all sorts. Many aircraft can be seen parked, awaiting passengers—the easiest to spot are the huge intercontinental airliners standing near the long-distance terminal at the south-west corner.

grew swiftly from simple adding machines to complicated computers that could store and use figures and facts in enormous quantities at lightning speed. Meanwhile scientists discovered how to cram masses of electronic circuits into tiny spaces, and by using silicon chips they were able to make the computers both smaller and more complicated. These machines could be programed to carry out more and more of the tasks of a human brain, and to do them quicker and more reliably, for they did not tire. Now whole factories were organised where the only workers were machines, apart from a few skilled technicians to service them.

Machines could do much more for men, and men were depending on machines much more, but machines had to be given fuel. Oil was needed, for it was so much easier to use than coal. Old oilfields were exploited more ruthlessly, surveyors drilled on land and under the sea to find new oilfields, and as the thirst for oil grew gigantically, so the most gigantic

The Fiat car company of Turin was among the first European manufacturers to use robots on a large scale in their factories. The car in this photograph is moved automatically into the correct position for the machine on the left automatically to work on it; no human beings are involved.

ships ever built ferried it over the oceans. Meanwhile scientists were trying to develop a new source of power – nuclear power. The force of the atomic bomb could be used to drive machines, if ways could be found to convert it into manageable electricity.

All this progress meant that the people of the industrialised countries were able to reap and mine and manufacture faster and bigger than ever before, and more every year. They soon learned to consume everything the world could yield, and to enjoy comforts and luxuries that were not available even to millionaires when the century began.

Standards of life were also being raised by astonishingly rapid medical improvements. There was a stream of new chemical products to arrest infection, heal wounds, drug those suffering pain or distress. Surgeons developed delicate techniques to operate on brains and hearts, even to replace defective heart valves with plastic copies or transplant hearts and kidneys from other people. The science of genetics advanced to the point where it seemed feasible even to create new forms of life and alter the genetic structure of human beings.

In the rich, 'developed' countries people now lived longer, and the average age of the population grew steadily older as doctors improved their methods of keeping the elderly alive. In Third World countries there was not enough money for the most advanced and difficult medical treatment, but there was real progress in dealing with diseases and conditions that had previously killed great numbers of people, including the young. Here, therefore, there was a steep, swift increase in the population.

More people demanded more food. Biologists and engineers worked hard to increase the food supply in many different climates. They tried to cultivate strains of plants that would offer higher yields, to find chemicals that would destroy insect pests, to improve irrigation, transport and housing. But it was hard to keep pace with the growing demands of what was coming to be called the 'population explosion'.

Just as the human race was crowding closer in a world that no longer seemed very big, the almost unbelievable notion that mankind might spread outside the world gradually became a reality. From the beginning of time people had known this world as the only one, though some may have dreamed of flying like birds, or spun fantasies about the moon and the stars.

The size of nations according to population 1980 *(the colours relate to the map on page 122)*

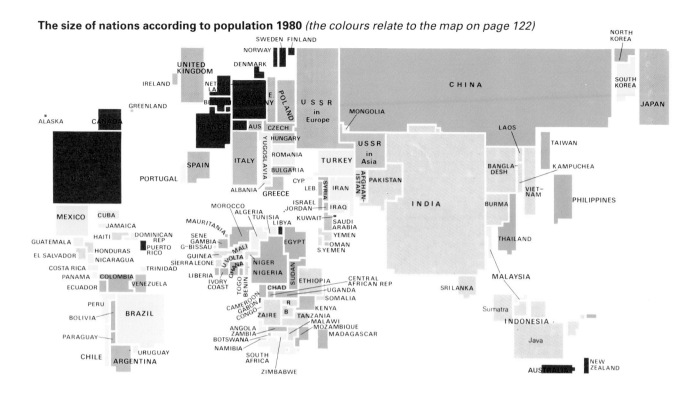

Since the opening of the century flight had ceased to be a dream, and now it was beginning to seem that the moon and stars were no longer beyond reach.

The instruments of space exploration began as instruments of war – Hitler's rockets. The USA and the USSR both saw how valuable such weapons could become and they had the means to experiment and develop rockets. This became as important as nuclear research in the Cold War arms race (page 111). Besides trying to make rockets that could reach an enemy thousands of miles away, both sides saw how useful it would be if a rocket could put some artificial satellite into space, so that it passed over the other's territory observing and sending signals. The USSR took a big jump forward on 4 October 1957, when it put into orbit Sputnik I – the name means 'travelling companion'. It was entirely mechanical, but next month Sputnik II flew successfully with the first space traveller from earth, a dog. The first human was a Soviet army major, Yuri Gagarin, who flew in a satellite weighing six tons on 12 April 1961. Thereafter both of the superpowers put

many satellites above the earth. Constantly circling the globe in many directions, they could watch and threaten. But satellites could also be used for peaceful purposes, gathering information about the weather and passing television messages around the world.

The superpowers were also competing to send up rockets with spacecraft that could reach the moon, the planets and even beyond, and send back information. The USA scored a great success in July 1969 when Americans reached the moon, explored parts of it and came safely back to earth; and the whole adventure could be witnessed as it was happening by millions of people watching their TV screens all over the world. Afterwards there were other successful flights to the moon. But in spite of such achievements, there were doubts about the value of the flights, and the USA stopped them while scientists studied the results. Instead, the USA sent unmanned spacecraft towards the more distant planets, with instruments to gather and send back information for the scientists. The USSR meanwhile spent more effort on building

The space age

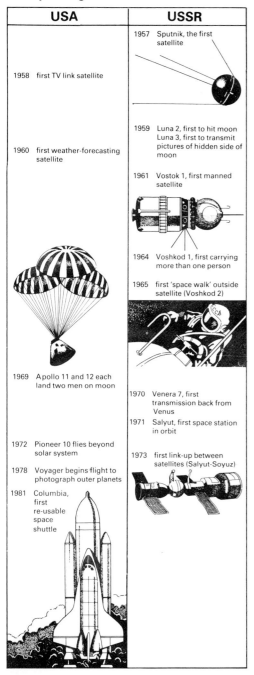

USA	USSR
	1957 Sputnik, the first satellite
1958 first TV link satellite	
	1959 Luna 2, first to hit moon Luna 3, first to transmit pictures of hidden side of moon
1960 first weather-forecasting satellite	
	1961 Vostok 1, first manned satellite
	1964 Voshkod 1, first carrying more than one person
	1965 first 'space walk' outside satellite (Voshkod 2)
1969 Apollo 11 and 12 each land two men on moon	
	1970 Venera 7, first transmission back from Venus
	1971 Salyut, first space station in orbit
1972 Pioneer 10 flies beyond solar system	1973 first link-up between satellites (Salyut-Soyuz)
1978 Voyager begins flight to photograph outer planets	
1981 Columbia, first re-usable space shuttle	

large satellites, flying laboratories where scientists could live and work in space for months. And here at last there seemed to be some prospect that the rival superpowers might co-operate in equipping and manning space laboratories, so that all the world might share their discoveries. Partly in order to transport people and materials to these laboratories, the USA developed a 'space shuttle', a machine that was rocketed out like a satellite, but flew back and landed like an airplane. This made its first flight exactly twenty years after Gagarin's, and as it landed millions of people watching on television wondered if they were seeing the world's first real spaceship.

The affluent society

'You've never had it so good!'

That was probably the most famous election slogan in post-war Britain. In many ways it was true when it was used in the late 1950s, but this was not due to the work of any one political party and it did not apply only to Britain.

All the industrialised countries were becoming richer, though some were doing much better than others and the USA was well in the lead. Americans believed in producing huge quantities and consuming just as energetically. People should buy, use and throw away. Things were not meant to last for long; why should they, when there would be improved models to be bought next year? And by constantly buying the latest, people not only kept factories and shops busy, but encouraged manufacturers to try to offer something new and better every year. This was the way to ensure progress. The two countries that were most successful in following the American road to riches were the two that had lost the war, Germany and Japan. Perhaps it was because they had been so utterly defeated that those nations felt that only a completely new start and unsparing effort could rescue them from ruin. The Americans who occupied their countries were ready to advise and assist them, for they preferred to make the Germans and Japanese prosperous and powerful friends rather than leave them poor and resentful. The result in both countries was what was called an 'economic miracle'. Twenty years after the war Japanese and West German factories were turning out quantities of cars, cameras, television equipment, up-to-date machines of every sort, establishing a reputation for excellent quality in the markets of the world, and becoming very rich.

If we were to take one thing as the symbol of the new prosperity, it would have to be the automobile. During the twenties and thirties the car had become a normal part of life, but in the fifties and sixties it came to dominate life in the 'developed' countries. Cars filled and choked city streets, wide highways were built so that they could speed across the country, and any family that did not own a car was thought poor or eccentric. Railway and bus services shrank as people preferred to travel in their own cars and send goods on huge, fast trucks. In some countries–Britain was one–the manufacture of cars and trucks became one of the most important industries, perhaps the key industry, because so many others prospered through selling such things as sheet steel, electrical fittings, safety glass or tires to the car-makers. Thousands more people earned a living in garages and roadside gas stations and restaurants, or in building and maintaining roads.

The car was the most obvious sign of what was called the 'affluent society'; the phrase meant a society where the people as a whole, not just a fortunate few, enjoyed an abundance of worldly goods. Telephones, refrigerators, washing machines and labour-saving gadgets of every kind were no longer for the better-off only, but common in ordinary homes. As machines did more to help them, people got higher wages and worked shorter hours, so they had more free time and more money to spend. They bought more, they went on holidays abroad–tourism became an important industry–and they wanted to be entertained.

In this society young people became more important. Like everybody else, boys and girls who had just left school were earning more, but they did not have to spend it like older wage-earners on families and homes. Children at school, too, were getting more pocket-money. Here was a vast new market, and manufacturers, advertisers, and entertainers saw it and invented a word to describe it: 'teenage'. They produced teenage clothes, teenage food and drink, and teenage fashions in music, like the 'rock' of the fifties. In some ways all this built up a separate teenage culture, different from the older sections of society, but to some extent society in general accepted teenage fashions.

As affluence increased and as people came to take it for granted that they should enjoy more leisure and pleasure, a new phrase appeared: the 'permissive society'. This meant a society where anybody was permitted to take his or her plea-

The 'motorway age' in Britain began when the first section of the M1 was opened on 1 November 1959. This is a view of the Gravelly Hill Interchange, near Birmingham, where the A38(M) joins the M6. The scale of this complex pattern of roads can be judged by comparing it with the nearby buildings, and we can speculate on what the people living in the houses thought of the environmental effects.

sure in whatever way he or she chose, as long as it did not harm anybody else. Permissiveness became most obvious in sexual matters. Britain, the home of Victorian morality, within a few years abandoned censorship of plays, permitted the publication of books previously classed as obscene, made divorce easier and legalised abortion and homosexuality. Of course this did not please everybody, and there were long arguments between those who said Britain was decaying and those who said society was becoming more humane and mature.

One thing was beyond argument: affluence and permissiveness were failing to make society calm and contented. Instead, violence of all sorts seemed to be increasing. In Britain, where the police had never needed weapons, armed crime began to increase; old people, formerly respected because of their age and weakness, became favourite targets of robbers; and the nation that used to boast of sportmanship and 'fair play'

left: 'Pop' music. Open-air 'rock' concerts attracted huge gatherings, mainly of teenagers. This view from the stage of the 1970 Bath festival shows the percussion instruments and electrical equipment used to enhance rhythm and volume; part of the crowd of 150,000; and the wire mesh barrier that protected performers from being mobbed by over-excited fans.

below: 'Pop' art. In 1967 Andy Warhol (born 1930) produced portraits of Marilyn Monroe, probably the most glamorised and advertised of all American film stars, who had died of a drugs overdose in 1962. The artist used visual tricks from film, television and advertising to make each 'Marilyn' look slightly different. He was deliberately using popular techniques on a popular subject, but perhaps it was to show how modern commercial methods could alter or even destroy a human personality.

became notorious by the seventies for vandalism and brutality among its football crowds. Other people just 'dropped out'; this was most obvious among young people in the USA who tried to cut themselves off from what they saw as the greed and false values of the affluent society. They formed their own small communities to lead more simple lives; but some of them used drugs to help them in their search for happiness, and ended as hopeless addicts. A few young men and women hated the wealth they saw around them so much that they tried to destroy the society that produced it. They used terrorism, robbery, kidnapping and murder; among the most notorious of these groups in the seventies were Germany's Baader-Meinhof gang and Italy's Red Brigades. One of the results of terrorism was to force governments to make strict security arrangements not quite in keeping with the spirit of a free society. It might easily antagonise people, especially if they were already feeling critical of the way society was being run.

The widest outburst of discontent in Western Europe occurred among the best educated of the young people in the summer of 1968. There were student riots and demonstrations in several countries, culminating in disturbances in Paris during May and June, which sparked off a general strike. But the movement died down without achieving much, and showed that although a great many intelligent young people were dissatisfied with the affluent society, they had few practical ideas about how to improve it.

A world of anxiety

In some of the richest countries worry was becoming a prevalent disease. It may have been the strain of always trying to keep ahead in ruthless business competition, or the unnatural rush and noise and tension of big-city life, but doctors found themselves supplying patients with sleeping pills and tranquillising drugs in vast numbers to enable them to face daily life. By 1980 it was calculated that one person in every ten in Britain would, at some time in his or her life, be treated for nervous or mental illness. Of course the reasons for these illnesses could be many and complex, but perhaps one of the factors was distress at the new dangers that seemed to be hanging over mankind.

Nuclear war was the most obvious danger. Both sides in the

Cold War went on stockpiling weapons and making them even more deadly, until they could destroy the human race several times over. No doubt it was very unlikely that any sane person would deliberately start a war with such weapons, but there were other dangers. False alarms occurred, when instruments seemed to be showing that the other side had launched missiles; so far the mistakes had always been spotted in time, but some day they might not, and a nuclear war might start by accident. Small nuclear weapons were invented, to be used on the battlefield in a 'limited' war; but perhaps this increased the danger. Such a war sounded less risky and was therefore more likely – but it could escalate into full nuclear war. All the time nuclear knowledge was spreading, and more countries were learning to make bombs. This obviously increased the risks. The most alarming prospect was that fanatics, terrorists or plain criminals might get access to such weapons. In many Western countries groups of people urged their governments to set a good example by refusing to have nuclear arms on their territory, but no government dared put itself at such a disadvantage against potential enemies. The best hope was for both the superpowers to agree to reduce their armaments, and

Some of the people who took part in an Italian anti-nuclear protest march from Perugia to Assisi, 27 September 1981. The meaning of the skeleton costumes is obvious. The different salutes – Communist, Fascist and the V sign of the Western Allies – may be intended to accuse all the ideologies of sharing responsibility for the nuclear danger. In 1981 there was a powerful revival of anti-nuclear movements throughout Western Europe.

on 5 August 1963 they and Britain signed the Test Ban Treaty, which nearly a hundred other states also signed within the next few months. This forbade testing bombs in the atmosphere, where lethal radiation could be released over a wide area, though underground tests were still allowed. It was a good beginning, but when the USA and the USSR began their Strategic Arms Limitation Talks to reduce the number and size of their weapons, they could not think of any way of guaranteeing each other's safety and ensuring that the disarmament was equal and genuine. Neither could risk trusting the other, yet they did not want to go on threatening each other. So the talks dragged on for years, with a small agreement from time to time, while both sides spent more and more fantastic sums of money increasing their armaments. The hopes and difficulties became very obvious during the 1970s. The decade began with the American President Nixon visiting both Moscow and Beijing, and then followed a time of 'detente', as it was called, when the tension eased. In 1972 the first SALT treaty was signed to limit long-range weapons, and in 1975 the Helsinki treaty was signed to try to guarantee peace and respect for human rights among all the nations of Europe, whatever their political systems. But still both sides went on improving their defences, then both superpowers fell into awkward situations which made them fear that their rivals were going to take advantage. By 1980 the old atmosphere of distrust was as strong as it ever had been.

Nuclear power seemed to many people dangerous even when used peacefully. What sort of devastation would ensue if there were a serious accident at a nuclear power station? Even more frightening than the explosion was the radiation, which could destroy people slowly and deform generations as yet unborn. The same peril lurked in the waste material from such plants, and it was not reassuring to be told by scientists that the waste would become safe after a thousand or so years. Few people were happy at the prospect of its being buried in their country or dumped in the seas around. Yet it seemed that sooner or later the industrialised countries would be compelled to accept nuclear power everywhere.

Fuel shortage was looming ahead. It was reckoned that people had used more of the world's fossil fuel resources in the twentieth century than in the whole of previous history. By the 1970s everybody knew that the world's supplies of oil, which had taken millions of years to form, would all be exhausted early in the next century, unless people stopped using it so lavishly. But the whole way of life in the industrialized countries had come to depend on endless supplies of fuel. If the oil were not available and no alternative fuel had been found, the whole affluent industrial civilisation would fall into poverty and squalor.

Pollution and exhaustion of the earth would still remain a problem even if the fuel problem were solved. The enormous growth of industry had meant that a correspondingly enormous amount of waste had been created. Some of it was chemical, pouring away in streams or rising in clouds into the atmosphere. It was disgustingly obvious that many rivers were already foul and poisonous because of the first Industrial Revolution, but the new poisons were worse. 'Environmentalists', people who felt strongly that the whole of man's environment desperately needed protecting, often managed to persuade governments, both local and national, to make stricter rules about industrial waste and to start cleaning rivers, but it was a slow and expensive process. Pollution in the air was harder to check because often it could not be seen or smelled, though some people feared that eventually it might prove the most dangerous form of pollution. Meanwhile there was the possibility that too much was being taken out of the earth. Some rare minerals might be used up. Land might be over-cropped to feed the expanding population, and the sea might be over-fished. Even cutting down tropical rain forests to provide more land for agriculture might make the situation worse, because it might have unforeseen effects on the climate of large areas of the globe.

Unemployment might still remain a problem even if the others were solved. With machines doing so much more work. human beings would lose their jobs altogether or would be employed for only a few hours each week. Would they be able to earn enough to live comfortably? Would they be able to spend their extra leisure happily, or would they become bored and restless? Would control over the machines belong to only a small number of clever technicians, and would they become the new ruling class, eventually? Meanwhile when trade slumped badly, as it did in the world-wide depression of the later 1970s, the shadow of unemployment hung darkly over millions of workers in the industrialised countries and was a much more pressing danger than nuclear and environmental hazards.

A view in one of the squalid favelas, or shanty towns, that cluster around the beautiful city of Rio de Janeiro. Throughout the Third World, as populations increased, millions of people moved to the cities from countrysides that could not support such numbers. So the urban populations began to expand enormously, most of the newcomers living in miserable suburbs that contrasted with the sophistication and wealth of the city centers. Brazil especially was full of contrasts —at one extreme a specially created modernistic capital, Brasilia, and at the other vast primeval rain forests where some tribes still lived a Stone Age life.

The power of governments to enforce obedience was becoming stronger as technology progressed. It became easy to spy on suspected people by using electronic 'bugs', to store information about everybody in the country in computers, and to 'get at' the population with propaganda, either openly hammering at them from all sides or subtly suggesting in, for example, their entertainments what they ought to think. Whether it wanted to or not, any government was obliged to make more and more regulations and to employ more and more officials, partly because all the technological changes created new conditions that had to be checked and made safe, partly because people were expecting the government to do more and more to look after them. Governments could not avoid taking more power. In 1949 the British novelist George Orwell tried to imagine what life could be like under total state control, when every citizen would be constantly watched on television by 'Big Brother' and must believe whatever 'Big Brother' decreed, even if the beliefs were contradictory; and when anyone who refused to obey would be 'corrected' by whatever torture he or she most dreaded. Orwell called his horrifying vision *1984*.

All these dangers were produced by the science and technology of the advanced industrialised countries, and it was in these countries that people showed most concern about the new problems. In the Third World people had something old and familiar to worry about – hunger. As we saw on page 130, the 'population explosion' meant that poverty and hunger were actually being made worse in many lands; the millions of desperately poor were increasing. How long could this go on before the poor majority of the world's population exploded against the rich minority? Some people saw this 'North–South' contrast as being the most urgent of all the problems that the world's leaders must solve.

These really were world problems. For the first time in history the human race as a whole was facing things that could change its condition, not slowly and patchily as in the past, but all together and quickly. There could be great benefits, or there could be total catastrophe. People had learned to create power that could achieve miracles; but it could, if wrongly handled, bring untold misery and even extinction to mankind. They would have to learn to live with that power, for there was no way of unlearning the knowledge that had produced it.

Two machines that changed the world in the twentieth century

THE AUTOMOBILE

1885–1914

BEGINNINGS: First practical gasoline-driven vehicles – *Karl Benz* 1885 and *Gottlieb Daimler* 1886. Widespread interest, quick progress—first major road race Paris–Marseilles 1895.

TECHNICAL DEVELOPMENTS: Many, rapid, important – e.g. pneumatic tires 1895 (Michelin); automatic lubrication 1901 (Lanchester); pressed steel chassis, honeycomb radiator, expanding clutch 1903 (Mercedes); electric lights and starter 1910–12.
By 1914, in most important respects, the car was *mechanically fully developed.*

MANUFACTURE: Mainly *small firms,* directed by enthusiastic engineers, with bodies added by coachbuilders.
Beginning of *mass production* – conveyor belt assembly 1913 (Ford).

EFFECTS: At first, merely *novelties* for enthusiasts and rich men; but usefulness soon recognised:
a. For people who had to move about in their daily work, e.g. farmers, doctors – especially in a big country like USA. Therefore first attempts to supply reliable *cheap cars* (Ford, Austin, Morris).
b. For *public transport and industry.* Therefore first buses (regular service in London 1905), taxis (in London 1903), trucks, tractors (Marion, Ohio 1898).

1914–18

CARS ADAPTED TO WAR: Huge expansion of manufacture, especially trucks. New types—armoured cars, tanks, Many thousands of people learned to drive and maintain cars.

1918–39

EXPANSION: The car became a normal part of daily life in industrialised countries:
a. *Private car* ownership greatly increased, with cheap 'popular' models, e.g. Model T Ford, 'Baby' Austin 7, 'Bull-nosed' Morris Cowley.
b. *Public service and commercial* vehicles completely replaced horse transport – buses, vans, ambulances, fire-engines etc. New specialised types, e.g. tankers, earth-movers.

TECHNICAL DEVELOPMENTS: *High performance* still led by luxury and sports cars, e.g. Rolls Royce, Bentley, Cadillac, Alfa-Romeo; and *speed records* – 1922, 130 mph (209 kph); 1929, 231.44 mph (372.5 kph); 1939, 369.7 mph (595 kph).

Driving made *easier and more comfortable*, e.g. synchro-mesh gears, independent suspension.

MANUFACTURE: The supply of cars, accessories and fuel became *major industries*; also road-building.
Stamping out car bodies from pressed steel ended need for separate chassis and expensive coachbuilding, made streamlining easier.

EFFECTS: In industrialised countries, began to change environment:
a. Convenient, cheap *mobility* for most people; frequent bus services; 'ribbon' development along roads.
b. Many deaths in road *accidents*, and traffic 'jams' in towns.
c. New *regulations:* driving tests, road signs and traffic lights, pedestrian crossings, speed and noise restrictions.

1939–45

THE ARMOURED FIGHTING VEHICLE DOMINATED land warfare – changed it from trench to blitzkrieg.

After 1945

EXPANSION: The car became necessary to normal life in industrialised countries:
a. *Private car* ownership increased enormously; huge sales of most successful cheap models, e.g. Volkswagen 'Beetle', British Motor Corporation 'Mini'.
b. *Road freight* greatly expanded; 'juggernauts'.

TECHNICAL DEVELOPMENTS: By now, mainly small refinements and *gadgets*; but together they greatly increased comfort, speed, economy.

MANUFACTURE: Production of vast numbers of standard models could be achieved only by *vast firms* – small firms swallowed by giants e.g. General Motors, British Leyland, Peugeot-Citroen. Oil companies likewise became giants, often multi-nationals. Motor industry now vitally important in many *national economies*, e.g. rise of German and Japanese industries, difficulties of British.

EFFECTS: Dominated daily life in industrialised countries and very important in Third World communications.
a. National *motorway networks*; very fast private and commercial transport; decline of buses and rail freight in some countries.
b. Increased *congestion* in towns; urban motorways and by-passes, one-way systems, parking meters, pedestrian precincts.
c. Accidents relatively fewer (considering increase in traffic). but new *fears of pollution* by fumes and noise.
d. Dependence on cars implied *dependence on oil* supplies.

THE AIRPLANE

1903–14

BEGINNINGS: First sustained, controlled flight in heavier-than-air machine – *Orville and Wilbur Wright* at Kittyhawk, North Carolina, 17 December 1903. Widespread excitement, experiments, attempts to improve.

TECHNICAL DEVELOPMENTS: Very rapid advances in ten years:
1909 – rotary engine (Gnome)
– first flight across English Channel (Blériot)
– first international air meeting, at Rheims.
1910 – experimental helicoptor (Sikorsky)
1911 – first practical seaplane (Curtiss)
1912 – first airplane with enclosed cabin (Roe)
1913 – first four-engined airplane, 'Le Grand' (Sikorsky)
– gyroscope automatic pilot (Sperry)

EFFECTS: Though they were becoming fairly reliable and their possible uses were much discussed, airplanes had in fact not been employed.

1914–18

AIRPLANES ADAPTED TO WAR: Scouting and bombing demanded development of both small, swift, agile machines and large, steady, long-range machines.

1918–39

EXPANSION: Increased capabilities of aircraft demonstrated by *pioneer flights:*
across North Atlantic 1919; Britain–Australia 1919;
across North (1926) and South (1929) Poles;
across Pacific, USA–Australia, in three 'hops' 1928;
over Mount Everest 1933.
Peaceful uses – growth of air lines, air mail.
Military uses – all governments saw need for efficient air forces.

World Air Speed Records
for manned flight, excluding seaplanes and rocket planes.

1906	25 mph	41 kph	1953	755 mph	1,215 kph
1912	108	174	1955	822	1,323
1922	223	359	1956	1,132	1,822
1932	294	474	1957	1,207	1,943
1939	469	755	1958	1,405	2,260
1945	606	976	1959	1,484	2,388
1948	671	1,080	1959	1,526	2,456
1952	698	1,124	1965	2,070	3,331

TECHNICAL DEVELOPMENTS: Much *experiment* and improvement in aerodynamic shapes, engines, construction methods and materials (light alloys, all-metal fuselages).
Vertical flight: autogiro 1923 (Cierva); practical helicopter 1940 (Sikorsky).
Jet propulsion: work begun independently in Britain and Germany 1937; first jet flight 27 August 1939, Heinkel He 178.
Great increase in size, speed, range, reliability; e.g. Junkers Ju 52/3 'Iron Annie' 1932, Douglas DC 7 Dakota 1933, British 'Empire' and US trans-Pacific 'Clipper' flying boat services, late 1930s.

EFFECTS: *Civil air transport* firmly established, with internationally agreed regulations; but still expensive, confined to rich usually. *Powerful air forces* built up by major powers; some tried out in war conditions, e.g. Spain 1936–9.

1939–45

AIR POWER A DECISIVE FACTOR IN WAR: essential part of blitzkrieg; glider and parachute attacks; devastation of cities; at sea, defeated battleships and submarines. Development of radar, jets, pilotless planes and rockets. Many thousands of people learned to fly and maintain aircraft.

After 1945

EXPANSION: Huge *increase in passenger* services; by 1970 4,356 million passenger miles (7,010 million km) flown annually on scheduled services throughout world, 2,416 million miles (3,888 million km) within USA alone.

TECHNICAL DEVELOPMENTS: Large, fast *jet airliners:*
1958 – first trans-Atlantic jet service, DH Comet
1970 – first high-capacity jet air-liner, Boeing 747 'Jumbo'
1976 – first supersonic intercontinental service, Concorde
Hovercraft: 1959 first cross-Channel service, Saunders-Roe SR1.
Vertical flight: not only great increase in helicopters, but first 'conventional' airplanes with VTOL (Vertical Take Off and Landing) – Hawker Harrier 1966.
Very high speeds of *military aircraft* – new shapes, including ability to 'vary geometry' in flight – partly replaced by unmanned *rockets*.
Spacecraft: first man in space 1961; first men on moon 1969.

EFFECTS: *'Shrinking' world* – all parts within easy reach of others for:
holidays (now normal for millions of ordinary people), business and political negotiations ('shuttle diplomacy'), warfare (combined with the threat of nuclear weapons).

9 The world balance of power

As the final quarter of the century began there was general agreement that the nations of the world must work together to solve the world-wide problems, but not on how this should be done. The UN had some influence, but when things became difficult every nation naturally put its own interests first. The UN could not do anything against either of the superpowers, but as long as they were roughly balanced in strength they would not risk a world war – though this did not prevent either of them backing one side or other in the local wars that kept on erupting in many parts of the world. But the balance did not remain still and steady, for both the USA and the USSR showed serious weaknesses at different times, and it appeared just possible that new superpowers might be forming.

Weaknesses of the superpowers

During the early years of the Cold War the American people were strongly patriotic and anti-Communist. When spies were caught and it was discovered that scientists had been passing atomic secrets to the USSR, the mood became near-hysterical. Senator Joe McCarthy seized the opportunity to stir up a 'witch-hunt' against 'Commies', and anyone thought to sympathise with them. People accused of 'un-American activities', no matter how well respected they had been before, had to attend Senate enquiries where they could be insulted and bullied by McCarthy and his assistants, and the whole show was in the newspapers and on radio. Though the USA had no prison camps like the USSR's, McCarthy could easily destroy reputations and ruin careers, and during the early 1950s he was the most feared man in America. But the Communist panic wore itself out; Americans increasingly felt ashamed of McCarthy's methods and doubted his motives. When the Senator died in 1957 the mood in the USA was already changing.

The USA boasted itself as the land of freedom, opportunity and wealth, as opposed to the tyranny and poverty of Communist countries. But many Americans, whole sections of the nation, did not share these blessings, and the most obvious section was the Negroes. It was almost a century since all slaves had been freed and declared full American citizens, but in many southern states blacks were still treated as an inferior race. They were segregated, kept apart from whites in trains, buses, restaurants, and sent to all-black schools. Whites would give them only ill-paid, menial jobs, and any black who

Senator McCarthy in action. One of his favourite tactics was to interrupt proceedings and try to unsettle and confuse opponents by suddenly raising points of order. The photograph shows him doing this during a Senate investigation into his criticisms of the US army, in April 1954. The way the army officers are looking at the senator may suggest what many Americans were coming to think of him.

March 1965 was a critical time for the blacks' Civil Rights movement in the USA. Violence broke out in Selma, Alabama, and a white supporter of the blacks was killed. Dr Martin Luther King believed, like Gandhi, in non-violent protest, so he led 4,000 of his supporters on a peaceful march from Selma to petition the state government at Montgomery. Here they are photographed in Montgomery; by carrying the stars and stripes they meant to show that they were loyal American citizens, but this may have seemed an insult to many Southern whites, for it was the flag of the Union that had beaten them and liberated their Negro slaves just a century before. Non-violent protests did not end the murders, but they seem to have done much to convince white Americans that King and his followers were right.

showed that he 'did not know his place' was likely to get a good beating, at the very least. It was not as bad for Negroes in other parts of the USA, but everywhere they were among the poorest, and it was rare to see a coloured person in a position of responsibility and authority. Now it seemed to many blacks that they had accepted the position of second-class citizens for too long, and that they must insist on getting their full rights. The Civil Rights movement, as it was called, spread rapidly among coloured Americans during the 1960s, and many whites had to agree that their cause was just. Other whites feared or despised blacks, and there was a great deal of violence, mainly in the southern states. Gradually the Federal government and the governments of the different states saw that they must take steps to guarantee that blacks really would be treated the same as white Americans. In 1968 the most famous Civil Rights leader, Dr Martin Luther King, who had always used his great influence to prevent violence, was shot dead by a white man. After this, few Americans cared to appear on the same side as the murderer, and it could be said that the Civil Rights movement had won.

But this did not restore unity to the USA. The blacks were

still poor. There were other racial minorities who claimed that they did not get fair treatment, like the Puerto Ricans, the American Indians and the Mexicans who came in their thousands as cheap labour into the south-western states. Many 'pure white' Americans agreed with them, especially young people, and it seemed as if a mood of general protest was arising out of the Civil Rights movement. It was vague and mixed up with dislike of the Vietnam war, fear of nuclear disaster and contempt for the greed, corruption and violence which, it was said, pervaded American life. When President J.F. Kennedy was assassinated in 1963 there were persistent rumours that, in spite of a massive enquiry and voluminous reports, the truth was being concealed by some government departments. Eleven years later President R.M. Nixon was forced to resign in disgrace after it was proved that he knew about a burglary in the offices of his political rivals in the Watergate building, Washington, and lied persistently in an attempt to 'cover up'. The Watergate scandal could be taken as the final proof that American public affairs were rotten.

The Soviet leaders, though, could not afford to feel smug. In the first place, their allies kept on objecting to Soviet interference. We have seen how Yugoslavia and China both broke with the USSR (pages 109 and 123) but there were other challenges which Soviet troops put down. The first serious rising was in East Berlin, June 1953, and the Soviet army had to use its tanks before the East German Communist authorities could regain control. The Hungarian revolt of October 1956 was much bigger, for it overthrew the government and the Soviet army had to launch a full invasion of Hungary. There was heavy fighting in the streets of Budapest, many Hungarians were killed and many thousands more fled to western Europe before the Soviet army sealed the frontier once more. Though the USSR was strong enough to ignore the reproaches of the United Nations (especially as the Suez war was distracting them at the same time – page 120) the whole world, including other Communists, had seen how the Soviet government treated independence movements. In 1968 came the 'Prague Spring' when the Czechoslovak Communist government itself tried to allow people more freedom to express their opinions. After a few months of discussions and arguments, the Soviet and other Warsaw Pact armies moved in with overwhelming force. But these unsuccessful attempts to gain more freedom taught both the USSR and other east European states to calculate their chances very carefully. Romania's government became skilled at ignoring advice from Moscow without ever going far enough to provoke a Soviet invasion, bearing in mind that the Soviet leaders were not eager to resort to force yet again. In 1970 groups of workers in Poland protested so vigorously about bad conditions that, though some were killed in street fighting, they forced the Prime Minister to resign. In 1980 Polish workers protested again, and this time formed a trade union, named *Solidarity*, which rapidly spread over the whole country and recruited vast numbers. Solidarity, by strikes and threats of strikes, forced the Polish Communist government to recognise it and to make several reforms. According to Communist ideas, a trade union must be part of the state organisation and can never strike against the state. What Solidarity was doing challenged the whole structure of Communist states; it was a dangerous idea that might spread. Yet the USSR and Poland's other neighbours, though they warned and criticised, stopped short of invading. It was the Polish army that took charge in December 1981, declared martial law and curbed Solidarity. The USSR had become very reluctant to be seen to be using force on her allies.

Some of the Soviet troops who put down the Hungarian rising. This photograph was taken in November 1956, and it seems that the Soviet officers did not approve.

There had been big changes inside the USSR. After Stalin's death in March 1953 the terror gradually eased as new leaders settled themselves in. Then, in February 1956, the new Secretary, Nikita Khrushchev, addressed the Party Conference, and astounded them with a long, bitter attack on the dead dictator and his fearful tyranny. What he said was true – they all knew it – but they had all been well trained to obey. After the first shock, the Party Conference decided that Khrushchev was the new master and joined in the rejection of Stalin. Did this mean that the Soviet peoples were now going to be free to do and say whatever they pleased? Thousands of prisoners were set free from labour camps. Artists and writers began to express what they really felt and thought, instead of what would fit the government's policies. Criticism spread, not only about Stalin, but about the Communist system itself. No Communist government could allow that.

People who took their liberty too far were arrested, tried for anti-Soviet activities, and sentenced to labour camp or to exile. Some were even classed as mad, and sent for treatment in mental hospitals. But though strict control was imposed once more, there was no such terror as had existed under Stalin. People with grievances dared to assemble in the street

The increased freedom of Soviet citizens after Stalin's death went only so far. For example, the government still kept a tight grip on foreign travel and emigration, and many Soviet Jews were forbidden to migrate to Israel. That was the point of this protest in October 1976 outside the London hotel where a Soviet scientific delegation was staying. But the very manner of their protest shows that the demonstrators appreciated that things had indeed changed since Stalin's reign of terror, and that it might be possible to influence the new Soviet leaders.

and complain openly, and so-called dissidents wrote books criticising the Soviet way of life – some of them were smuggled to Western countries and published – without risking torture and death. Alexander Solzhenitsyn, who became famous for his writings on the labour camps and who persisted in criticising the system, was merely expelled from the USSR, and the internationally known nuclear scientist Andrei Sakharov was exiled to a provincial town – though several of his less famous friends were sent to labour camps. Like the American government, the Soviet government knew that it could not simply stamp out criticism from its own people, though the Kremlin had powers to sway public opinion that the White House lacked.

Both superpowers were weakened by economic ailments, too. In the later 1970s the USA suffered as badly as the other industrialised Western countries when the oil-producers raised their prices (page 125), and the depression in trade re-

minded people of the dark days of the thirties. But the USSR was in no position to rejoice at this evidence of the failure of the capitalist system, because its tightly planned economy was slowing equally serious defects of its own. Soviet food production invariably fell badly short of what was needed and expected, and only by purchasing large quantities of grain from the USA could the USSR feed all its people. Of course both of them refused to let their difficulties prevent them from keeping up their arms race, and they both remained tremendously strong military powers.

Even superpowers were not all-powerful, and by coincidence both the USA and the USSR at the same time in the same part of the world got into entanglements that embarrassed and shamed them.

Iran was a poor country which was becoming very rich because of its oilfields. Its ruler, the shah, used the riches he gained from the oil to build up a very large, well-equipped army and to try to force modernisation on his people, rather as Ataturk had done in Turkey in the 1920s and 1930s. Many of the shah's Western ways seemed wicked and immoral to a large section of the nation, who were deeply devoted to the Shia branch of Islam. The shah used his army and secret police ruthlessly to smash any opposition, and the USA supported him – because he was strong, because he disliked the USSR just to the north of Iran, and because he produced the vital fuel. In 1979 it turned out that the shah was not as strong as he seemed. Religious leaders stirred up demonstrations and riots against his government, the army began to hesitate about shooting their brothers in Islam, and the shah fled. It was a successful revolution, but it owed little to Communist help. The *ayatollahs* who led the new republic were Muslim teachers and preachers whose burning purpose was to enforce strictly the laws and customs of their religion. In November 1979 a fanatical crowd of young Islamic revolutionaries stormed into the US embassy in the Iranian capital, Teheran, and captured almost all the staff. This was completely against international law and the UN condemned it, but the Iranians cared nothing for the rest of the world. They held the American diplomats for over a year, threatening to try them as spies. After several humiliating failures the USA negotiated their release in January 1981; a superpower had been powerless against a small country that had imprisoned and threatened her representatives.

Humiliation for the USA. Islamic revolutionary students, after storming the US embassy in Teheran, lead out blindfolded American diplomats, 4 November 1979.

Humiliation for the USSR. Islamic resistance leaders with a tank captured from the Soviet occupying forces near Herat, 11 January 1980.

In Afghanistan, next to Iran, the USSR had gained influence, and Communists had formed the government. But the Afghan Communists proved troublesome friends to Moscow. They were unruly and incompetent, and while they quarrelled among themselves Afghanistan became more disorderly and the tribesmen murdered more Soviet advisers and technicians. It had to be stopped. In December 1979 Soviet troops entered Afghanistan, set up a new government and tried to enforce order throughout the country. They had underestimated the tribesmen; fierce and independent, among their mountains these men could usually hold their own against Soviet tanks and aircraft. They were also Muslims, and when they claimed to be fighting a holy war against the godless Communist invaders, the Soviet government had reason to feel anxious about the effect this might have on the millions of Soviet Muslims who lived in Central Asia, not to mention Muslim countries of the Third World that the USSR had hoped to win over. The UN condemned the Soviet invasion of Afghanistan but was unable to take any action; and all that the USA and her allies could think of was a half-hearted boycott of the 1980 Olympic Games, which were being held in Moscow, and a few ineffective trade restrictions. Yet the USSR remained in a very awkward position as long as the Afghans remained rebellious.

While both of the superpowers showed signs of being in difficulties, they still remained the only two giants in the world. Was it possible, though, that others could be growing big and strong enough to equal them?

Possible new superpowers: China

China was the most obvious country in the world to be a superpower. It had the largest population, probably the longest continuous history of civilisation, and now it had an energetic and determined central government. The Communists under Chairman Mao Zedong had a much tighter grip on the huge country than any previous government, but before they could make a great impact on world affairs they had to rescue China from the poverty that made her weak.

Mao had succeeded in almost impossible tasks before, as when he led the Long March (page 59), but now he undertook the greatest of all – to modernise Chinese agriculture and industry at the same time, in a few years of Herculean effort. The 'Great Leap Forward' began in 1958, and was to double both food production and manufactures. Within a couple of years it became plain to everyone that it was a miserable failure; years later, after Mao's death, the Chinese government revealed that many millions died of starvation during the Great Leap. It was true that the weather and the harvests were bad, and that just about this time the USSR was withdrawing aid (page 123); but the real cause of disaster, it seems, was that Mao himself had badly misjudged what his people could manage to do.

Mao could not be wrong. He blamed the failure on lack of revolutionary enthusiasm among his people, and set about curing this with the 'Cultural Revolution'. This would root out traditional Chinese ways of thinking, which were still strong among people who had grown up before 1949. So he relied on young people to change the country's culture. From 1965 onwards he and his most trusted colleagues encouraged teenagers to form bands of 'Red Guards' who believed unquestioningly in Mao's doctrine of endless revolution. Once people lost the feeling that they were all striving to bring about more changes, he said, they would settle down into a traditional, conservative sort of society, where some would establish their families as 'haves' and most would only get along as 'have-nots'. The Red Guards looked for anyone who did not seem to them to be a keen enough revolutionary, especially if he or she were in a senior position. Managers, teachers and government officials were interrogated, criticised, insulted and punished; it was a total reversal of the age-old Chinese custom of courtesy and respect to the old. It was a kind of mob rule, but all the members of the mobs carried the same little red book, *The Thoughts of Chairman Mao*, and Mao made sure that the police and the courts backed up what the Red Guards did. Thousands of 'counter-revolutionaries' were killed, far more sent to be 're-educated' by living for years on peasant communes, where professors and artists spent all their time tilling the ground or tending the pigs, often with painful and humiliating spells of 'education' by Red Guards. This was no less than an attempt by Mao to alter the whole character and civilisation of the Chinese people. It was even more ambitious than the Great Leap Forward, and it also failed.

Gradually the fury of the Red Guards cooled. They found it hard to keep their enthusiasm at fever pitch for months and years, and some of them grew ashamed of their own behaviour. It seems likely that most Chinese, even if they did venerate Mao, resented being told what to do by adolescent gangsters. Besides, Mao was very old by now; was he really in control of what was being done in his name? Around the aged leader the most powerful Chinese Communists plotted and prepared. Mao died in 1976. His wife and her friends, who had been behind the Cultural Revolution, tried to seize power, but they were arrested and imprisoned by other Communist leaders. They were nick-named the 'Gang of Four', blamed for everything that had gone wrong during the past few years, and in 1980 put on trial and sentenced to long terms in jail.

All this time China was very much a closed country. Few foreigners were welcome, for the Chinese wanted to be able to support themselves without depending on any outsider. Already in 1954 Chinese scientists knew how to produce nuclear power, and there were vast resources in people and materials, but with the failure of both the Great Leap Forward and the Cultural Revolution, by the early 1970s it did not seem very prudent to go on treating both the USA and the USSR as enemies. Just about this time President Nixon of the USA was trying to ease the Cold War by visiting other leaders, including the Soviet ones, so Mao invited him to Beijing, too. This was the beginning of a slow and cautious movement towards co-operation between China and the USA, which Nixon's disgrace and Mao's death did not stop. The main reason was that they both distrusted and feared the USSR, but there were other reasons. China wanted machines and advice to help her to set up her new industries, while the USA and other Western industrial countries were eager to sell their goods. So the chief

Mao's widow on trial. Jiang Qing (on the right) and some of her associates listening to the charges being read. Though some of the accused were broken-spirited and submissive, Jiang Qing remained defiant throughout the trial. She and her friends received long prison sentences.

The 'little red books' of the Cultural Revolution. In this cover picture from a Chinese propaganda magazine for November 1966 young Red Guards joyously brandish their copies of 'The Thoughts of Chairman Mao'. It was this book that provided the inspiration and the excuse for whatever they did.

capitalist countries of the world, partly for commercial reasons, became friendly with the biggest Communist country in the world; and the Chinese Communists, with ideas of world revolution that made Soviet Communism seem feeble, welcomed the capitalists. One result of this in world politics was that the USA ceased to insist that the Nationalists on Taiwan were the true government of China (page 110), and the Communist government at last was allowed to take the Chinese seat in the Security Council of the UN.

Was it a sincere attempt at friendship on both sides? Were they merely using each other? Was it a threat to the USSR? Probably the answer to such questions would be known only when China grew strong enough industrially to rank as a superpower herself; this would take a long time, and many things might change in that time.

Possible new superpowers: Islam and the Arabs

The Islamic civilisation was not, like the Chinese, the way of life of one great ancient empire. It was based wholly on the Muslim religion, and nationality had nothing to do with this – at least, officially. On the other hand, the Islamic peoples did occupy one large, clearly recognised part of the world and, though they had often been rent by religious strife between different sects and by wars and conquests, they had never

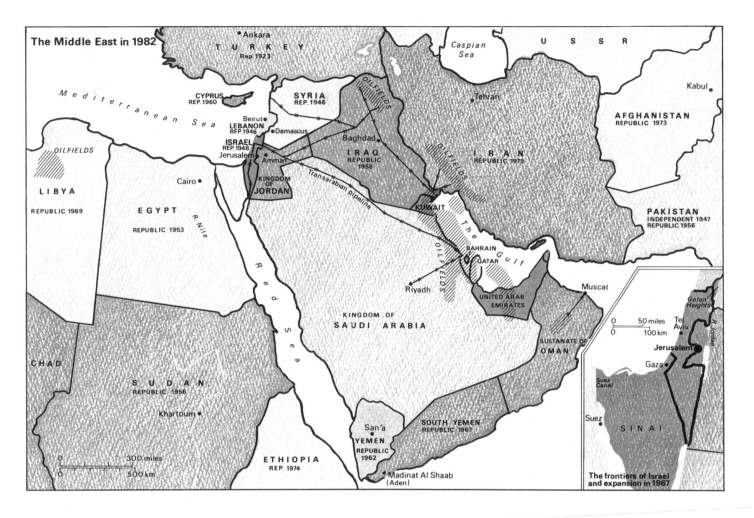

The Middle East in 1982

altogether lost the ideal of being united under the caliph, Muhammad's successor, the Commander of the Faithful. There had never been a time when there had not been religious revivals going on in some parts of the Islamic world, and the preaching of the duty to wage *jihad*, the holy war, against enemies of the true faith. Even during the centuries when Islamic countries became poor and weak, the old spirit never died altogether.

The Arab peoples occupied the middle regions of the Islamic world. Despite their importance in the history of Islam, they had been divided and oppressed for centuries (page 54). It was not until after the Second World War that all the Arab nations became independent (page 120) and then they were given a new sense of unity by the creation of a common enemy, the new Jewish state of Israel.

One result of the Nazi slaughter of millions of Jews in Europe was to strengthen Zionism (page 55). It was natural for those who survived the death camps to want to get far away from the scenes of their nightmare, to want at all costs to live in a country of their own; and most other people felt that after all the Jews had suffered they had a right to peace and safety. But, as thousands of them poured into Palestine, the Arabs saw it as an invasion of their own land. Why should they, who had not persecuted the Jews, be expected to pay the compen-

147

sation for the crimes of the Nazis? The fighting between Jews and Arabs in Palestine grew worse, with indiscriminate terrorism on both sides; the British occupation force, caught in the middle, was helpless to restrain them. The United Nations, who had taken over from the League the final responsibility for the mandate, could think of no better solution than to divide Palestine between Arabs and Jews, which satisfied neither side, and to tell the British to leave, which they were only too glad to do. This was 1948. Not only the Palestinian Arabs, but forces from neighbouring Arab countries advanced against the tiny new Jewish state, which called itself Israel. They were confident of destroying it, but what happened was entirely different. The Israelis defended themselves with skill and determination far beyond anything the Arabs had expected. Sullenly the attackers drew back, while many thousands of Palestinian Arabs fled as refugees to camps in neighbouring Arab countries. But the Arab states, which had formed a loose association called the Arab League in 1945, refused to make peace or to recognise that Israel had any right to exist. Though active fighting stopped, Israel remained, small but very strong, surrounded by enemies.

Israel's strength lay partly in the quality of the people who settled there. Many of them were highly intelligent, educated and experienced, well able to use the most modern machinery of both peace and war. They had plenty of this machinery, and money, because so many people in Western countries were supporting them; some of these people were themselves Jews, but many were non-Jews who felt that they ought to help a nation that had been so cruelly treated in Europe. It soon became obvious that the USA was Israel's greatest supplier and protector, which may have had something to do with the importance of Jewish voters in American elections. But perhaps the most decisive factor in Israel's success was that so many of the Israelis knew that if they did not win they would cease to exist; yet God, they believed had brought them back to their own land after two thousand years and did not wish them to fail again. Twice, in 1956 (page 120) and in 1967, they attacked the Arab neighbours whom they suspected of planning to attack them, and each time they scored spectacular victories and seized more land.

Israeli victories, though, brought real peace no nearer. By occupying such Arab territories as the west bank of the Jordan and the Gaza strip the Israelis became rulers of bitterly resentful Arab populations, and new Israeli settlements in those areas increased the hostility. All the time Palestinian refugees were living miserably in their camps just across the border in Lebanon, Syria and Jordan, and as the years passed without any real improvement many of them decided that terrorism was the only way of forcing other people to pay attention to them. By the late 1960s many of the terrorists were young people who had spent all their lives in the camps. The bombings and shootings that followed, both in Israel and other countries, shocked people everywhere and were condemned even by some Arab governments. They also proved to the rest of the world that the 'Palestinian problem' was not going to fade away quietly, and that the Palestine Liberation Organisation (PLO) would have to be taken seriously in any permanent peace settlement.

The Arab countries, however, were not nearly as united as they sometimes claimed, and they lacked the industry and technical knowledge that the West was supplying to Israel. Some Arab countries appealed for help to the USSR, and the Soviet rulers were pleased to get the chance to gain influence in the Middle East. In October 1973, equipped partly with advanced Soviet weapons, Egypt and Syria suddenly attacked Israel, and this time the Egyptians won the first battles. Then the Israelis recovered, the USA sent in fresh supplies, and it began to look as if Israel might be victorious again. At this point other Arab states stepped in – the oil producers (page 125). They raised the price of oil and threatened to stop supplies altogether to the Western countries that befriended Israel. The effect was dramatic. The USA and her allies in western Europe quickly decided to use their influence to bring about peace, on terms that favoured Egypt slightly. The Arabs had discovered that they held a decisive weapon.

Did this mean that the Arabs, or perhaps the Islamic peoples as a whole, were now to be a major force in the affairs of the world? It soon appeared that while the OPEC countries (including non-Arab states) were ready to enrich themselves by charging more for their fuel, they could not agree for long. The increase in oil prices set off a bad slump in trade all over the industrialised West. As it went on, some oil producers were for ruthlessly squeezing as much as they could, while others, led by Saudi Arabia, argued that it would be stupid to destroy the West's prosperity. Every meeting of OPEC was divided on this question.

When the Ayatollah Khomeini's followers drove out the Shah and set about 'purifying' Iran, many women gave up 'corrupting' Western fashions and resumed more traditional Islamic costume. But this did not mean that they were weak and helpless; they were ready to fight with modern weapons, and this photograph shows some of them training in a Teheran suburb, December 1979.

Other divisions, some of them old ones, also made it hard for Islam to act as one power in the world. There were frontier feuds that sometimes burst into fighting, like that between Iran and Iraq, or Morocco and Algeria. There were governments of all types; old-fashioned kingdoms and emirates, parliamentary republics, military dictatorships, some that combined elements of different types, some that were near-Communist. There were longstanding feuds within countries that blazed into revolts and civil wars, like the struggle of the Kurds for independence in Iraq and Iran, or the conflict between Christian and Muslim communities in the Lebanon. In all this confusion, some parties looked for help to the USSR, others to the USA and Western Europe.

Eventually, even hatred of Israel was not enough to bind Arab countries together. Egypt, the largest of Israel's neighbours, had borne the brunt of the wars, though she was poor. President Anwar Sadat decided that Egypt could not go on spending her resources indefinitely on warlike preparation. The USSR was helping, but in return wanted too great a say in Egyptian affairs. Anyway, it was time to admit that Israel had lasted long enough to be a fact of life, and the USA would never let it be wiped off the map. So in 1978 he travelled to Israel in person and suggested a permanent peace settlement. Everybody was astounded, the USA was delighted, the other Arab countries were enraged and branded Egypt as a traitor. With the USA urging them on and offering help, Israel and Egypt began a series of negotiations and partial agreements which restored most of Sinai to Egypt. But they did not settle the problem of the Palestinian refugees, nor the Israeli occupation of the west bank of the Jordan; they did not bring much safety to Israel; and they added to the arguments and quarrels among the Arabs.

Nevertheless, the Islamic nations emphasised their common Muslim faith as much as ever, perhaps more. As we saw (page 143) the 1979 revolution in Iran was religious. In Saudi Arabia advisers and technicians from the West were generously welcomed to help in modernising the country, but only on the strict understanding that neither they nor the modernisation would impair the old traditions and laws of Islam. Every leader of an Islamic country, no matter what his political beliefs might be, took care to proclaim his faith in Islam. Obviously there was the possibility here of a mighty force, but it seemed unlikely that the Muslim countries could ever put aside their quarrels and become a great power in the world.

Possible new superpowers: Western Europe

The century had begun with Europe dominating the world, and for three or four centuries past Europe had been the great power-house of the world. Europe had sent out the explorers and colonisers who had linked the different parts of the world together. Europe had created the Industrial Revolution that had transformed and was still transforming human life. Both the superpowers had sprung from Europe. But Europe had apparently tried to destroy itself in two terrible wars, and nearly succeeded. In 1945 eastern Europe lay under the control of the USSR, while western Europe leaned heavily on the USA for support and protection.

Could western Europe regain anything like its former strength? Much would depend upon the leadership of the two western European countries that were still recognised as major powers, Britain and France. Britain had the advantage of not having suffered defeat and occupation, and of being slightly removed, by the English Channel, from the dangers and disputes of mainland Europe. Britain's wartime Prime Minister, Churchill, who had been so uncompromising in his resolve to destroy the Third Reich, was one of the first to call for reconciliation among the nations of Europe, including the German people, now that Nazism was crushed. But he was no longer Prime Minister, and the new government was preoccupied with setting up the welfare state and with the change from Empire to Commonwealth (page 120). Also, the British people on the whole seemed to have very little interest in Europe; after six years of war they were tired and mistrustful of foreign entanglements. So Britain did not take the lead, but reverted to her old attitude of cautious reserve.

Among the French there was an old and widespread belief that France was naturally the leader of Europe, that French civilisation was the finest and that France was the pre-eminent military power. The succession of defeats by Germany since 1870 had only made some French cling more obstinately to this belief, and loathe the Germans. It was taken for granted by many people all over Europe that French and Germans were natural enemies, like cat and dog. But some statesmen saw things more hopefully. Surely, they argued, French and Germans must now realise that all they had managed to do was to ruin each other and Europe, but that if they had the sense to work together as the two strongest nations in western

The two who changed the politics of Western Europe

General Charles de Gaulle of France, 1890–1970. Professional soldier. Escaped from collapse of Third Republic, 1940, founded Free French. On liberation of France became head of provisional government, 1944–6. Founded Gaullist party; constantly proclaimed the greatness of France. Recalled to settle Algerian crisis, 1958; established new constitution (Fifth Republic) and became president, 1959–69. Under him France became dominant in Western Europe by working with West Germany, excluding Britain from EEC and asserting independence of US protection and influence.

Dr Konrad Adenauer of West Germany, 1876–1967. Professional lawyer, member of Centre Party. Mayor of Cologne, 1917–33; dismissed and imprisoned by Nazis. After collapse of Third Reich, 1945, became Mayor of Cologne again, founded Christian Democratic Union Party, was elected president of Parliamentary Council 1948–9. On foundation of Federal Republic became chancellor (until 1963) and foreign minister (until 1955). Under him West Germany achieved her 'economic miracle', established a democratic system, and was accepted once more as a leader in Western Europe.

Europe (Germany was already showing signs of revival), with their smaller neighbours, they might still be able to count for something in world affairs. They must try to think of themselves more as Europeans, less as French or Germans. It was a French statesman with a German name, Robert Schuman, who proposed in 1950 that France and Germany should pool their resources of coal and iron. Other countries were interested, and the result was that on 18 April 1951 France, West Germany, Belgium, the Netherlands, Luxemburg and Italy signed the agreement setting up the European Coal and Steel Community.

The Community succeeded so well that the members decided to extend it to cover industry, agriculture and trade generally, and on 25 March 1957, the six countries signed the Treaty of Rome, setting up the European Economic Community, often known as the Common Market. Though it was confined to economic matters, many people made no secret of their hopes that in time the Community would grow into a full federation of all western Europe – it might prove symbolic that the treaty was signed in Rome. The members prospered. Though no other country quite achieved the 'economic miracle' of West Germany, all shared in the growth of trade and industry, and in the protection given to farmers, who were guaranteed high prices to ensure an ample food supply.

Britain was now in a dilemma. She wanted to keep her trade links with other parts of the world, and especially her arrangements with members of the Commonwealth, but did not want to be cut out of Europe. Yet she had lost the opportunity of joining the EEC early enough to have a say in framing its regulations. In 1959 Britain was one of seven countries that set up the European Free Trade Association to balance the Common Market, but it was not very effective and in 1961 Britain applied for membership of the Common Market. She was not allowed in. President de Gaulle of France objected that Britain had too many ties overseas, but it was obvious that he also feared that Britain might challenge the leading position that France had gained in the EEC. After this rebuff British uncertainty about Europe continued. De Gaulle died and in 1973 Britain, along with Ireland and Denmark, joined the EEC; but there was so much opposition in Britain that a referendum, the first in British history, was held to confirm that the majority of the British people were willing to join. (In Norway a similar referendum went the other way, and Norway stayed out.)

The EEC had its difficulties. As it grew, it produced a big 'civil service' of its own, based in Brussels, which in turn produced a mass of complicated rules and regulations, at vast expense. Some policies had absurd results, most obviously the Common Agricultural Policy, which paid farmers to produce much more than was needed, so that the Community was left with beef and butter 'mountains' and wine 'lakes' which it had to sell outside the Common Market at a great loss. There were problems when the interests of individual member countries clashed with Community rules. Here Britain was soon in serious difficulties, largely because her industries were not doing nearly as well as those of the original members of the EEC and she could not afford to pay as large a share of EEC expenses as she had promised – even though newly discovered oilfields in the British part of the North Sea brought in a considerable amount of money. Despite all setbacks, though, the EEC grew. It set up the European Parliament, with members

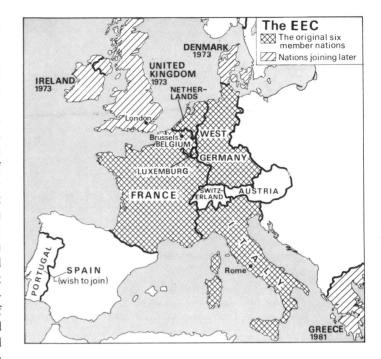

elected from all nine countries; this was mainly for discussion, and had little real power – but in time it could become very influential. Some members began to work towards a common currency for the whole EEC. As new countries applied to join – Greece (admitted 1981), Spain and Portugal – the EEC more nearly represented western Europe as a whole.

Another sign of a desire for unity appeared in the Christian religion, when an 'ecumenical movement' began among the separate Churches. While statesmen were trying to repair the damage that past enmities between their countries had left, churchmen tried to bridge the gulfs that the Reformation had opened between fellow-Christians. Catholics and Protestants began to hold joint services occasionally and some Protestant Churches which had once split apart now re-united. For the first time since the Reformation there was elected in 1978 a non-Italian Pope, the Polish John Paul II, and he embarked on a series of visits to all parts of the world, in startling contrast to the former custom that the Pope stayed in Rome. Still deep divisions remained, however. In Northern Ireland, when trouble flared up again from 1969 onwards, the people split once more according to the old labels, Protestant majority and

Catholic minority, though there were many other causes of discontent and violence mixed in with it. Some Christians believed that their religion obliged them to plunge into politics, or to send help to revolutionaries in Third World countries, and a few even saw a resemblance between Christianity and Communism. Others held that Churches that meddled in politics were forgetting their true tasks, and many believed Communism to be fundamentally anti-religious. There was further disagreement within Churches about how far it was right for them to go in giving up old customs and ideas. The movement towards Christian unity had many exceptions.

There was also a movement away from unity within several European countries. People of some regions felt that they were different from the others, and that the government and its bureaucrats, remote in the capital, did not care about them. In many cases these people had once been independent, but had been swallowed to form parts of larger nations. There were parties set up to demand self-government for the Welsh and Scots in Britain, the Bretons in France, the Basques and Catalans in Spain. In Belgium the Flemings and the French-speaking Walloons behaved like two separate nations, and the north and south of Italy were so different that their people sometimes seemed to resent being linked in one state. Perhaps all this was pointing towards setting up federal systems of government, such as the West Germans already had, and perhaps ultimately there might be one large federation of western Europe; but a great many deep-rooted national loyalties would have to be modified if anything like this should ever take shape.

Even allowing for all the obstacles, western Europe seemed to have the best chance of becoming the third great power in world affairs. It was as advanced scientifically and technically as the two superpowers, unlike China and Islam, and, although it was not under one government like China, it worked much more effectively and peacefully than the Islamic world. Standing between the USA and USSR, a strong western Europe might be able to guarantee peace between the two. But this was all speculation. As the final two decades of the twentieth century opened, western Europe remained under the protection of the USA in NATO, and eastern Europe with the USSR in the Warsaw Pact; the future of mankind still depended mainly on the balance between them.

The superpowers and the Cold War

The tables on pages 154–7 show the main events as they occurred, year by year. Relations between the superpowers were not always the same; sometimes they got along in a fairly tolerant way, but at other times the gap between them widened almost to complete enmity. There is no way of measuring this accurately, but in the central space between the columns of the USA and the USSR there is a rough indication of how far apart they seemed to be at various times.

The introductory notes on these two pages should help in picking out the main developments.

The forties and before

1917 was a turning point for both of them:

The USA entered the Great War; this marked the start of her role as a world power.	The Russian Revolution brought the Bolsheviks to power, which led to the USSR becoming the center of world Communism.

During the twenties and thirties both were somewhat withdrawn from international affairs:

The USA resumed an 'isolationist' attitude, trying to avoid becoming committed in other nations' relationships. Yet she had great influence economically and culturally. She continued to grow into the world's greatest industrial power, despite the 1930s' depression.	The USSR, as the only Communist power, was suspicious of all others and distrusted by them. She had considerable unofficial influence through Communist Parties in other countries. Under Stalin's Five Year Plans there were great efforts to become strong industrially and militarily.

During the early stages of the Second World War both were neutral:

The USA was openly sympathetic to the Allies, and US aid did much to save Britain from collapse after the fall of France.	The USSR made an agreement with Germany, which provided the opportunity to expand in eastern Europe.

The fifties

Each side in the Cold War was determined to stand firm. The USA and her allies were richer and technically more advanced, but the USSR and her allies had large populations and resources still to be tapped.

During the fifties the USA prospered. Wealth and population went on growing and most people were strongly anti-Communist. Her wealth made it possible for the USA to spread her influence world-wide, helping any government threatened by Communism and building a network of warning stations and military bases. This was 'containment' of Communism, as practised notably by Secretary Dulles.

Meanwhile the USSR began to catch up with the USA in advanced technology, and helped China also to begin modernising. After Stalin's death Khrushchev soon became the new leader and the idea of 'peaceful co-existence' with capitalist countries was put forward.

The position in Europe was being consolidated on both sides, and some attempts to revolt in eastern Europe were sternly suppressed by the USSR without the West being able to intervene.

There seemed more scope for competition among the newly independent states in Asia and Africa. Both sides offered aid here, and sometimes supported rival political parties inside them. On the whole, the new states remained friendly with their former rulers and this was to the advantage of the USA. The USSR found its opportunities in assisting revolutionary movements, and made the most of such Western blunders as the Suez invasion.

During the decade both sides were enlarging their stores of devastating weapons, and it became obvious that a full-scale nuclear war would probably destroy both superpowers and the rest of humanity too.

The sixties

As the decade began hostility continued to build up, and the installation of a young and apparently liberal president in the USA, John F. Kennedy, made no difference. Soon the most dangerous confrontation of the Cold War came, the Cuban Missile Crisis. After that, both sides were anxious to reduce the tension.

Both leaders soon went; Kennedy was assassinated, and Khrushchev was forced to retire. The question of bases in foreign countries became much less important as missiles were developed of such range and accuracy that the superpowers could devastate each other from home bases. In addition, both of them had other preoccupations. The USA was drawn into a costly, inglorious war in Vietnam. The USSR's ideological dispute with China grew into a venomous quarrel, and there were frontier clashes. Besides, the USSR needed time to build a navy.

For Western industrialised countries, most notably West Germany and Japan, this was a time of economic growth and increasing wealth; though the material welfare did not prevent dissatisfaction and restlessness among many young people.

In Asia and Africa decolonisation was largely completed during the sixties, and the new states were beginning to be recognised as part of a new force in world affairs, the Third World. Though poor, they included the greater part of the world's population and had a growing majority in the UN. They wanted help in solving their economic and social problems from anyone willing to provide it, either capitalist or communist, but this did not mean necessarily that they were willing to accept interference or control.

In the Middle East the Six Days' War made it appear that the USA and her allies were committed to helping Israel. Arab countries such as Egypt therefore accepted more aid from the USSR, though they sometimes remained suspicious.

The seventies

The prestige of the USA seemed to be waning: failure in Vietnam, the Watergate scandal, finally the seizure of US diplomats in Teheran. The USA also suffered, like all industrialised countries, from the severe recession in world trade after 1973. The USSR did not undergo such humiliations, but it had to face a growing attitude of independence among its allies in eastern Europe, particularly Romania and Poland. Soviet food supplies were still very unsatisfactory, and only large wheat imports from, ironically, the USA averted the threat of famine year after year.

Both sides bore crushing expenses as they went on building up their stocks of weapons. Both would have preferred to spend less, and feared that the dangers of a catastrophe, perhaps accidental, were becoming ever greater. In the early part of the decade they tried to create a new spirit of reasonable understanding – 'detente' – and to limit their most destructive weapons; but by the end distrust was as strong as ever.

China now began to take a more active part in world affairs, and to turn towards the West for trade and technical assistance, especially after Mao's death. Chinese distrust of the USSR seemed intense, yet China remained completely Communist.

The Middle East also was increasingly important in world affairs, as the Arab-Israeli war of 1973 led Arab oil-producing states to discover what a stranglehold they could exert on industrialised countries. At the same time there was a strong revival of Islamic custom in many countries and a reaction against some Western standards of behaviour.

The influence of the Third World generally was increasingly obvious, and causing the industrialised nations to realise that, despite the economic depression, they must do more to earn the goodwill of the poorer parts of the world.

The superpowers and the cold war: the 1940s

USA	Year	USSR
Japanese attack on Pearl Harbor.	**1941** **Entry into World War.**	German invasion – 'Operation Barbarossa'.
Untouched by war; huge production; became great military power.	**1942**	Enormous losses; complained of too little help from western Allies.
Advanced in Pacific, North Africa, Sicily and Italy.	**1943** **The turn of the tide.**	Began to push back Germans, apparently with little help from Allies.
Invasion of western Europe by US and British forces.	**1944**	Invasion of eastern Europe by Soviet forces.
Western Germany and Austria occupied by USA, Britain and France. USA produced and used atomic bomb. US occupation of Japan.	**1945** **Europe divided** **'Summit' meetings at Yalta and Potsdam made only temporary arrangements.**	Eastern Germany and Austria occupied by USSR. Soviet frontiers extended westwards. Encouragement and support for Communist and allied parties to take control in
Churchill's Fulton speech – 'Iron Curtain'.	**1946**	Poland, Yugoslavia, Albania; Bulgaria, Romania, Hungary.
USA promised help to any country resisting Communist pressure ('Truman Doctrine'). Marshall Aid begun; formation of Organisation for European Economic Co-operation (OEEC).	**1947**	Communist Information Bureau (Cominform) set up to co-ordinate work internationally.
Formation of Organisation of America States (OAS). Airlift to Berlin.	**1948** **Berlin crisis**	Communists seized power in Czechoslovakia. Yugoslavia expelled from Cominform. Blockade of Berlin.
Formation of North Atlantic Treaty Organisation (NATO). Foundation of German Federal Republic. Anti-Communist victory in Greek civil war.	**1949**	Formation of Council for Mutual Economic Assistance (Comecon) in Eastern Europe. Foundation of German Democratic Republic. Communist victory in Chinese civil war. Soviet atom bomb tested.
UN help for South Korea, with USA taking lead. Atomic spies discovered; McCarthy 'witch-hunt'. Work begun on hydrogen bomb.	**1950** **Korean War**	North Korean invasion of South Korea. Chinese help for North Korea.

The superpowers and the cold war: the 1950s

USA		Year	USSR
	Peace treaty with Japan, which became one of the Western powers.	**1951**	
	US hydrogen bomb tested. US nuclear-powered submarine begun.	**1952**	
J.F. Dulles US Sec. of State; policy to 'contain' communism everywhere.		**1953** **End of Korean War.**	Death of Stalin; first moves towards policy of peaceful co-existence. Soviet hydrogen bomb tested. Rising in East Berlin suppressed by Soviet forces.
Formation of South-East Asia Treaty Organisation (SEATO): USA, Britain, France, Australia, New Zealand, Pakistan, Thailand, Philippines.		**1954**	
Western Allies ended occupation of West Germany, which joined NATO.		**1955** **Austrian Peace Treaty** **All occupying powers agreed to withdraw, and Austria to be left independent and permanently neutral.**	Formation of Warsaw Pact.
Suez Crisis; USA supported UN condemnation of Britain, France and Israel.		**1956**	*Hungarian Crisis;* Soviet forces crushed revolt in Budapest. Riots in Poznan, Poland. Soviet aid to China extended.
USA promised help to preserve independence of any state in Middle East ('Eisenhower Doctrine'). Arabs saw this as a move to protect Israel.		**1957**	Sputnik; USSR took lead in 'space race'.
US intervention to keep order in Lebanon.		**1958**	Khrushchev renewed moves towards peaceful co-existence.
Formation of Central Treaty Organisation (CENTO): Britain, Turkey, Iran, Pakistan. Castro's revolution in Cuba.		**1959**	Eisenhower–Khrushchev summit meeting at Camp David. Repeated Soviet demands for a German peace treaty, all rejected by West.
US economic pressure against Castro regime. Formation of Organisation for Economic Co-operation and Development (OECD): OEEC countries plus USA and Canada.		**1960**	U2 incident – US spy plane shot down over USSR. Maoist Communism condemned by Russian Communist Party.

The superpowers and the cold war: the 1960s

USA	Year	USSR
'Alliance for Progress'; scheme for economic co-operation among American nations. 'Bay of Pigs'; failure of US-backed attempt to invade Cuba. US advisers sent to help South Vietnam forces.	**1961**	Berlin crisis when West rejected Soviet proposals; Berlin Wall built. Gagarin's flight; USSR still ahead in 'space race'.
US blockaded Cuba until missiles were withdrawn, but promised not to interfere again.	**1962** Agreement on peaceful co-operation in space. **Cuban Missiles Crisis.**	Soviet missiles installed in Cuba; withdrawn after US blockade.
Assassination of Kennedy.	**1963** 'Hot line' set up, direct telephone link between White House and Kremlin. **NUCLEAR TEST BAN TREATY** forbade all testing above ground.	Breakdown of talks in Moscow intended to settle ideological differences with China.
	1964	USSR began to expand navy. Fall of Khrushchev. China produced its own atom bomb.
US land and air forces sent in strength to the Vietnam war.	**1965**	
Withdrawal of France from military side of NATO.	**1966**	
USA now seen to be totally committed to protecting Israel.	**1967** Six Days' War	Arabs became more willing to see USSR as a friend. China produced its own hydrogen bomb.
'Tet offensive' in Vietnam seriously shook confidence of American public. Widespread student unrest in Western Europe.	**1968** **Nuclear Non-Proliferation Treaty** attempted to stop spread of nuclear weapons to countries that did not already possess them.	Czech government's attempt to be more liberal – 'Prague Spring' – ended by Soviet occupation.
The first landing on the moon; USA now leading in the 'space race'.	**1969**	
Powerful anti-Vietnam war protests in USA; demonstrators shot at Kent State University.	**1970**	Pro-Communist government elected in Chile.

The superpowers and the cold war: the 1970s

USA agreed at last that Communist China should have the Chinese seat on the UN Security Council.	**1971**	

1972 Beginning of detente – US President Nixon visited Moscow and Beijing. West German Chancellor Brandt began policy of reconciliation with East European states *(Ostpolitik)* leading to treaties with USSR and Poland. Salt 1 Agreement – Strategic Arms Limitation Talks produced first attempt to control major weapons.

USA withdrew from Vietnam. Pro-Communist government in Chile overthrown by military coup. 'Yom Kippur' war led to increase in oil prices in West.	**1973**	
Watergate scandal in USA; disgrace and fall of Nixon.	**1974**	Emperor of Ethiopia overthrown by military coup, paving way for Marxist government.
Inflation and trade recession, first set off by oil crisis (1973) continued and grew during the later 1970s in USA and other Western industrialised countries.	**1975 Helsinki Conference agreement guaranteed frontiers and human rights throughout Europe.**	Communists (pro-USSR) took over the whole of Vietnam. Khmer Rouge Communists (Maoist) captured Cambodia (Kampuchea). Marxist government in Mozambique.
	1976	Marxists won civil war in Angola. Death of Mao; but relations between China and USSR did not improve.
	1977	
USA deeply involved in peace talks between Israel and Egypt leading to	**1978**	
Camp David agreement.		
US embassy staff held hostage in Iran.	**1979**	Soviet forces moved into Afghanistan.
USA and allies boycotted Moscow Olympic Games and imposed mild economic sanctions to show disapproval of USSR in Afghanistan.	**1980**	Revolution in Nicaragua; apparent growth of Communist influence in Central America.

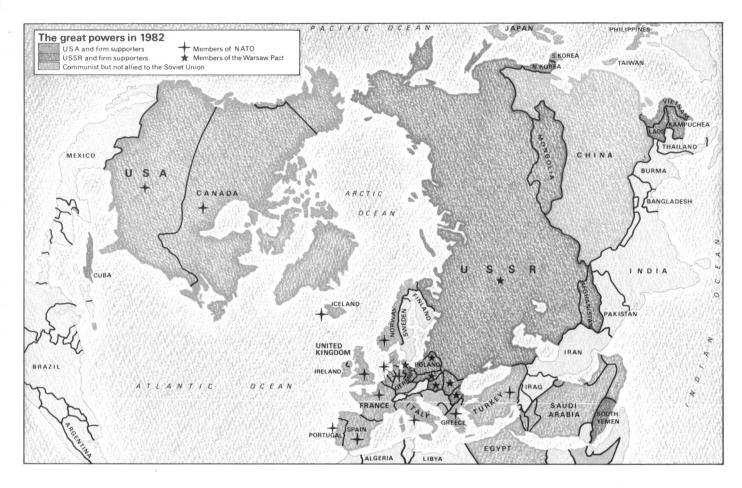

The great powers in 1982

- USA and firm supporters
- USSR and firm supporters
- Communist but not allied to the Soviet Union
- ✛ Members of NATO
- ★ Members of the Warsaw Pact

As the world entered the last score years of the century its peace depended on the balance of strength between the superpowers and their allies. This balance was firstly in nuclear weapons, which they dared not use and dared not be without; secondly, therefore, in 'conventional' armed forces that might be used without causing a nuclear holocaust; and thirdly in economic resources needed to pay for the enormously expensive armaments. It was extremely dangerous and wasteful, and if it succeeded in deterring big wars it did not prevent a large number of small wars.

Could a better system be devised – perhaps by the UN?

The United Nations

Founded 1945 by the Allies at San Francisco Conference to provide a more effective substitute for the League of Nations. Official beginning, 24 October, 'United Nations Day'.

Aims stated in United Nations Charter (111 articles). Similar to those of the League in attempting to safeguard peace.

In addition they proclaimed the freedom and equality of all people and stressed the need for social and economic improvements.

In 1948 the UN adopted the Declaration of Human Rights (30 articles).

Membership originally the Allies (51). Soon extended to include others, and increased enormously as colonies became independent:

1955   76 members
1965   120 members
1975   144 members

In theory every nation, large or small, ought to be a member, but there could be disputes, as for example the rival claims of the Beijing and Taiwan governments to represent China.

Structure

SECURITY COUNCIL: 11 members (later 15) –
5 permanent (Britain, China, France, USA, USSR), the others elected by the General Assembly for two-year terms.
Always in session.
Right of veto for permanent members.

GENERAL ASSEMBLY: all member states represented equally, irrespective of size.
One session per year. Two-thirds majority required for any resolution demanding action on an important matter.

SECRETARIAT: as with League of Nations, but larger because of increased membership and additional projects undertaken by UN and its subsidiary bodies.
Secretary-General elected for five-year term, eligible for re-election. Chief executive officer, not only in charge of administration but often conducting important negotiations; therefore very influential.

Special Committees and associated bodies:

Three principal subsidiary organisations –
Economic and Social Council: to co-ordinate regional and specialised organisations.
Trusteeship Council: to look after the former League mandates.
International Court of Justice: continuation of Hague Court.

Specialised Agencies –
Educational, Scientific and Cultural Organisation (UNESCO)
Food and Agricultural Organisation (FAO)
International Bank for Reconstruction and Development
International Civil Aviation Organisation
International Labour Organisation (ILO)
International Monetary Fund (IMF)
International Refugee Organisation - replaced by High Commission, 1951
International Telecommunication Union
Universal Postal Union
World Health Organisation (WHO)
World Meteorological Organisation

Commissions for different regions of the world and for special topics such as
refugees   human rights   status of women
population   statistics   drugs

Funds –
International Children's Emergency Fund (UNICEF)
Special Fund; set up 1957 to help to finance projects in poor countries.

Headquarters built in New York.

opposite: *The United Nations Building, New York. Built in modernistic style and ready for use in 1952, it covers six blocks in Manhattan which are legally classed as UN territory. In both style and location it suggests significant contrasts with the headquarters of the League of Nations (page 96).*

What the UN has achieved in settling international disputes has varied according to the attitude of the superpowers. When one or both supported UN action, it has sometimes been strong and effective. The UN can only intervene within any country if it is requested to do so by that country's government.

Successes	*Failures*
	1948–9 Palestine: both Arabs and Jews rejected UN proposals and fought; UN did help to arrange truce, however.
1950–53 Korea: UN forces saved South from invasion by North – because USA gave lead and USSR accidentally failed to veto.	
1956 Suez: Britain, France and Israel obliged to withdraw; UN force sent to observe.	1956 Hungary: USSR ignored all protests about the way she suppressed the rising.
1960–63 Congo: UN forces and negotiators helped to prevent the republic from falling to pieces.	1965 Rhodesia: illegal regime after UDI prospered in spite of UN condemnation and blockade (until 1980).
	1967 Israel: UN observers expelled by Egypt, so could not intervene when Israel attacked. Thereafter Israel (with US support) ignored UN condemnations of her treatment of occupied territory.
1970s 'North-South': steady increase in awareness of richer members of UN ('North') about importance of helping poorer members ('South').	1970s Namibia: continued refusal by South Africa to follow UN wishes in bringing the mandated territory of South-West Africa to independence.
	1979–80 Iran: refusal to release US hostages. Afghanistan: refusal of USSR to withdraw.

Useful routine work went on, as under the League but on a bigger scale. Special emphasis on aid to 'under-developed' countries . Some allegations, however, of bureaucratic wastefulness and inefficiency, e.g. in cultural activities and in distribution of relief to poor areas.

The United Nations Organisation, *whatever may be said of its failures, has* **survived** *much longer than the League of Nations did.*

Why?

Can it be explained simply as an improved organisation or as a change in the conditions of world affairs generally?

1 *The veto* prevented the Security Council from being able to get into a position of hopeless confrontation with a major power.

2 *UN forces* were raised with the approval, or at least without the disapproval, of the major powers, and were therefore less likely to meet formidable opposition.

3 *The rivalry* of the two superpowers meant that even if one of them blocked the wishes of the UN as a whole, the other would support the UN; therefore the UN was less likely to look absurdly weak.

4 *World public opinion* was more of a reality as both education and communications brought the parts of the world closer together, and sometimes governments – especially the superpowers – were unwilling to lose sympathy by defying the wishes of the UN.

5 *Nuclear weapons* made the strong nations very fearful of bringing about a big war, though there was no such limit on small-scale wars in which their vital interests were not in question. Thus the decades after 1945 saw many wars, but all of them relatively limited.

In 1982 the Secretary-General's annual report stated, with bluntness never used before, that the UN was powerless. Most obviously, it had failed to stop Argentina and Britain from fighting over the Falkland Islands, and Israel from invading Lebanon. Later, a special session on disarmament proved to be no more than a theatre for propaganda speeches by the world's most powerful politicians. And the UN Environmental Conference could only warn that the continuing growth of population, pollution and waste of natural resources would probably become a world crisis by the end of the century.

List of Maps and Diagrams

Index

Acknowledgments

Illustrations in this volume are reproduced by kind permission of the following:
pp 5 (Blériot), 8, 10, 16, 23, 48 (bottom), 53, 57 (bottom) 74, 85, 102, 104, 142 BBC Hulton Picture Library; p 6 photo Mrs Ginsberg; pp 6, 7 from the collection of the Victoria & Albert Museum, London; p 9 The Ulster Museum; p 11 © archives SNARK; pp 13, 29, 63 (top), 64, 65, 66, 106, back cover Novosti Press Agency; pp 17, 20, 69, 71 The Mansell Collection; p 18 (left) National Gallery, Prague; p 18 (right) Tate Gallery, London © ADAGP; p 19 Philadelphia Museum of Art, The Louise & Walter Arensberg Collection © ADAGP; pp 25, 26, 27, 28 (right), 32, 57 (top), 76, 82 Imperial War Museum, London; p 46 David Taylor; p 47 (top) Geffrye Museum, London; p 48 (top) Cunard Line Ltd; p 51 The Atkinson Art Gallery, Southport; p 52 Tennessee Valley Authority; pp 58, 146 *China Reconstructs*; p 72 Gallerie des 20 Jahrhunderts, Berlin; pp 73, 75 Institute of Contemporary History and Wiener Library; p 77 Bundesarchiv, Koblenz; p 89 (top) US Navy Department; p 89 (bottom) The Auckland Collection; p 95 Official US Air Force photo; p 96 Swiss National Tourist Office; pp 108, 112, 114, 124, 134 (top), 135, 140, 141, 143, 144, 146 (top) Popperfoto; p 116 Keystone Press Agency; p 121 United Press International photo; p 129 British Airways; p 130 Fiat Auto UK; p 133 Aerofilms; p 134 (bottom) Tate Gallery, London © SPADEM; p 137 Süddeutscher Verlag; p 149 MEPhA; p 158 United Nations Information Centre.

Maps, diagrams and drawings by Reg Piggott, John Blackman and Leslie Marshall

front cover: *The founder of Fascism, Benito Mussolini, firm-jawed and steel-helmeted on a badge of the Fascist youth organisation Balilla. The inscription round the top is the first part of Mussolini's famous three-fold command:*
If I advance, follow me;
If I fall, avenge me;
If I retreat, kill me.
The badge measures 3.8 cm (1.5 in) across.

back cover: *The Diamond Jubilee of the Communist Revolution – the military might of the Soviet Union parades through Red Square, Moscow, on 7 November 1977. The photograph is taken from the ramparts of the Kremlin, and the cubical building in front of the Kremlin wall is Lenin's tomb, where the Soviet leaders take the salute. From the facade of GUM, Moscow's main department store, on the opposite side of the square, a huge portrait of Lenin faces his tomb and his successors.*